SATHER CLASSICAL LECTURES

Volume Forty-one

THE JUSTICE OF ZEUS

THE
JUSTICE
OF ZEUS

by HUGH LLOYD-JONES

UNIVERSITY OF CALIFORNIA PRESS

BERKELEY, LOS ANGELES, LONDON   1971

UNIVERSITY OF CALIFORNIA PRESS
BERKELEY AND LOS ANGELES, CALIFORNIA

UNIVERSITY OF CALIFORNIA PRESS, LTD.
LONDON, ENGLAND

© 1971 BY THE REGENTS OF THE UNIVERSITY OF CALIFORNIA
ISBN: 0-520-01739-0
LIBRARY OF CONGRESS CATALOG CARD NUMBER: 71-121190
PRINTED IN THE UNITED STATES OF AMERICA

To Marcelle and Anthony Quinton

Wer die Grösse dieses Unterschieds zwischen Menschen und Göttern bedenkt kann sich nicht wundern, wenn das Dasein der Götter in vielen Stücken einem andern Gesetze folgt als das der Menschen. Das ist es, was das engherzige Urteil hervorgerufen hat, dass es um die Sittlichkeit der griechischen Götter bedenklich stehe.

WALTER F. OTTO

Preface

THIS BOOK contains, very much as they were delivered, the text of the six lectures I gave as Jane K. Sather Professor of Classical Literature at the University of California, Berkeley, during the fall term of 1969, together with a short final chapter. A set of lectures is not the same thing as a monograph, and I make no attempt to offer a systematic treatment of the large subject indicated by the title. The most fully documented history of the concept which the Greeks called *Dike* is that of Rudolf Hirzel, supplemented to some degree by Victor Ehrenberg; the best account of *Dike* as a political concept is that of J. L. Myres; and for the origin, cult and attributes of Zeus one should consult the learned work of A. B. Cook.

I chose to speak about *Dike* because it seems to me a central concept of the early Greek religious outlook, and therefore one well suited to allow me to express certain views about that outlook in general. It can mean "justice," or at least can indicate some kinds of justice, but it can also mean the divinely appointed order of the universe. It follows that "the justice of Zeus" is not quite the same as "the early Greek view of justice." I have tried to sketch the nature of this concept, starting with the Homeric epics and going as far as the end of the fifth century. For this purpose the literary evidence is the most valuable, and almost all this book is concerned with it.

One of the many pleasures of giving the Sather Lectures is

that of addressing an audience which includes not only classical scholars of different kinds and ages but scholars trained in other disciplines and other interested persons. I therefore chose a topic about which I felt eager to address the general reader, as well as my academic colleagues, and I have done my best to present the lectures in a way which he will understand. I make no pretence of offering a full bibliography, and the notes are meant simply to elucidate the text; at least half of them consist of references to ancient authors.

The book is written from a point of view markedly different from that of most writers of the intellectual history of the period in question, with what some may find the surprising exception of the late Walter F. Otto. It abounds with expression of disagreement, and I am uncomfortably conscious that many of these relate to scholars to whom I am in various ways obliged; disagreement, as all scholars know, is by no means always a token of disesteem. I cannot pretend to a warm admiration for the writings of the late Werner Jaeger; but towards many of the scholars from whom I have dissented I feel very differently. For example, my rejection of the views about "the discovery of the mind" associated with the names of Hermann Fränkel and Bruno Snell must not be taken as indicating disrespect for those distinguished scholars; and the same applies to my reservations about the view of early Greek ethics expressed in A. W. H. Adkins' interesting book, *Merit and Responsibility*.

The modern scholar most often quoted in these pages is E. R. Dodds, and without his Sather Lectures (*The Greeks and the Irrational*, 1951) my own could hardly have been written. Since, at the age of sixteen, I was taken to hear him lecture on the *Bacchae*, I have found his work a constant stimulus and inspiration; and I hope no reader will find my frequent disagreements, particularly with the first two chapters of his Sather Lectures, a sign of disrespect.

I have much for which to thank my hosts at Berkeley; they not only caused me by their gracious invitation to write down ideas which might not otherwise have been worked out, but also did everything possible to make my stay with them agreeable. In particular, I wish to express my gratitude to Professor W. Kendrick Pritchett and Mrs. Pritchett, whose hospitality to me was fabulous. I would also like to thank Professor and Mrs. J. K. Anderson, Professor and Mrs. T. G. Rosenmeyer and many others, both students and professors, inside and outside the classical department; and I would like to record my gratitude for the delightful company of Mr. and Mrs. Stephen Goldstine.

Sir Maurice Bowra has read through my draft, parts of it more than once, and has given me much encouragement. The whole book has been read through and discussed in detail by Professor George Devereux, and has greatly profited from his unique combination of classical scholarship and expert knowledge of psychology and anthropology.

HUGH LLOYD-JONES

Christ Church, Oxford
17 March, 1970

P.S. I am deeply grateful to those friends who helped me with the proofs. Professor G. S. Kirk and Mr. D. M. Lewis both did much to improve the book. Later Professor Dodds with characteristic generosity read the draft and supplied most valuable comments. "I stressed the element of change in Greek beliefs," he writes, "you stress the element of continuity; we are both of us right, though both of us at times exaggerate the partial truth we are stressing."

H. L.-J.

Christ Church, Oxford
18 January, 1971

Principal
Abbreviations Used

Adkins, *MR* . . . . . .A. W. H. Adkins, *Merit and Responsibility: A Study in Greek Values* (Oxford, 1962).

Dodds, *GI* . . . . . .E. R. Dodds, *The Greeks and the Irrational.* Vol. 25, Sather Classical Lectures (Berkeley and Los Angeles, 1951; paperback ed. 1963).

Guthrie, *HGP* . . . .W. K. C. Guthrie, *A History of Greek Philosophy,* I-III (Cambridge, 1962–1969).

Latte, RGAG . . . .K. Latte, "Der Rechtsgedanke im archaischen Griechentum" (*Antike und Abendland* 2, 1946, 63f.= *Kleine Schriften,* 1968, 233f.)

Lesky, GGM . . . . .Albin Lesky, "Göttliche und menschliche Motivierung im homerischen Epos," *SB Heidel. Akad.,* Ph.-Hist. Kl. 1961, 4 Abh.

Lesky, "Homeros" . . .*Idem,* in Pauly-Wissowa, *Real-Encyclopädie,* s.v. "Homeros."

Lesky, *TDH*² . . . . .*Idem, Die tragische Dichtung der Hellenen* (2d ed., Frankfurt, 1964).

Nilsson, *GGR* I² . . . .M. P. Nilsson, *Geschichte der grie-chischen Religion* I (Munich, 1941; 2d ed. 1955).

Otto, *GG* ³ . . . .W. F. Otto, *Die Götter Griechen-lands* (Frankfurt, 1929; 3d ed. 1947). Translated by Moses Hadas, *The Homeric Gods: The Spiritual Significance of Greek Religion* (New York, 1954).

Rohde, *Psyche* . . . .Erwin Rohde, *Psyche* (London, 1925).

Schmid, *GLG* . . . .W. Schmid and O. Stählin, *Ge-schichte der griechischen Literatur* (Munich, 1929–48).

VS . . . . . . .H. Diels, *Die Fragmente der Vor-sokratiker* (6th ed. rev. by W. Kranz, Berlin, 1951).

Von Fritz, *AMT* . . . .K. von Fritz, *Antike und moderne Tragödie* (Munich, 1962).

Von Fritz, *GG* . . . .*Idem, Die griechische Geschichts-schreibung* Bd. I Text and Bd. I Anmerkungen (Berlin, 1967).

Wilamowitz, *Glaube* . . .U. von Wilamowitz-Moellendorff, *Der Glaube der Hellenen*, I-II (Berlin, 1931–32).

Contents

SATHER CLASSICAL LECTURES

Volume Forty-one

THE JUSTICE OF ZEUS

I

The *Iliad*

SOME OF the most celebrated historians of Greek thought hold that in their origins religion and morality were wholly separate.[1] I am not now concerned with the truth or falsity of their opinion, though I remark in passing that to the latest investigators of the origins of religion the subject seems far more difficult and obscure than it did to their comparatively recent predecessors.[2] What concerns me is that some of them find that in the *Iliad,* the earliest document of Greek civilisation which we possess, the association between the two has reached only a very elementary stage. Dodds, for example, has written that he finds "no indication in the narrative of the *Iliad* that Zeus is concerned with justice as such." [3] Chantraine does not go as far as Dodds in this direction; he believes that Zeus maintains a kind of order in human society, but that with the exception of one isolated passage he never acts in order to enforce a moral law.[4] Other scholars go further than Dodds; Adkins, for instance, holds that "the gods as portrayed generally in the Homeric poems are far from just." [5] "Though right triumphs in the main plots of both *Iliad* and *Odyssey*," he writes, "it does not do so because it is right." Adkins does indeed find in the Homeric epics, in particular the *Odyssey*, evidence of the process by which the gods, and Zeus in particular, were made into agents of morality. But he thinks that this process remained incomplete until long after Homer; and even at the peak of its development he does not consider that it fulfilled

adequately the purpose for which it was commenced, that of
lending a special sanction to the co-operative as against the competitive virtues, to *dikaiosyne*[6] as against *arete*. Adkins points
out that the main ethical terms of praise in Greek, *arete* and the
corresponding adjective *agathos*, denoted originally and long
afterwards competitive qualities—valour, skill, and other ac-
complishments—and that co-operative virtues like *dikaiosyne*,
justice or righteousness, in Homer's time and for long afterwards failed altogether to enjoy the same prestige. Attempts
were made to remedy this state of affairs by making Zeus an
agent of justice and by incorporating *dikaiosyne* into the notion
of *arete;* in the striking phrase of Dodds the Greeks passed
from "shame-culture" to "guilt-culture." [7] But these failed, according to Adkins, because the gods manifestly did not punish
all offenders against justice and because ordinary usage resisted
the attempt to make righteousness into an integral part of virtue. Even as late as the fourth century before Christ, in Adkins'
view, the Greeks lacked an adequate concept of moral responsibility.

To begin with I wish to enquire what part, if any, is played
by justice or righteousness in the *Iliad*, and if it does play a part
there, what kind of justice or righteousness it is. First it will
be necessary to examine the view that Zeus is not concerned
with justice, or that he is not concerned with the justice that
assigns to each what he deserves. But even if we find this to be
correct, the investigation will not be at an end; for it might still
be that the human actors in the poem subscribed, all or most
of them, to certain moral notions; and in order to discover
whether this is so or not, we shall have to examine not simply
their moral terminology but also their behaviour and the manner in which the poet chooses to present it. One of the most
damaging sources of error about early Greek morality has been
the assumption that in order to study the moral notions found
in a work of art or in a society it is enough to list and analyse
the words indicating moral concepts which occur in it. The
scrutiny of such words is certainly an important part of such

an investigation; but the investigation will not be complete until the study of moral terminology has been supplemented by a study of the actions performed in the book or the society in question and the attitudes shown towards them by those who have performed and those who have described them. Also we shall need to distinguish the ancient meanings of the words indicating moral concepts from the sense assigned to them in later antiquity, and from the meanings attached in modern times to the words generally thought to correspond with them.

The action of the *Iliad* takes place on two planes, a human and a divine, which are closely linked to one another by the various ways in which the gods influence human behaviour. The Greek notion of the divine, it can never be said too often, differed utterly from the Jewish or Christian notion. Between men and gods there is no comparison in point of beauty, happiness and power. The gods lie for ever, and meet with little but good fortune; men either meet with nothing but ill fortune or at best are given a mixed lot; after death, their existence in Hades will hardly be an existence. Zeus may be father of gods and men in the sense that he is their ruler; but men in general are not the children of Zeus. Homer says nothing of their origins; the first poet who does says that they were created out of stones.[8] Their special protector in Greek myth after Homer was not Zeus but Prometheus, one of the early generation of gods which that of Zeus supplanted. In the *Iliad,* as in all early Greek poetry, the gods look on men with disdain mingled with slight pity. "I should not be sensible," says Apollo to Poseidon when he meets him in the battle of the gods, "if I fought with you on account of wretched mortals, who like leaves now flourish, as they eat the fruit of the field, and now fade away lifeless." [9] "Nothing," says Zeus himself, "is more wretched than a man, of all things that breathe and move upon the earth." [10]

Miserable as men are, the gods are jealous of their own superiority, and are quick to punish even the least action which may seem to challenge or deny it; they treat men as the nobles of an early stage of a rural society treat the peasants. "Never shall they be like each other," says Apollo as he pushes down Diomedes from the wall of Troy, "the tribe of immortal gods and the tribe of men that walk upon the earth." [11] The gods have their favourites among men, who are the children of gods or their descendants. Even these favourites must walk warily; it is dangerous to provoke a god, even if another god has encouraged one to do so and for the moment can be trusted to protect one. By the aid of gods, men can achieve great triumphs; but such aid never comes except to the valiant, the god-descended, and even they cannot, like the heroes of the Old Testament, leave all to the god, but must exert themselves to the best of their ability.[12] Further, the gods, like the heroes themselves, demand that men render them the honour due to them, their *time,* and on any who fail to do so they take a terrible revenge. If Niobe speaks slightly of Leto,[13] if Oeneus omits, whether through forgetfulness or ignorance, a sacrifice due to Artemis,[14] if Agamemnon offends Apollo by refusing to release the daughter of his priest,[15] the god will show no mercy. From a modern point of view, or indeed from that of Plato and many subsequent Greek thinkers, such gods are monstrously unjust. But for Homer, and for later poets also, they are perfectly within their rights; Aeschylus does not blame the conduct of Apollo towards Cassandra nor Sophocles that of Athene towards Ajax. The early Greek concept of order required that each god and man should receive his proper *time;* and besides meaning justice, *dike* meant the preservation of the established order.[16]

One god, even in the *Iliad,* is in a different position from that of all others with regard to justice. The order of human communities is safeguarded, in the last resort, by kings; the gods too have their monarch. In the *Iliad* Zeus is supreme among the gods, quite as much as in any later poet. All the rest together cannot pull him down from heaven to earth;[17] he can force even the mightiest gods, Poseidon, Hera, and Athene together, to bow to his authority. He exercises a vague general control over events, and since his thought is identical with future happenings, the future can be known by him or by whoever knows his mind. *Moira,* one's "portion," is in the last resort identical with the will of Zeus; when Hera reminds him that he cannot save his son Sarpedon[18] she is only warning him that he cannot sacrifice to a sudden whim his own settled policy.[19] How far is that policy determined in accordance with justice?

In Dodds' view those who think that Zeus in the *Iliad* is concerned with justice as such "confuse the punishment of perjury as an offence against the divine *time* and the punishment of offences against hospitality with a concern for justice as such." [20] Zeus in Homer possesses three of the functions later closely associated with that of protecting justice; he is protector of oaths (*Horkios*), protector of strangers and of the law of host and guest (*Xeinios*) and protector of suppliants (*Hikesios*); the last two functions are in their origins practically identical. Those who break an oath or injure a stranger have offended against the *time* of Zeus, and are punishable by him. When Menelaus kills the Trojan Pisandros, he declares that the Trojans have not feared the grievous wrath of loud-thundering Zeus, Zeus Xeinios, who will one day destroy their lofty city, they who have carried off his wife together with much property.[21] That may explain why at the very outset of the war Zeus has sent to the Achaeans two omens that guarantee their final triumph; has he done that merely as protector of the law of host and guest, or has he some general concern for justice? When both sides agree to settle the issue between them by a single combat between Paris and Menelaus and Paris is defeated, the Trojans treacherously break the truce. Agamemnon declares that Zeus will unfailingly destroy the Trojans, however long it may be before his inevitable punishment overtakes them.[22] Is that merely because Zeus is the protector of oaths and compacts, or does he out of a concern for justice punish the guilty?

If we go through the surprisingly few instances of the word *dike* and its cognates to be found in the *Iliad*,[23] we find comparatively little evidence bearing upon this problem. In epic δίκη first means a judgment given by a judge or an assertion of his right made by a party to a dispute. It may be "straight" or "crooked." Zeus by *dike* makes the *themistes* straight; kings by *dike* sort the *themistes*. The use of the word as "right" or "custom" occurs only in the *Odyssey*. Only once in each epic does it occur in a general or abstract sense. There is, it is true, one passage which if taken at its face value makes decisively against Dodds' view, and which Chantraine acknowledges to be the sole exception to his rule that Zeus in the *Iliad* does not act to ensure distributive justice. The scene as Patroclus pursues the fleeing Trojans[24] is compared to that caused by an autumn storm sent by Zeus to punish men "who by violence pronounce in the market-place crooked judgments and drive out justice, having no care for the concern of the gods." The words recall a well-known passage of the *Works and Days*,[25] and the convenient explanation of their apparently unique character has been to dismiss them as an "interpolation" based on Hesiod, or as the work of a late poet influenced by Hesiodic notions.[26] True, the passage coheres well enough with the doctrine of the *Litai,* the spirits of entreaty, set forth by Phoenix in the embassy to Achilles; but that passage too is regarded by some scholars as a late addition to the *Iliad,* whose theology is not consistent with that found in the older and more authentic portions of the poem. For various reasons, most of which have been clearly set forth by other scholars, I find these opinions unconvincing.[27] I find them all the more so because I hope presently to show that the doctrines expressed in the simile of the flood and in the speech of Phoenix are in fact perfectly consistent with the theology of the *Iliad* as a whole.

But for the present we must consider the attributes of Zeus. He derives them from the attributes of kings as they were known in early times.[28] One important function of a king in Homer is that of protecting the *themistes*—customs, usages, principles of justice.[29] A king is one to whom Zeus has given the sceptre and the *themistes,* that he may take counsel for his people;[30] the Achaean chiefs "protect the *themistes* that come from Zeus," [31] as Sarpedon protects Lycia "by his judgments and his strength." [32] In the underworld of the *Odyssey* the great king Minos gives justice among the dead; that is he does not judge them for their acts committed upon earth, but settles their disputes. [33] The justice which the kings dispensed was a rough reciprocal justice, summed up in the line from a lost epic which the emperor Claudius was fond of quoting, "If he suffers as he did, straight justice will be done." [34] Since it is from Zeus that kings derive the *themistes,* and since his attributes were obviously based on theirs, it would be strange if he had not, as they had, the function of protecting justice. Offenders against oaths or strangers were considered as offenders also against the *time* of Zeus, and since a god punished offenders against his *time,* were punishable by him. Was the same true of all offenders against justice? Whether the justice that Zeus champions in the *Iliad* is in all respects similar to modern notions of justice is of course another matter.

To know the nature of Zeus' justice, we must examine his attitude towards the most important problems concerning right and wrong that are debated in the *Iliad.* Let us take first the quarrel between Greeks and Trojans caused by the abduction of Helen and the theft of property that accompanied it. "Right triumphs," says Adkins, "but not because it is right." [35] If we survey the issue solely from the viewpoint of the politics of Olympus, we may well conclude that Zeus' natural partiality for the Trojans is overborne by a powerful combination of gods who for reasons of their own are bent upon the Trojans' ruin. But if we consider the matter from the viewpoint of the human actors in the drama, we must remember the pledge given to Agamemnon at the beginning of the war, the certainty of Menelaus that Zeus Xeinios will punish the abduction of his wife, the certainty of Agamemnon that Zeus Horkios will punish the treacherous breaking of the truce by Pandarus. Can we really feel certain that the eventual triumph of the Greeks has no connection with the undoubted truth that Paris provoked the quarrel by abducting Helen? That is hinted in the last book of the *Iliad,* and the old fashion of dismissing the passage as an "interpolation" is now less popular than it once was.[36]

In terms of Olympian politics, Zeus seems to fall in with the will of the preponderant party among the gods, just as an earthly monarch might decide an issue in accordance with the wishes of the most powerful among his nobles. In terms of human action, his decision is in accord with the basic principle of justice, that the aggressor must be punished. Is this accord merely a coincidence? Anyone who accepts the argument I have put forward to show that the protection of justice must have been one of Zeus' attributes from the earliest times will hardly think so.

Let us now test this conclusion by a consideration of the central episode of the *Iliad,* the dispute between Agamemnon and Achilles which begins in Book I and is settled only in Book XIX. It will be necessary to examine not only the part played by Zeus in relation to this dispute, but the moral attitudes towards it of the human actors and, if possible, those towards which the reader is inclined by the suggestions of the poet himself. If the notion of Zeus' justice which I have outlined is correct, we shall expect to find implicit in the poet's treatment of the action a view of justice or righteousness not out of harmony with that notion. Much of what I say may seem obvious and familiar. But recent studies of Homer, particularly in English-speaking countries, have been so much concerned with the historical background of the poems, with the problems of their composition and transmission and with other matters apart from their content[37] that there seems to me some warrant for a discussion of the central problems of the plot of the *Iliad* as it exists. In the attempt to analyse the moral attitudes implicit in the poem, we shall need to guard against assuming that Homer was always more interested in these than in the emotions of his heroes. The indispensable framework which the received morality provides must not be treated as though it were itself the main subject of the poem.

Before starting I must say a word about theories which if true would rule out the possibility that the *Iliad* is a poem in which justice or righteousness plays any significant part. By an analysis of words used by Homer to describe facets of the mind or mental processes, Hermann Fränkel has argued that Homer had no coherent, articulated concept of the self; Bruno Snell and his followers[38] have tried to show that Homer has no cognisance of any concept denoting the psychic whole, of any notion that might correspond to our word "soul." "Psychic organs such as the *noos* and the *thymos*," Snell maintains, "are at the mercy of wizardry, and . . . men who interpret their own mental processes along these lines consider themselves a battleground of arbitrary forces." [39] When Homer describes a mental process leading up to what we should call a decision, he is incapable, according to Snell, of describing it properly, because he lacks a word denoting the psychic whole which might decide. That theory, by depriving Homer's characters of all responsibility for their decisions, would make it impossible for the *Iliad* to be a poem dealing with great moral issues, a poem set against the background of definite moral attitudes.

Snell is complaining, it has been pointed out, that Homer lacks the concept of will;[40] no wonder, since it is a concept of considerable sophistication. Does this lack make him incapable of describing a decision? Albin Lesky's sound treatment[41] helps me to save many words here. The pattern of a right decision, it has long been recognised, is provided by a passage in Book XI.[42] Odysseus is cut off and surrounded by the enemy; for a moment he considers flight, but in the end decides to stay and fight it out. "What is to become of me?" he says, "Great harm is done if I flee for fear of their numbers, but it is yet worse if I am taken alone; for the other Greeks have been frightened away by the son of Kronos. But why does my *thymos* say these things to me? No, I know that cowards leave the battle, but that he who excels in fighting must stand firmly, whether he is struck or strikes another." For a moment the person facing the alternatives weighs them in his mind; then he remembers the knowledge of the principles of right behaviour on such an occasion which he possesses, and this memory determines his course of action. A wrong decision, as we shall see presently, occurs when the decider's passions prevent his *thymos* from functioning correctly; his passions have been set in motion by the action of a god. It is important to observe that when a human action, whether right or wrong, is put down to the action of a god, that does not mean that the human actor is not held to be responsible for his decisions. Agamemnon can to some extent mitigate his shame at having caused a disaster by his quarrel with Achilles, but that does not cause him to deny responsibility and withdraw his offer of compensation; Achilles knows that his obstinacy was due to *ate* sent by Zeus, but none the less feels responsible for the death of Patroclus.[43] In each instance, also, the divinely motivated act can also be fully motivated in human terms; the part played by the god can always be subtracted without making nonsense of the action.

This double motivation and double responsibility, human and divine, has always been difficult to grasp. The old view that the divine part in human action represented a mere *façon de parler,* died hard; in recent times it has been defended by such scholars as Martin Nilsson and Paul Mazon.[44] But the most prevalent modern view of the question has been shaped by the tendency begun by Nietzsche and carried further by his friend Rohde to correct the error made by the old classicism when it denied proper emphasis to the irrational features of Greek thinking. Scholars now rightly insist that the Homeric religion is real, and that the gods and their activity must be taken seriously; also, they have become aware that early Greek thought retains many primitive survivals. In consequence some of them have gone too far in the new direction, believing that or acting as if Homer's world were itself primitive and depriving his human characters of all power of decision and mental independence. That is a tendency which has to be resisted.[45] If we strike a proper balance, we must acknowledge that Homer's gods are effective and his religion real, but that his human characters are free to decide and are responsible for their decisions.

Let us now examine the quarrel between Agamemnon and

Achilles that is the central incident of the *Iliad*. In the opening
lines of the poem, the Muse is exhorted to tell of the quarrel
of Agamemnon and Achilles, of how it caused many deaths,
and how the design of Zeus was fulfilled. Clearly it was Zeus'
purpose that many should perish. It is not reasonable to argue
that the author of the *Iliad* is here imitating the author of the
Cypria, who made Zeus cause the war in order to relieve the
earth of its excess of population;[46] but the idea that this was
why Zeus caused wars may well have existed at a very early date,
as this passage might be taken to suggest. But the immediate
cause of the quarrel is the action of Apollo, who punishes the
Achaeans for Agamemnon's rejection of his priest's appeal for
the return of his daughter by sending plague. Though the
plague ceases on the return of Chryseis, during the debate over
her return there has occurred the quarrel that will prove so
disastrous.[47]

Unwillingly Agamemnon agrees to renounce Chryseis, but he
demands another prize of equal value. Had he been dealt with
tactfully he might have been induced to forget this suggestion;
but instead of leaving it to others, such as Nestor, to lead him
away from it, Achilles becomes angry. This causes Agamemnon
to make the fatal assertion that he will rob one of the other
chieftains of his prize to compensate himself for the loss of his
own.[48] Achilles furiously reminds the king that he is here not
in his own quarrel, but in that of Agamemnon and his brother,
and that though his share in the fighting is greater than theirs,
his booty is much less. Concern over property, even human
property, would hardly have troubled the antagonists so much
were it not that in their society one's share in booty reflected
one's degree of *time*. Their quarrel is over *time* and only sec-
ondarily over property.

Achilles threatens to leave for home at once, and Agamemnon angrily replies that he is free to go, since he has others who
will show him *time,* and particularly Zeus himself.[49] Achilles,
he says, is the one among the chiefs whom he most hates, since
at all times contention (*eris*) and battles and war are dear to

him. If Achilles has mighty strength, that is something that a god has given him. That attempt to belittle his opponent's chief asset is ineffective; the gifts of the gods, as Paris reminds Hector,[50] are to be made the most of. Some modern interpreters ought to be surprised at Agamemnon rebuking Achilles for loving only battles and war, since in their opinion all Homeric heroes cared for little else. But Agamemnon means to say that there are virtues other than the martial, and in these Achilles is deficient. Later, soon after their reconciliation, Achilles will virtually admit this charge; and he will curse *eris* and *cholos* (anger), the powers which have caused the disastrous quarrel. Agamemnon ends his speech by positively asserting that he will take away Briseis, and only the dramatic intervention of Athene prevents Achilles from drawing his sword and instantly dispatching him.

Taking the goddess' advice, Achilles now abuses Agamemnon with great violence.[51] Yet when he accuses him of cowardice and of avarice he is being unjust; Agamemnon, like Achilles himself, has acted out of wounded pride. Now Achilles solemnly swears that the day shall come when the Achaeans shall miss him when they are perishing in great numbers before the man-slaying Hector. At this point[52] Nestor, the person best qualified by seniority and prestige to settle the dispute, makes his intervention, but by this time both antagonists are too angry to listen to his good advice.

Adkins[53] holds that Agamemnon as the more powerful chieftain has the right to take Briseis if he will, and only comes to regret it later because it has led to a military disaster. That is not how Nestor during his attempt at mediation views the matter. He does indeed start by warning the two quarrellers that nothing could better please the enemy than their dispute; but he goes on to point out to each in what way he is acting wrongly. Noble as he is, he says, let Agamemnon not take the girl, but leave her with the owner to whom the Achaeans originally gave her; and let not Achilles quarrel with the king, since a king to whom Zeus has given glory has greater *time* than other men.

Achilles may be stronger and have a goddess for his mother, but Agamemnon is mightier (*pherteros*), since his subjects are more numerous. He ends with a solemn appeal to both parties to restrain themselves; Achilles should put a stop to his *menos,* Agamemnon should let go his anger.

This speech of Nestor's may contain no mention of an abstract notion of justice, but justice is what Nestor is aiming at; he wishes to settle the dispute by persuading each participant to accord to the other his proper *time.* Had Nestor and not one of the disputants been the king, they would have been obliged to follow his instructions. But the quarrel is one in which the king, whose duty it is to give justice to his subjects, is himself a party, so that the human machinery for securing justice cannot be set in motion.

However, Achilles is not in the position of an ordinary vassal of Agamemnon. First, he is the son of Thetis, whose influence with Zeus is exceptionally great, even for a goddess; the Achaeans are in no position to do without the tremendous military power which Achilles commands. Faced with a difficulty, a Greek will first pray to a god; but he must then reinforce the god's action on the divine plane by applying on the human plane whatever effort he is capable of making. Achilles and his contingent withdrew from battle, and with the aid of Zeus their absence swiftly leads to a severe reverse. In terms of the politics of Olympus, Zeus flouts for the time being the wishes of the Achaean supporters among the gods to do honour to Achilles and thereby fulfil his special obligation towards Thetis. He does not act, Adkins complains, because he respects justice; but we must observe that just as in decreeing Troy's eventual destruction he is fulfilling not only the wishes of the pro-Achaean gods but also the demands of justice, so in acceding for the time to the wishes of Thetis he is ensuring the triumph of Achilles in a dispute in which Achilles is undoubtedly in the right. But that is not all there is to Zeus' purpose, as we shall see later.

During the second book Agamemnon tests his men's readiness to fight by proposing to return home, and is alarmed when many of them seem inclined to take him at his word. During the debate that follows, Thersites reproaches him with having dishonoured Achilles, "a much better man than himself"; it has been observed that Thersites echoes many of the arguments used by Achilles in Book 1.[54] Thersites is soon silenced, but in the conversation with Nestor that follows Agamemnon declares that Zeus has made trouble for him. He gives as instance the quarrel with Achilles, actually admitting that he himself provoked it. If they could once agree together, he says, the fall of Troy could not be long delayed.[55] It is not always remembered that Agamemnon admits responsibility for the quarrel at this early stage.

At that time the situation is not yet critical, but by the time of the Achaean assembly at the beginning of the ninth book, the army has been heavily defeated, and the need for the return of Achilles has become imperative. Agamemnon in his opening speech[56] blames Zeus, who has made him the victim of *ate* and of *apate* (deception); that is true, but according to the rules it is no excuse for his own disastrous mistake. After Diomedes has rebuked Agamemnon for his lack of courage, Nestor tactfully proposes adjourning the assembly and holding a banquet so that the chiefs may discuss the most important issues in private; at this banquet he persuades Agamemnon, without much difficulty, to offer atonement to Achilles. Adkins[57] maintains that atonement is offered only because of the military reverse, and that moral issues do not enter into it. Now suppose Nestor and the other chiefs had thought Agamemnon justified in taking Briseis, but had become convinced because of the military situation that Agamemnon must be persuaded to offer atonement to Achilles. Nestor would have said, "Son of Atreus, in your quarrel with Achilles everything you said was right; but Achilles is much loved by Zeus, and without him we shall be driven into the sea; for the army's sake swallow your pride and offer him atonement." That is not what Nestor does say. What he says is, after leading up to the point with infinite tact, "I was right from the start, when I advised you not to take away Briseis;

but you, giving way to your mighty *thymos,* dishonoured a mighty man, whom even the gods honour." Moral error and mistake are in Greek thinking often not easy to distinguish; but it seems fair to say that Nestor tells Agamemnon that in the quarrel with Achilles he was in the wrong. Since Agamemnon has already admitted this, it is not surprising that he at once tells Nestor that he agrees with him;[58] he has been governed by *ate,* obeying his baneful mind. The custom of Achaean society requires that Agamemnon's regret be expressed in material terms, and he describes the enormous compensation, enough by itself to make its owner a prince of some importance, which he will offer to Achilles. "All this I will give him," he says, "if he will cease from his wrath. Let him be won over—it is Hades who is not to be appeased nor to be won over, and that is why he is the most hateful to men of all the gods—and let him meet my wish, in so far as I am more a king, and claim to be greater by birth." [59] The argument that one should give way to one who is more a king has been used by Nestor, as well as by Agamemnon himself, in the first book, although the ambassadors are not stupid enough to use it while they are pleading with Achilles. It appears that it is one to which some weight is meant to be attached, and the same is true of the argument that a man should not remain obdurate in the face of pleading, which will occur again later.

"The fact that Agamemnon has incurred social disapproval for his failure," writes Adkins[60] "gives the transaction an appearance of 'quiet morality' which it does not possess. The only aspect of *arete* in which Agamemnon has fallen short is success in war; the quieter virtues are so much less important that Agamemnon does not see the transaction in this light at all." To say that is to neglect the clear implications of what is said both by Nestor and by Agamemnon. Even in a heroic society, in which feelings of shame and not feelings of guilt do the main work of morality, the so-called quieter virtues are essential, above all loyalty, without which not even a gang of thieves, let alone an army, can hope to operate successfully.

It will already be clear that I am not one of those who regard the ninth book as the late addition of a post-Homeric poet;[61] certainly there seems to have been an earlier version without Phoenix, but that may have been, as some have argued, an earlier version by the poet of the ninth book himself, whom I identify with the "monumental composer," or as I prefer to call him, Homer.[62]

After drawing Achilles' attention[63] to the extreme gravity of the military situation, Odysseus reminds him of the advice his father Peleus gave him before he left for Troy, "restrain the mighty *thymos* in your breast, for friendliness is better, and abstain from mischief-making *eris,* so that the Argives may honour you, both young and old." Peleus, it would seem, was able to appreciate some at least of the "quieter virtues." Achilles, says Odysseus, is forgetting this advice; let him now abandon the anger caused by his aggrieved *thymos* and accept the great gifts which he is offered. Even if Achilles cannot forgive Agamemnon, he continues, let him pity the other Achaeans, who will honour him like a god.[64] If he does, he will win great glory; for now Hector, elated by his triumph, will come near the ships, where Achilles may catch and kill him. Before appealing to his love of glory, Odysseus has appealed to him to pity the Achaeans; they deserve his pity because as a partner in the expedition he owed them a debt of loyalty.

The other speakers add no new arguments to those of Odysseus, but help to bring out more vividly the emotional implications of the arguments already used. Phoenix too[65] urges him to subdue his *thymos.* Even the gods, whose *arete, time,* and power are greater than those of men allow themselves to be persuaded; like Agamemnon in the discussion before the sending of the embassy, he thinks obduracy in itself an evil. *Ate* is strong and moves swiftly over the earth to wreak havoc among men; after her slowly come the *Litai,* prayers or Entreaties, repairing the damage she has done. Achilles should do them honour, daughters of Zeus, as they are made by a transparent piece of allegory; and in illustration he tells how Meleager lost by his obduracy the gifts he should have been given for defending Calydon from the Curetes.[66]

Of the three ambassadors Ajax has most in common with Achilles, and it is his short speech[67] that makes most impression on him. He reproaches Achilles for having put into his breast a *thymos* that is savage, and for paying no regard to the *philotes* (dearness, or friendship) of his companions, who have honoured him beyond all others. It is the accepted thing in such a case, Ajax insists, to accept a proper offer of compensation; men have done so even for the life of a brother or a son. The *thymos* which the gods have put into Achilles is unrelenting and cruel.[68]

A moment before[69] Ajax has said that it is Achilles himself who has put his present *thymos* into his breast, but there is no real inconsistency. Zeus has indeed sent *ate* to take away his *phrenes*, Zeus has indeed put into his breast such a *thymos* as Ajax has described. But Achilles cannot evade responsibility for the decisions which he takes under the influence of this *thymos;* he himself, as well as Zeus, has put it there.

The speeches of Phoenix and Ajax bring out the situation in all its concreteness against the background of ethical assumptions which the speech of Odysseus has already supplied. There exists a code of behaviour according to which a man is thought to be acting unreasonably if he rejects an offer of compensation, provided it is sufficient to ensure him the proper degree of *time*. Achilles' behaviour is particularly unreasonable, since he is placing his grievance before the claims of friendship and loyalty. When Phoenix makes the *Litai* daughters of Zeus, it is partly because he wishes to lay stress on their importance, as later Pindar will call Gold the child of Zeus and Euripides, again in a special context, will say the same of love.[70] But it is also because when the *Litai* are rejected it is to Zeus that they go for their redress, just as in Hesiod's *Works and Days*[71] *Dike,* when she is being maltreated, cries out to Zeus and he punishes her oppressors. The affinity between the doctrines has lent colour to the suggestion that the ninth book is a late addition to the

Iliad which shows the influence of Hesiod, or at least of the morality current in the Hesiodic world. Whether Homer— the monumental composer of the *Iliad*—was earlier or later than Hesiod is not so easy to determine as most people have usually assumed; many of the differences between them could as easily be explained in terms of social or of geographical separation as in terms of time.[72] But whatever the chronological relation between the *Iliad* and the *Works and Days*, it is not safe to assume that the moral climate of the two poems is altogether separate and distinct. It must be admitted that the concepts of Zeus as the protector of oaths and as the champion of strangers, hosts, and guests are present in the *Iliad*, and I have argued that they are not easily separated from the concept of Zeus as the protector of justice which Hesiod in the *Works and Days* so explicitly puts forward. With that concept the doctrine of the *Litai* has obvious affinities.

The note of strong disapproval struck by Ajax is of great importance. He drives home far more effectively than either of the other speakers that according to accepted moral standards Achilles, who until now has been in the right in his dispute with Agamemnon, has now put himself in the wrong, and this is presently confirmed by the round condemnation of the conduct of Achilles by Diomedes.[73] In his answer to Ajax, Achilles cannot help showing much sympathy with what Ajax has said. "Ajax, Zeus-descended son of Telamon, lord of peoples," he says,[74] "in all things you have seemed to speak in accordance with my *thymos*. But my heart swells with anger when I remember what happened, how the son of Atreus treated me with despite among the Achaeans, as though I had been an immigrant without honour." In conclusion, he does not repeat that he will return home next day, but simply says that he will take no part in the fighting till Hector shall attack the ships of his own followers.

When Achilles admits that all Ajax has said is in accordance with his own *thymos*, he is recognising the strength of Ajax' argument, and in effect acknowledging that he is right; but since his *thymos* is swelling with anger, he cannot bring himself to act upon his knowledge. Let us consider the decision of Achilles in the light of the decision of Odysseus in Book XI not to run away, but to stay and fight the enemy.[75] Like Odysseus, Achilles knows, as he admits to Ajax, what he ought to do; however, the anger that makes his heart swell is, despite the advice given him by his father and recalled by Odysseus, too strong for him. Later, in Book XIX, Achilles will describe his behaviour in theological terms and in a way different from but not inconsistent with his description of it here; we shall come to that passage presently.

Towards the end of Book XI,[76] Achilles sees Nestor escorting a wounded man out of the battle and sends Patroclus to verify his guess that it is Machaon. Nestor seizes the opportunity to persuade Patroclus to use his influence over Achilles. Nestor's long narration of his own past triumphs is designed to arouse Achilles' appetite for glory, but both at the beginning and at the end of his speech he asks whether Achilles feels no pity for his friends.[77] "You are impossible," says Patroclus to Achilles when he finally returns to him,[78] "may I never be visited by such anger as that which you guard, you who are terrible in your *arete*. What good shall any born later get from you"—here Patroclus is using one of Nestor's arguments—"if you do not save the Argives from ruin they do not deserve? Pitiless man, the horseman Peleus was not after all your father nor Thetis your mother, but the gray sea bore you and the steep rocks, so relentless is your purpose." If Achilles has in mind his mother's prophecy that he will die early if he continues to fight, let him send Patroclus in his place, as Nestor has suggested.

Achilles replies[79] that he is in no way moved by the prophecy, and we must believe him; though in his reply to Odysseus he has used the prophecy as an additional reason for not giving way to the ambassadors, fear of death by itself would never have caused him to withdraw from battle. But grievous pain comes over his *thymos* and his heart, he says, when Agamemnon tries to damage a man that is his peer and take back his prize, "as though I had been an immigrant without *time*." But now he says that all this belongs to the past, and that his anger could not have lasted for ever. True, he has said that he will not cease from anger until the fighting reaches his own ships; but now let Patroclus put on his armour and lead the Myrmidons into battle. He must save the ships from being burned and must obey Achilles' instructions, that he may win great glory for Achilles and that the Greeks may restore Briseis and bring great gifts with her. Once the ships are safe, Patroclus must return, otherwise the *time* of Achilles will be less, and some god may intervene to help the Trojans. Clearly Achilles is eager to secure the greatest possible amount of *time;* he wishes to avoid the fate of Meleager, who returned to battle only when the Curetes had actually set fire to Calydon, and so lost the great gifts that he would otherwise have received. He says nothing of pity for his friends as a motive; and his wish that all Trojans and Greeks except Patroclus and himself may perish shows that Nestor has been wrong in arguing from his interest in the identity of the wounded man escorted by Patroclus that he feels pity. But it is clear that Patroclus himself feels pity, and argues strongly that Achilles ought to feel it. The obligation to feel pity is bound up with loyalty. But Achilles is still restrained from returning to the battle by the dire pain that comes over his *thymos* when he remembers Agamemnon's insult.

Let us now return to the plan of Zeus which the poet has told us in the opening lines of the poem was accomplished. In Book VIII [80] Zeus has told Hera that Hector shall not cease from battle until Achilles shall return to the war after the fight for Patroclus' body, and in Book XV [81] he tells her in more detail what course events are destined to take. In promising Thetis that he will honour her son by giving the Trojans victory till he returns, Zeus has granted Achilles a favour which he will bitterly regret. For the Trojan victory will lead to the death of Patroclus, sent into battle by Achilles himself. That in turn will lead, Zeus says to Hera, to the death of Hector, and soon after to the fall of Troy. Had Patroclus remembered the orders of Achilles and returned to camp after driving the Trojans from the ships, he would have escaped death; but, in the words used by the poet at this point, the purpose of Zeus is always stronger than that of men. Achilles has had his wish granted, only to have it recoil on him with bitter irony; Aeschylus in his Achillean trilogy[82] will make him apply to his own case the fable of the eagle who recognizes on the arrow that has brought him death some feathers of his own. When we consider the nature of the plan of Zeus, we understand why Agamemnon can exclaim that none of the gods is deadlier than Zeus.[83] Yet neither Agamemnon nor Achilles can complain that Zeus has been unjust; according to the terms of Zeus' justice, each has got what he deserved.

When Achilles learns of Patroclus' death, he has no wish to survive unless he can avenge it upon the killer.[84] This attitude has often been considered to be that of a savage. Hector has killed Patroclus not in a private quarrel, but in the course of a war. Achilles feels a strong desire to appease his own feeling of guilt. He has been of no use, he says, to Patroclus nor to any of those friends of his whom Hector has slain—here at last he admits feeling pity for the Achaeans—but supreme as he is in battle he sits here a useless burden on the earth.[85] Not that this emotion is his only reason for wanting to kill Hector. If vengeance is taken upon his killer, Patroclus will receive great *time;* the word *timaoros,* meaning "protector of someone's *time,"* is regularly used in tragedy to mean "avenger," and this attitude is certainly as old as Homer's time. All Achilles can now do for Patroclus is to do him funeral honours and to kill Hector. In war he is supreme; in counsel, he now admits, others are his betters; and he utters a curse upon two powers that have been his ruin, *eris* and *cholos.* Death in the end is not to be avoided; even the mighty Heracles died at last; meanwhile, let him win glory and give the Trojans cause to know that he has returned to battle. Achilles speaks of glory, for the time to win it has arrived; but the glory is only incidental. He finally sacrifices his life not for glory, but out of remorse for his responsibility for the death of Patroclus.[86] In Homer's world loyalty to an individual friend, like loyalty to the group, is not insignificant; I suppose loyalty to one's friends counts as a co-operative virtue. Achilles' insistence on honouring Patroclus by giving Hector's body to the dogs is clearly contrary to the prevailing standards. When he rejects Hector's plea that his body be returned, Hector warns him that the gods may hold this act against him when the time comes for him to perish at the Scaean gates at the hands of Paris and Apollo. The "unseemly" actions he performs on Hector's body[87] are disapproved of by Apollo, who reproaches the other gods with abetting "the deadly Achilles, who has no righteous mind, nor can his intention in his breast be turned aside, but like a lion's his purposes are savage, a lion's who yielding to his mighty strength and his proud spirit goes against the flocks of men to take his meal." Thus Achilles has destroyed pity, and he lacks *aidos* which does men great harm or great good. ". . . This is in no way to his honour or his good; let him take care that noble as he is we do not feel *nemesis* against him." [88] Zeus sends Thetis to tell Achilles that the gods are angry with him, himself most of all.[89] But in sending Iris to tell Priam to ransom Hector, he tells her that Achilles will accept the offer, "for he is not foolish or aimless or wicked, but will in all kindness spare a suppliant." [90] Speaking of Achilles' treatment of Hector's body, Apollo has said that he has no righteous *phrenes;* Zeus also deplores his treatment of the body, but denies that he is *aphron,* without *phrenes.* Clearly his treatment of the body is condemned, although Zeus' account of his character is correct, as his conduct towards Priam later proves.

In the assembly of Book XIX, Achilles formally lays aside his anger[91] and Agamemnon makes an apology for his conduct.[92] He has been blamed for the disaster, he says, but he was not guilty (*aitios*); it was Zeus, and his portion, and the Erinys that walks in darkness who in the assembly put savage *ate* into his mind. No one is proof against *ate,* not even Zeus himself, and to prove it Agamemnon tells how Zeus himself was caused by *ate* to give to Eurystheus the privilege he had designed for his son Heracles. That helps Agamemnon to save face, but it does not cancel his responsibility; and he gives orders for the immediate payment to Achilles of the vast compensation he has offered him.

Soon afterwards, in his brief speech made before offering sacrifice,[93] Achilles in turn gives a theological explanation of his conduct during the quarrel. "Father Zeus," he says, "great are the *atai* which you send to men. Never would the son of Atreus have for so long stirred the *thymos* in my breast, nor would he have taken the girl against my will in his stubbornness; but Zeus wished death to come to many of the Achaeans."

Along with the account of how he made his decision which at the time of the embassy Achilles gives to Ajax, this shows how a disastrous error is conceived as happening. *Ate,* sent by Zeus, takes away the *phrenes* of the person concerned; as a result his *thymos* is rendered uncontrollable, his heart swells with *cholos* and the knowledge of how to make a right decision which he possesses is rendered ineffective. The gods put a fierce *thymos* in his chest[94] but at the same time he himself puts it there.[95] Like Agamemnon, Achilles blames Zeus, but he does not deny his own responsibility.

The *Iliad* contains several other instances of the operation of *ate* which conform to the same pattern. Patroclus, we have seen, neglects the command of Achilles to return to camp once he had driven the Trojans from the ships, "because the purpose of Zeus is always stronger than that of men." Hector forgets that the guarantee of success given him by Zeus through Iris in Book XI [96] was to last only until nightfall and rejects the advice of Pulydamas to order a retreat to the city after Achilles has returned to battle. His wits and those of the other Trojans have been taken away by Athene;[97] later, when he is confronted with the infuriated Achilles, it is the fear that the Trojans will reproach him with this error that prevents him from trying to escape.[98] In one instance the god is not content with invisibly prompting the wrong decision, but appears in person to bear down the resistance of the human agent. This happens after the duel between Paris and Menelaus in Book III; Aphrodite has rescued Paris from certain death and carries him to Helen's chamber; then in the form of an old woman she summons Helen to go to bed with him.[99] Helen, as we know from her conversations with Priam and with Hector, is tormented with regret for her elopement, and now expresses horror at the suggestion; but the goddess, casting aside the pretence that she is not herself, with dire threats forces her into submission. Priam has tried to console Helen by telling her that it is not she, but the gods who are to blame, and in a sense this is the truth; but according to the rule the human agent must take the responsibility even for a god-prompted decision.[100] The human agent knows what is right, but the god overbears his will. In the other instances the god acts by working on the agent's passion, but in that of Helen a kind of allegorical picture is given of this process. If the part of the gods in these disastrous decisions was removed, the working of human passions that determine them, *eros, eris, cholos,* would still be manifest. That does not mean that the working of the gods is not real, or the religion not genuine; it is the great merit of those who have reasserted the importance of the irrational element in Greek thought to have insisted on this important truth. At the same time the divine motivation could be dispensed with and the human decision be the same. When the old classicism and in our time scholars like Nilsson called the divine machinery a mere *façon de parler,* they were not being quite as unintelligent as it has become the fashion to suppose. During the early stages of the epic tradition, the Homeric way of representing reflection and decision doubtless corresponded to men's cultural beliefs.[101] How far they still did so when the *Iliad* took its final form is a question that will be worth asking.

I cannot express more clearly the difference between my view of the place occupied by religion and morality in the *Iliad* and that taken by some recent critics than in terms of an expression borrowed by Dodds from modern anthropologists. In contradistinction to other cultures which are "guilt-cultures," he has called the culture described by Homer a "shame-culture." [102] A useful definition of these terms known to me is given by the anthropologist J. K. Campbell.[103] "Both guilt and shame," he writes, "are internal states of conscience, but whereas shame is concerned with a man's failure to approach some ideal pattern of conduct, the reference of guilt and personal sin is to the transgression of interdicted limits. Shame relates to failure, especially in comparison with the achievement of others. It has an external sanction in the social abandonment which in some degree always accompanies public shame. The sense of guilt, on the other hand, is the consequence of acts which defy the commandments of God, whether they concern the relations between man and God, or social responsibilities that follow from common membership in a group. An act may, of course, provoke both a sense of guilt and a sense of shame. Which term will be used depends on whether the act is more generally regarded under the aspect of transgression, or of failure to live up to an ideal pattern of behaviour." My only objection to this definition is that it restricts the use of the word "guilt" to a religious use. I should include among the acts which cause men to feel guilt not simply acts which defy the commandments of God, but acts which defy the commandments of a social group, in fact laws and general standards of behaviour.

Generally speaking, it is easy to tell whether a given culture must be considered in a general sense a guilt-culture or a shame-culture. Clearly the countries around the eastern Mediterranean which were formerly under Turkish rule and also those of China and Japan are shame-cultures, while those of the United States, England, and other countries where Protestantism is or has been strong are guilt-cultures.[104] But I know no example of a culture of the one type which does not contain elements of the other also, and I doubt whether it is possible to point to a specimen of either type which is totally without an admixture of the other. In Andalusia and in modern Greece, for instance, a shame-culture based on the concepts of pride and honour is found together with a strong belief in Christianity, a religion which especially in its Protestant but also in its Catholic form must make any culture which accepts it to a great extent a guilt-culture. These terms are relative, and can only be used as very general descriptions of the societies to which they are applied. Dodds of course recognises that this is so; but I wish he had not called the second chapter of his book "From Shame-Culture to Guilt-Culture," thereby obscuring the fact that in general Greek culture continued to be a shame-culture until well after the fifth century.[105]

An argument of a general nature, which the particular case of Homeric Greece serves to confirm, suggests that from the start a shame-culture must contain elements of guilt-culture. A culture which contains any form of social organisation must set some value on the essentially co-operative value of loyalty; as another anthropologist puts it, "Duty, in the first instance, is for those with whom we share honour." [106] It may be hard to name an equivalent of "duty" or "loyalty" in Homeric Greek, but if the word is lacking the thing is not. The dispute between Agamemnon and Achilles is over honour; but even in a shame-culture disputes of honour must be settled by authority, unless anarchy is to prevail. Had such a dispute arisen between two lesser persons, the king would have settled it in the light of the *themistes,* the principles of justice given to kings by Zeus. In this case, the king is a party to the dispute; therefore Achilles has to assert his rights by the withdrawal of his services. In doing so, he is justified; by depriving him of his prize, Agamemnon has neglected an obligation implicit in his whole relation to the partners in the expedition, that he will respect the *time* of his subordinates. Later when he refused atonement Achilles puts himself in the wrong; his swelling *thymos* prevents him from satisfying the demands of loyalty to his friends and the general principle that a man should not remain obdurate. Much of the tragic effect resides in the tension between the demands of individual honour and those of loyalty to the group.

Like men the gods also have their king, whose attributes are based on those of human rulers. He is, as earthly kings should be but often are not, able to dominate his subjects by the threat of force; he is able to settle disputes among them and impose his will. Being father of gods and men, he rules over men also. To men living in their own communities he gives justice through their kings; strangers, who fall outside these communities, are under his protection in his capacity of Xeinios. His concern to punish offenders against justice originates from the concern to punish offenders against his particular *time* that is felt by any god. He defends the established order (*dike*) by punishing mortals whose injustices disturb it, and at the same time by sternly repressing any attempt of men to rise above the humble place where they belong. If according to Achilles[107] Zeus gives some men good and evil mixed and others unmixed evil, that is a mark not of his injustice but rather of his justice. What is just for mortals is not necessarily what mortals want. In the *Iliad* the plan of Zeus is accomplished; the actions of gods and men all finally conduce to the fulfilment of his will.[108] An incidental consequence of that fulfilment is that, just as the Trojans will finally receive rough justice in return for their aggression against Menelaus, both Agamemnon and Achilles receive rough justice for their injustice to each other and the rest of the Achaeans perpetrated during their quarrel.[109] Zeus himself, in furthering his plan, has caused them to commit those injustices by means of *ate;* how can it be just that Zeus should punish them? Already in Homeric times that question caused much perplexity.

II

The *Odyssey:* Hesiod:
Early Lyrics

FEW PEOPLE doubt that the *Odyssey* is a poem in
which Zeus and Justice play an important, and indeed a pre-
ponderating part: and few doubt that its theology is in some
important ways different from that of the *Iliad.* Soon after the
opening of the poem,[1] Zeus in the assembly of the gods comments on the death of Aegisthus, the murderer of Agamemnon,
at the hands of his victim's son Orestes. Mortals, he complains,
blame the gods for sending them evil, but in truth they themselves through their wicked recklessness have to endure pains
beyond what is fated.[2] When Aegisthus was plotting to make
love to Agamemnon's wife and kill her husband, the gods even
sent their messenger Hermes to warn him of the inevitable
consequences, but Aegisthus rejected the warning and has now
paid the penalty. This speech of Zeus implies a belief radically
different from that found in the *Iliad.*[3] There the god puts evil
ideas, no less that good ideas, into men's minds; that is how
men's *moira,* the portion assigned them by the gods, comes to
be fulfilled. When the god wishes to destroy a man, he sends
Ate to take away his wits. But now Zeus denies that the gods put
evil ideas into the minds of men, and even claims that they
warn men against the evil ideas they themselves have thought
of.

"Placed where it is, at the very beginning of the poem," says Dodds, "the remark sounds . . . programmatic":[4] and in the *Odyssey* as a whole the programme which it announces is carried out. In the first half of the poem, the companions of Odysseus are warned by Tiresias[5] of what will happen if they slaughter the cattle of the Sun; in the second half, the suitors are warned first by the old man Halitherses[6] and later by the prophet Theoclymenus[7] of what will happen if they persist in their wooing of Penelope. Gods often put good or clever ideas into the minds of men; Athene, for example, is constantly inspiring Odysseus with such notions; but evil ideas the gods never inspire. It is true that the human characters sometimes blame the gods for their misfortunes, but the poet, unlike the poet of the *Iliad,* never in his own person blames the gods; when Helen blames Ate, sent by Aphrodite, for her elopement[8] or Odysseus blames Ate, sent by Zeus, for his having fallen asleep on the island of the Sun,[9] the reader is not obliged to accept their point of view. The survival of Odysseus and his triumph over the suitors are the reward of *arete.* He has indeed offended one powerful god, Poseidon, but not by an action which in the eyes of Zeus and Justice is a crime; he blinds his son Polyphemus in self-defence. Polyphemus has ignored the *themistes* and scorned the gods,[10] but Odysseus has been guilty of no worse offences than indiscretion in insisting on exploring the country of the Cyclopes and vanity in telling his defeated opponent his true name. In persecuting him, Poseidon is not punishing the guilty, but pursuing a private feud after the fashion of the Olympians. Odysseus enjoys the special protection of Athene, the closest of the gods to Zeus. This is because he fulfills the requirements of heroic virtue;[11] he has made regular sacrifices to the gods, he is as kind as a father to the people they have given him to rule, and with consistent good sense he has avoided overstepping the bounds which the gods set to human action. The conduct of the suitors, like that of Aegisthus, has been the opposite, and so they pay the penalty.[12]

As much as in the *Iliad,* Zeus is supreme among the gods;[13]

he sends men good or bad fortune,[14] and does so according to their deserts. Mortals are the feeblest of all creatures nurtured by the earth. They are totally dependent on the good or bad fortune sent them by the gods. While good fortune lasts they persist in thoughtless optimism; if bad fortune comes, their only resource lies in endurance,[15] and they must say to their hearts, as Odysseus so often does, "Endure now, you have endured worse than this in the past." Great stress is laid on Zeus' protection of strangers and suppliants. The gods visit the cities of men to observe their *hybris* and *eunomia;* Zeus Xeinios resents evil done to a stranger;[16] strangers and beggars are under Zeus' care;[17] even beggars have their own gods and Erinyes.[18] A suppliant is entitled to respect even from a god;[19] a stranger or a suppliant counts as a brother.[20] Polyphemus, we are told expressly, is punished for his disregard of an appeal made in the name of Zeus the protector of suppliants;[21] the suitors fail to respect strangers, suppliants or heralds, and so they perish.[22] Even fame is twice said to depend on men's behaviour,[23] though we are so often assured by modern writers that it depended only on their valour.

If this prevailing tone is really the late introduction of a "moralising" poet, he has done his work thoroughly; only in a few places, such as the mention of the poisoned arrows for which the young Odysseus asked Ilus the son of Mermerus or that of the skill of Autolycus in theft and with the oath,[24] do memories of an unregenerate past survive.

This unquestionable difference between the moral climate of the two Homeric poems has seemed to some to prove that the *Iliad* is the earlier, for they assume it to be due to an ethical development that must have taken place between the writing of the *Iliad* and that of the *Odyssey.*[25] But we cannot really be certain that the difference may not as well be due to a difference in outlook between two contemporary poets or schools of poetry, or even to a difference between the artistic purposes aimed at in the two epics.[26] We may here recall one difference between the poems which Reinhardt penetratingly observed

and characterised.[27] All characters and actions of the *Iliad* can
be regarded from more than one point of view; not even Henry
James is more sensible of the complexity of moral situations
than the author of this poem. Achilles and Hector, Helen and
Agamemnon are not easily to be classified as good or bad; the
issues between Greeks and Trojans, between Achilles and Agamemnon are not (despite the considerations regarding justice
mentioned in my first lecture) easily to be seen as conflicts between black and white. In the *Odyssey,* moral issues are infinitely simpler; not only during the adventures narrated by
Odysseus, with their marked element of folktale, but even in
Ithaca, where daily life is depicted with such great naturalism,
good and bad and right and wrong are separated almost as
clearly as in a Western film. True, one or two characters have
an intermediate status; there are the suitor Amphinomus, to
whom Odysseus gives good advice that is not taken, and Phe-
mius and Medon, who keep company with the suitors against
their will; but these exceptions hardly do more than heighten
the contrast between black and white. It seems most unsafe to
conclude that the comparative moral simplicity of the *Odyssey*
is due simply to ethical progress made by the Greek world in
the interval between the composition of the two poems. The
truth is that the *Odyssey* is not an epic poem of the same kind
as the *Iliad.* It is a poem linked with the true heroic epic
through the person of its hero and other characters, yet containing a strong element of folklore and distinguished by a
marked moralising strain, conducive to the triumph of the hero,
and a happy ending, from the tragic character of the other epic.
The difference in theology and morality between the two poems
reflects a difference in style and purpose, and is of no value in
fixing their temporal relation to each other.

The main theological difference between the epics lies in the
Odyssey's rejection of the belief that a god may suggest wicked
or foolish, as well as good or wise, actions to the minds of men.
But since in the *Iliad* the human agent must always be held
fully responsible for his action, even though a god has caused

him to perform it, the Odyssean modification of the doctrine exemplified in the *Iliad* is of strictly limited significance.[28] It is just the modification of the *Iliad*'s theology that we might expect to find in a poem whose aims and methods differ from those of the *Iliad* in the way in which those of the *Odyssey* differ. If in both epics the terms generally translated "good" refer primarily to skill or excellence, that does not mean that justice or righteousness has not considerable importance. Even in a Christian community, in which the primacy of the so-called co-operative virtues is officially acknowledged, those who are clever, strong or powerful tend to receive more commendation, except from the devout, than those whose excellence is purely moral.

As in the case of the *Odyssey*, so also in that of the Hesiodic epics, we must take care while studying the author's theology to keep in mind his special viewpoint and the purpose of his work. Hesiod was not himself a *basileus,* a member of the local aristocracy which he denotes by this Homeric term. He was a peasant farmer, dependent for justice on those whom Zeus had entrusted with the function of guarding the *themistes;* and when he found that justice was denied him, he naturally reproached the *basileis* with their failure to carry out their duties. He spoke with authority which he claimed was conferred upon him by the Muses; pointing out that they are Zeus' daughters, he argues that poets, no less than *basileis,* have special authority derived from Zeus.[29] Defeated in a lawsuit by Perses, who according to Hesiod has bribed the *basileis* to give an unjust judgment, he admonishes his brother with having violated the ordinances of Zeus himself. Zeus' justice, Hesiod says, demands that a man shall earn his living by honest work and not by trickery; and he goes on to justify his claim by describing from their very origins the relations between gods and men.[30]

In Jewish and in Christian mythology, men, or at least the elect people, are the children of the great god; in Greek religion Zeus may be called "father of gods and men," but that is because he is their ruler and according to some creation myths he is responsible for men's existence. He is their father in that he wields the power associated with the headship of a family; they are not his children in the sense that he regards them with a father's love.[31] In his myth of the successive ages, Hesiod represents Kronos, Zeus' father, as kindly towards the men of that golden race which existed while he ruled the universe; even the men of the inferior races which succeeded are regarded with partiality by the nephew of Kronos and cousin of Zeus, Prometheus. During the golden age men did not have to work, but were sustained by the earth without effort of their own, living exempt from pain and sickness. In the Prometheus myth, men at first lived without pain and hardship; then Prometheus, the special patron of men, angered Zeus by deceiving him and so enabling men to keep for themselves the best share of any beast which they sacrificed to the gods. To punish Prometheus, Zeus deprived men of fire; but Prometheus stole it back, hiding it in a hollow fennel-stalk. That led Zeus to create the first woman, through whose folly all kinds of plagues were let loose upon the earth; since then, Zeus has concealed from men the means of getting an easy living, so that they have had to work.[32]

Unlike Prometheus, Zeus has no special partiality for men. But Hesiod and other early Greek writers do not reproach Zeus for this; deeply pessimistic as, by Jewish or Christian standards, their view of the position of mankind must appear, their literature is not filled with railings against "whatever brute and blackguard made the world." [33] Unlike the author of those words, they had not been told in childhood that they had immortal souls and would eventually live for ever, and they would not have thought it reasonable to expect Zeus to have their interests at heart in preference to his own. Still, neither their awareness of this favor nor their knowledge that Zeus punished crime prevented ordinary men in early Greece from greeting Zeus with the same kind of affectionate familiarity as the other gods. "Rain, rain, dear Zeus," says the ancient Attic prayer.[34]

The various accounts of the creation of mankind given by the early Greeks harmonise with the comparatively humble view of the human situation and prospects which they held. In Hesiod's myth of the ages,[35] the first two races of men, the golden and the silver, are created by the gods, the former in the time of Kronos, the latter presumably later; the next two, the race of bronze and the heroes, are created by Zeus; nothing is said about the fifth, the race of iron, to which Hesiod and his contemporaries belong. The myth of the races cannot safely be taken as representative of Greek belief; it is a highly individual invention, made to demonstrate a theory, which found few echoes in later tradition. It has often been observed that among the five races the heroes are the odd race out, and the obvious explanation of this is that the heroes were too firmly established in ordinary belief to be omitted, so that Hesiod had to spoil the symmetry of his myth in order to include them.[36] The early Greek belief was that some men of the present time were descended from heroes, themselves descended from the gods through their unions with mortal women. The origins of the large nucleus of ordinary men and women were variously accounted for; Homer says nothing on the subject. The Hesiodic *Catalogues*[37] told the story of the great flood which wiped out one early race of men. After the flood, the earth is repopulated through Deucalion; according to the author of the *Catalogues* and other early writers, his father was Prometheus. Deucalion was the father of Hellen, the eponymous ancestor of the Hellenes; Hellen in turn was the father of Dorus, Aeolus and Xuthus, who represent the three principal divisions of the Hellenic race. Not all men after the flood were descended from Deucalion and his wife Pyrrha; Deucalion repopulated the earth by collecting stones, which Zeus turned into men, as in another legend Aeacus repopulated the earth with ants.[38] Later Prometheus himself was said to have created the first men from clay; this story seems not to occur before the fourth century.[39] All these legends cause most men to be created from inferior material, and in those stories in which some men have a divine ancestor, that ancestor is not Zeus but Prometheus. Belief in creation myths of this kind fits exactly with the prevailing attitude in early Greek poetry; they are in keeping with its modest assessment of the importance of mankind in the universe.

Zeus has no special partiality for men, but according to Hesiod he has given them the gift of justice, so that they do not live in a state of permanent war with one another, as beasts do. In a remarkable fragment of a lost play of Aeschylus, Justice herself explains the origin of her connection with Zeus.[40] When Zeus overthrew his father Kronos, he had Justice on his side, for his father had given him provocation; since then, Justice has sat beside his throne. The Aeschylean Justice is going only a little beyond what is related by Hesiod, for Hesiod tells how Ouranos was ousted from the throne of the universe by Kronos, Kronos in turn by Zeus, and also how Justice sits beside the throne of Zeus and tells him of the evil purposes of men. He causes the just to prosper and he punishes the unjust, sending thirty thousand immortal watchers to observe their actions and chastening those of whom his daughter Justice makes complaint. The unjust man's family after him will be punished for his actions, just as the just man's will flourish. Zeus' justice requires not only that men be just in their dealings with one another, but that they remember their subordinate station, and do not try to obtain a share in the privileges of the immortals. In the past, Zeus and the gods have destroyed four races of men, and in the future Zeus will destroy the present race of men also as a punishment for having offended against his laws. Zeus benefits men by forcing them to be just to one another, but at the same time his justice keeps them in their proper station.

The claim that Hesiod *introduced* the ideal of justice, though reiterated by many respected authorities,[41] must be rejected. Hesiod in the *Works and Days* applied to his own circumstances the doctrine of Zeus, justice and the responsibilities of the *basileis* which can be seen most clearly in the *Odyssey*, but which is already present in the *Iliad*; nor could Hesiod have appealed for justice as he does unless her authority had already been recognized. In the *Theogony* he set it in the context of the universal order guaranteed by Zeus, whose origins he now explained. In that poem Zeus after overcoming the last dangerous threat to his power by conquering Typhoeus marries Themis and becomes the father of Dike together with Eirene, Peace, and with Eunomia;[42] the notion of *eunomia* connotes both the possession of good laws and the disposition to obey them.[43] Mythological genealogy was for Hesiod a means of expressing his beliefs about the universe and the way in which Zeus governed it, and this family was no doubt his own invention. Still, by means of it he expressed an opinion which was also held by the authors of both the *Iliad* and the *Odyssey*.

This examination of the development of ethical concepts has so far thrown no light on the chronological relation to one another of the epics ascribed to Homer and Hesiod,[44] neither has it provided safe evidence for the development of ethics from one of these epics to another. But when we come to the transition from the age of epic to the age of lyric, from the eighth century to the seventh, shall we not come to very different conclusions?

Most of the best modern authorities discover a marked change in spiritual climate between the epic and the lyric age. Writing both some forty years ago, and from somewhat different points of view, Pfeiffer and Snell [45] both find the characteristic note of the age of lyric in the heightened sense of *amechanie,* of the helplessness of mortals in the face of the difficulties of life. At the outset of the archaic age Dodds is struck by the presence not of a different belief but of "a different emotional reaction to the old belief";[46] he finds "a deepened awareness of human insecurity and human helplessness (*amechania*), which has its religious correlate in the feeling of divine hostility." [47] Dodds recognises that even in the Homeric poems the view taken of man's position is not one of unmixed optimism. "Yet, for all that," he writes, "Homer's princes bestride their world boldly; they fear the gods only as they fear their human overlords; nor are they oppressed by the future even when, like Achilles, they know that it holds an approaching doom." [48]

Dodds allows that the actual religious belief at the beginning, at least, of the archaic age was not substantially different from that found in Homer. We have seen how in the *Odyssey* Zeus denies that the gods put evil ideas into men's minds, and that nowhere in the poem does the poet say they do. It has often been remarked that the theology of Solon, who wrote not long after 600 B.C., is virtually the same as that of the poet of the *Odyssey,* nor is the view of the relations between gods and men presented by most poets in the intervening period very different. Dodds finds that the main difference lies in the emotional attitude.

We must, I think, allow for certain factors in the situation which make that emotional attitude seem more different than it really is. In the Homeric poems, and more especially in the *Iliad,* the world of gods as well as the world of men lies open to the poet's vision. Although the ultimate purposes of Zeus are there, as everywhere in Greek poetry, inscrutable to men, the gods often mingle with the heroes and communicate their purposes directly, as well as through the medium of dreams and prophecies. The actions of the gods, although incalculable, are not therefore so mysterious as they would seem if the heroes lacked the special contact with the gods which they possess. Another factor that makes the emotional atmosphere of the lyric age seem different results from the basic difference between epic and lyric poetry. The very nature of lyric and elegiac poetry renders it natural for the poet to use it to express his personal feelings, and since he is human his feelings will often be determined by his perplexity in the face of the problems with which life confronts him. In a short poem meant for recital before a small audience and dealing with the events and emotions of the poet's life, it is not surprising if feelings of sadness or despair loom large, especially in a culture whose religion offers no easy consolation. We talk of the lyric age, but lyric poetry did not come into existence with Alcman and Archilochus. It must have been composed much earlier, nor can we safely assume that earlier lyrics, simple as they may have been, were written only for use in worship and never gave expression to personal emotions.[49]

Even in the surviving epics, where the main actors are heroes, less prone to give way to despair than the common run of humanity, desperation at the hard lot of the individual, of the community or of mankind in general is not uncommonly expressed. Pfeiffer in the article I lately quoted [50] has himself stressed certain affinities in this respect between the epic and the later poetry. In the last book of the *Iliad* Apollo blames Achilles for his excessive grief for the dead Patroclus; others, he says, have lost a loved one, but have ceased from lamentation, for "the gods have given man a *thymos* that can endure." [51] These words are in the mind of Archilochus when in the elegy written after some of his friends have been lost at sea he reminds Pericles that "against evils that cannot be cured the gods have given strong endurance." [52] We have already seen that the notion of endurance is a prominent motive of the *Odyssey,* where again and again in desperate circumstances Odysseus exhorts his *thymos* to endure. When Archilochus speaks to his *thymos* in the same fashion, he describes it as "thrown into turmoil by troubles that are hard to deal with." [53] He adjures himself to face his enemies in battle and to preserve moderation in victory and defeat alike; he does not surrender to despair, nor does he resist the troubles that beset him less bravely than one of Homer's heroes. When he reminds himself what kind of a pattern shapes the concerns of men, he is doing in a different way what Achilles in his words to Priam near the end of the *Iliad* has already done before him.

We are accustomed to being told that Archilochus "revolted against traditional values to a degree far transcending the particular issues of his time"; the explanation for this, some scholars think, lies in his illegitimate birth and in the various difficulties he had to face. The first verses we read that are not epic are said to transport us to a new world: Archilochus begins a line with the words "I am"—it is the poem in which he claims to be the servant of Ares and the possessor of the Muses' gift,[54] and we are told in words I apologise for not being able to put into English, "er stellt sein Ich frei heraus": we are also told that he addresses his *thymos* directly, as though that were new, and as though Archilochus were the first Greek to write a lyric poem. When he tells how in order to escape death in battle he threw away his shield,[55] we are told that he is rebelling against the Homeric code of honour. But those who tell us so seem to be confusing the Homeric code of honour with that of the Spartans typified by the mother who said "with your shield or on it"; do they imagine that the Homeric Odysseus, faced with the choice between abandoning his shield and being killed or captured, would have kept his shield? [56] Archilochus says that no one who is dead is given proper respect or fame, that men try to please not the dead but the living, and that the dead are always as badly off as possible.[57] We are told that he is revolting against the Homeric notion that a brave man must sacrifice all things, even life itself, to fame. The utter misery of the dead is hardly an unhomeric notion; when Odysseus, saluting Achilles in Hades, calls him the most fortunate of all men, Achilles replies that he would rather be a serf on earth than rule over the dead.[58] In any case, Archilochus is not saying that fame is an empty notion; he is saying, as the second sentence shows, that living men do not accord it when they should, since they are more eager to carry out the wishes of the living, who can reward them, than the wishes of the dead. Archilochus says he does not care for a general who is tall, takes long strides, is proud of his curly hair and shaves carefully; he prefers a short man with bandy legs who is steady on his feet and full of courage.[59] But the idea that a man's appearance is no guide to his performance in action is as old as the account of the Greek embassy to Troy before the start of the war that Antenor gives to Helen in the third book of the *Iliad*.[60] Odysseus, he says, was shorter than Menelaus and when he first rose to speak gave the impression of inexperience by his downcast gaze and his way of holding the sceptre fast without moving it. He seemed ill-tempered and unintelligent, but once he had begun to speak, the effect was very different. One of the few heroes whose good looks are stressed is Paris, who though not a coward is not one of the most effective fighters. The great Tydeus, according to his son Diomedes, was small of stature, but a fighter;[61] it is against the background of these passages that we must read Pindar's words when he describes his patron Melissus as being "contemptible in appearance, but formidable when he joined battle with the spear," and adds that Heracles was "small in body, but unbending in spirit."[62] When Archilochus stresses the supremacy of Zeus,[63] the helplessness of mortals to achieve anything without divine help,[64] the alternation of good and bad fortune and the unending mutability of human fortunes,[65] he is echoing the belief found in Homer, and the words in which he adjures himself to remain courageous in the face of difficulties resemble those used in similar situations by Odysseus. Faced with injustice, the fox in his fable appeals to Zeus;[66] that fox stands for Archilochus himself. His violence against his enemies is no evidence for his lack of self-control by the standards of the seventh century, whatever Pindar may have felt about it in the fifth.[67] Hating one's enemies was, according to the ethics of the time, a merit, and even the virtuous Solon two generations later prayed that he might taste sweet in the mouths of his friends and bitter in those of his adversaries.[68] Even had Archilochus been born in wedlock, I doubt whether his treatment of his enemies would have been more courteous. Page has lately demonstrated that the style and language of Archilochus' elegiac verses is closely modelled upon Homer;[69] much the same is true of his opinions regarding the gods and their government of the universe, and also of his attitude regarding the human condition. When he calls himself the servant of Enyalios and one that possesses the gift of the Muses,[70] he is seeing himself in Homeric terms; when he adjures himself to stand fast against his enemies, he does so in words that deliberately recall the words of Odysseus. Let no one suggest that I am denying the originality and individuality of the great poet Archilochus; I wish simply to point out that they are asserted not only, for the most part, in Homer's language but also within the framework of Homer's beliefs and attitudes. They will be best appreciated not by means of anxious attempts to demonstrate that Archilochus made a distinctive contribution to the development of theology, ethics or psychology but by the study, so far as the remains permit it, of his poetic aims and methods.

Another author often quoted as exemplifying the new *amechanie,* the desperation, supposed to be characteristic of the lyric age is Sappho. Sappho is above all else a poet of love, and so often describes the despair of unsatisfied longing for the beloved being. When she calls Love "a bitter-sweet irresistible creature," [71] the use of *amachanon* is pounced on by the chroniclers of early Greek ethical development as proof that she suffered from the same psychic complaint as other poets of her time. Like other early poets, Sappho knows that power and immortality belong only to the gods, and that men can enjoy moments of happiness only when the gods grant them. Like other early poets, she entreats the gods to grant her wishes, knowing that they may do so, but that she cannot count on their compliance. Naturally the gods she most often prays to are Eros and Aphrodite: sometimes they grant her prayer; if they refuse, like Archilochus she must endure.[72] Like the other poets she laments the coming of old age,[73] but that is hardly a peculiarity of the age she lived in. She is a woman and her spiritual world is narrow; but so far as it extends, it coincides with a part of the spiritual world described by Homer. Sappho in one great poem shows herself aware that Homer presents one female character, Helen, whose devotion to love is equal to her own.[74]

Alcaeus yields just as little evidence to the seeker after ethical development. Like all the early poets, he stresses the power of Zeus, who can dispose all things as he will and without whom not even a hair can be moved.[75] He believes that Zeus punishes the wicked, as the recently published Cologne fragment clearly shows.[76] It is better for a community, he says, to stone a member who has provoked divine punishment than to risk sharing his fate, and following a post-Homeric epic he illustrates it from the case of the Greeks who took Troy, who might have escaped the disastrous storm that overtook them while returning had they punished Ajax the Locrian for his rape of Cassandra in the temple of Athene. The civil war on Lesbos, he says in another poem, has been caused by one of the Olympians, who has led the *demos* to Ate and given longed-for glory to Pittacus; we must remark that Alcaeus here adopts an Iliadic rather than an Odyssean or Hesiodic view of divine motivation. This return to an earlier belief should be irritating to those who insist on linear development, but they can of course blame it on this poet's well-known reactionary tendencies. Where Archilochus would have exhorted his companions to practise endurance, we are told, Alcaeus merely urges his to drink deeply and forget their cares. We happen to have evidence—and if we had not, we could easily have surmised it—that Archilochus did not despise the efficacy of wine as a promoter of endurance; neither did Alcaeus, but the soothing power of wine does not exhaust the social and symbolic significance of the symposium in early aristocratic societies, as is now generally recognised.[77] When the poet warns his companions of a coming struggle, urges them to remember earlier trials and exhorts each of them to win glory and not disgrace his ancestors, he like Archilochus is deliberately viewing the contemporary situation in a Homeric light. He and his friends, like their ancestors, are good,[78] Pittacus and other enemies, like their ancestors, are bad;[79] that is to say, his friends are defending *Dike* as the guarantor of a particular social order. The *Dike* that has this function is not therefore devoid of moral significance; Alcaeus like other noblemen believes that *noblesse oblige,* and for him "goodness" connotes moral as well as social attributes.

The aspect of human resourcelessness that vexes Mimnermus, at least in the surviving fragments, is the impermanence of youth and love, which poets must have deplored even before Homer. Like Semonides of Amorgos,[80] he laments their passing in language full of Homeric echoes;[81] the comparison of the generations of men to leaves comes from the speech of Glaucus to Diomedes in the sixth book of the *Iliad*,[82] the fates of death which stand always beside us from the speech of Sarpedon to Glaucus in the twelfth.[83] Zeus, Mimnermus says, gives all men much evil,[84] just as Achilles in the last book of the *Iliad* says that Zeus gives to men two parts evil to one part good. Like Archilochus before him and Theognis after him, he shows contempt for public opinion, a characteristically aristocratic sentiment[85] customarily glossed over by those who thumb through the poetry of this period for evidence of the increased importance of the *polis*. His hedonism, like that of Alcaeus, is perfectly compatible with the ability to strike a martial note in most impressive fashion.[86]

Like Mimnermus, Semonides of Amorgos[87] echoes the language in which Homer speaks of the ephemerality of man in order to urge his friends to enjoy life while it lasts. What prevents them from doing so, he says, is hope, which causes them to plan many projects which the certainty of old age and death at the finish renders vain. The same doctrine is stated more explicitly and at greater length in the first and longest of the iambic fragments.[88] Zeus determines all things and men have no intelligence, yet each man is confident that he is on the point of attaining riches or success, and so persists in vain endeavour until old age or death comes upon him.

Hope plays just the same part in the account of human life given by Solon in the great poem that begins in Hesiodic fashion with an invocation of the Muses which is designed to establish the poet's claim to speak with authority as the servant of the daughters of Zeus.[89] Men delude themselves about the nature of their gifts and capacities and devote themselves to favourite plans in the expectation that effort will command success, forgetting that mortals receive good or bad according to their god-given portion and that what the gods send cannot be avoided.[90] The purpose of the gods is inscrutable,[91] Solon says elsewhere, and no man is altogether happy or exempt from toil.[92]

Good or bad fortune from Zeus, Solon believes, depends on innocence or guilt; he strongly insists that the guilty man is always punished, either in his person or through his descendants after him. We have seen that that belief was not new in Solon's time. Unlike Alcaeus, Solon takes an Odyssean and not an Iliadic view of divine motivation;[93] he denies that the gods put evil thoughts into men's minds, and puts the responsibility for action fairly and squarely on the human agent. He himself, like all men, wishes to help his friends and harm his enemies, but he has no wish for prosperity gained by injustice, for it is bound to bring misfortune. *Arete* is permanent, wealth is not, and no man needs more than he can use. For Solon, *Arete* obviously has a moral element. What is new and important is the way in which this ancient doctrine is applied to the current political situation. Men must not blame the gods for their misfortunes; Zeus and Athene are protecting Athens, but danger comes from the greed of the citizens, especially those who possess most, to gain yet more.[94]

There is no point in trying to distinguish a Hesiodic Dike, who acts only through human judgments and through external visitations of the gods, like plagues and famines, and a Solonian Dike, immanent in the working of the universe. We have seen that even in the *Iliad* Zeus' justice may act through the judgments of kings who are his agents, but may be made manifest in the actual working of events. To early Greek thinkers for whom the gods were manifest in the natural working of the universe, such a distinction would not have been important. Having in mind Hesiod's account of how Power and Violence, as well as Dike, stand by the throne of Zeus, Solon claims that in his legislation he has harmonised justice with these divinities.[95] Remembering, again, how in Hesiod Dike is the sister of Eunomia, Solon declares that his own *thymos* tells him to teach the Athenians how much good results from Eunomia and how much ill from Dysnomia; the promptings of his thymos have the authority given to him by the Muses.[96] We now recognise that in the view of the ancients a poet's originality was not diminished by his use of old material, but rather displayed in his ingenious adaptation of that material to his own purposes; what is true of poetic technique is also true of thought. It is no disparagement of the achievement of the great statesman and political thinker to point out that the doctrines he puts forward come to him from Hesiod and from Homer.

Another poet whose poetry relates closely to the life of the *polis* is Tyrtaeus, but he is not connected with it in the way some scholars have supposed. According to him, it has been maintained, "there is only one standard of true *arete*—the state. Whatever helps the state is good, whatever injures it is bad." [97] In fact no such doctrine is stated either in the famous elegy about *arete*[98] or elsewhere in the fragments of Tyrtaeus. The view that the supreme kind of *arete* is martial valour, which is upheld at the beginning of fr. 9, would hardly have surprised the poet of the *Iliad,* nor would the poet who wrote of Hector have been surprised at hearing that martial valour was a good in which the *polis* and the whole *demos* had a share. Valour is praised in this poem not only because the community to which the writer belongs has to be made to realise that it must fight or starve, but because valour leads to honour. The man who dies in battle after fighting bravely is mourned for by young and old alike; his tomb is pointed out and his descendants enjoy distinction; his name is not allowed to perish.[99] If a man is driven from his city and his rich fields, he is reduced to beggary,[100] but the worst thing about this beggary is the disgrace. Tyrtaeus wrote, it is true, to exhort the Spartans to fight bravely for their community, but that community was ruled by aristocratic principles, and his poetry appeals above all to the sense of honour of its individual members. Not only his language but his ideas are strongly reminiscent of the *Iliad*; his tone closely resembles that of the Ionian elegist, Callinus of Ephesus. When Jaeger claims that Tyrtaeus was trying to substitute a city-state morality for an aristocratic morality in Sparta,[101] he has failed to notice that in Sparta the two kinds of morality were not distinct.

In Sparta the community was forced by military necessity to remain united under aristocratic leadership, but in other places the old aristocracy was challenged by tyranny, often promoting class war for its own purposes. How much of the Theognidean corpus is by Theognis will never be determined, but for the present purpose the question is not important, since the moral attitudes shown in the poems of the collection are more or less consistent. Its moral tone is very like that of other Greek poetry of the time. The gods are prayed to, piety is enjoined, parents and strangers are to be respected,[102] friends should be helped and enemies damaged,[103] falsehood and insincerity are strongly disapproved of.[104] Strong stress is laid on the mutability of fortune;[105] men are *amechanoi*,[106] and all power rests with the gods, who send *ate* or profit to men at their pleasure.[107] They punish crime, sometimes early but at others late;[108] they can make evil seem good to those they have decided to destroy.[109] One couplet says that mortals must not contend with immortals nor plead a cause against them,[110] but in two remarkable passages the injunction is disregarded. In the first of these,[111] Zeus is reproached with allowing the wicked to flourish while good men suffer poverty, the mother of *amechanie;* in the second,[112] the poet complains of the god's injustice in visiting the sins of the guilty fathers upon the heads of their innocent children. It is significant that this was probably written just when the belief that men were punished in the next life for the sins of this was beginning to spread.

As for Alcaeus, so also for Theognis; his own friends and associates are good, his enemies bad. Perhaps the most striking instance of the use of *agathos* in a non-ethical sense occurs in a passage in which Theognis laments that men who till lately lived outside the city and wore goatskins are now good and men who until lately were good are now bad.[113] Here the poet boldly uses the word good to mean "belonging to the prevailing group," which has now come to consist of those who until lately were termed bad. This is not his usual usage, for he generally reserves the title good for his own party; but until the recent revolution that party had always retained power, so that though good usually means "belonging to the party of the nobles," it can also be used abnormally to mean "belonging to the party in power."[114]

However, a close examination of the poems shows that the words meaning "good" usually connote certain moral qualities apart from or in addition to power, social status and martial prowess. In particular, the *agathos* must possess loyalty,[115] a virtue to whose importance in aristocratic societies I drew attention in connection with the *Iliad,* but whose necessity to such societies when they are threatened needs no explanation. The *kakos* or *deilos* does not know the principles, the *gnomai,* of good and evil;[116] he cannot be made *esthlos* by taking good advice,[117] and so remains shifty and untrustworthy.[118] He is particularly prone to *hybris*.[119] Unlike the *esthlos* he lacks self-control and will be unable to endure pain or hardship.[120] Endurance, almost as much as loyalty, is a leading theme of these poems, as it is of the *Odyssey* and, it appears, of the poems of Archilochus.[121] When the poet wishes for no other kind of *arete* but *eudaimonia,*[122] he is offering a variant of the commonplace that success and not skill is what counts, so that *arete* here is probably not ethical. But far more often we find him preferring, as Solon does, poverty with *arete* to wealth with *kakia,*[123] although for him poverty is one of the worse of evils.[124] The famous couplet which asserts that all *arete* is contained in justice comes immediately after one which expresses a preference for honest poverty over ill-gotten wealth.[125] Adkins[126] finds the statement about justice "sudden" and "amazing"; but if it is remembered that the writer, like Simonides,[127] would probably have denied full *arete* to the man who was *apalamnos,* unable to defend his interests, and also that he believed that the unjust were punished by the gods, I do not find it specially surprising. It is by no means uncommon for people to identify moral goodness with membership of a particular social group, though in our own time the most conspicuous instances are furnished not by aristocratic societies but by believers in the cult of the common man or the working class. It is hardly fair to assume that because Theognis often makes this identification his conception of goodness must have lacked a moral element, and in fact we have seen that it is not so. Further, he did not consistently deny the moral qualities implied by goodness to his enemies; in one place he declares that one has a duty to praise even an enemy if he is good,[128] a sentiment that we find uttered, and with great emphasis, by another firm believer in aristocracy, Pindar.[129]

Simonides in his few extant fragments presents the traditional Greek world picture with great clarity. Men are at best feeble creatures;[130] no man is exempt from toil;[131] the gods can easily deceive them;[132] the gods alone can know the future;[133] all men die at last.[134] *Arete* comes only with toil, and it can be given only by a god;[135] the two statements are not inconsistent, for in Greek religion both effort and divine favour are needed for success.[136] Goodness as a general characteristic can be predicated only of a god, never of a man, who may be overcome by a turn of events which leaves him helpless. When a man fares well, he is good; when he fares ill, he is bad; and as we know from Homer and many later authors, no man's fortune is entirely good. In the celebrated poem written for the Scopadae,[137] does the word "good" denote a co-operative or a competitive excellence? Direct indications in the text are lacking, but it seems to me rash to insist that the word implies only a competitive kind of goodness. At this period, as the evidence from Theognis indicates, the word is used vaguely to denote either kind of excellence or, more often, both together. When Simonides says that the good man will do, if he can help it, nothing ugly,[138] his conception of goodness is at least partly a co-operative goodness. Simonides says he will be content with a man who is not *kakos,* nor excessively incompetent (*apalamnos*), and who knows justice that benefits the city, a healthy man.[139] The mention of justice seems to me to indicate that the goodness he has in mind is more than a mere skill. The case for this view derives some support from a fragment published in 1959 and conjecturally assigned to Simonides.[140] Few can possess *arete*, says the poet,[141] for it is not easy to be good; one is constrained against one's will by the irresistible desire for gain, or by the mighty urge of Aphrodite, or by quarrels that spring up rapidly. Greed, passion or hatred surely do not prevent men from being skilful, but rather from being good in the moral sense.

Few authors seem at first sight to provide more material to those who maintain the inadequacy of the early concept of moral goodness than Pindar. "The gods watch the doings of men and take their own part in them," writes the most sympathetic of his modern interpreters, "but they are not for Pindar guardians of morality except in certain spheres which belong to them and where any infringement of their rights is a personal affront." [142] Our examination of the *Iliad* has shown that it is from this very notion that a god is affronted by any infringement of his rights within a particular sphere that the concept of Zeus as the champion of justice first developed. The same truth may be illustrated from the works of Pindar. When Coronis becomes the victim of Ate and incurs the vengeance of Apollo,[143] the god is punishing an offence against him within his own particular sphere; the same could be said of Zeus' punishment of Tantalus for giving nectar and ambrosia, the food of the gods, to his human friends.[144] However, Zeus punishes Ixion partly for his attempt to seduce Hera, but partly for having been the first to shed the blood of a relation; in his case, he is punishing ingratitude, and so acting as the champion of justice.[145] Further, we must note how often and how emphatically the gods, and Zeus and Apollo in particular, are identified with order, peace and harmony, in contrast with the forces of brute strength and violence. In the first Pythian Ode violence is typified by the monster Typhos, who lies beneath Mount Etna breathing fire, the deadly enemy of Zeus who has subdued him; later in the poem it is implied that Hieron owes his triumph to Zeus and that his defeated enemies, the Carthaginians and Etruscans, resemble Zeus' enemies.[146] So too in the eighth Pythian ode Hesychia, Quiet, daughter of Justice, is contrasted with the brutal force of Porphyrion and the other giants conquered by Zeus and the gods. Dike herself, as in Hesiod, is the daughter of Zeus by his early marriage with Themis, and the sister of Eunomia and of Eirene.[147] Of course the word *dika* can be used by Pindar in a relative sense, as when he says "each approves his own *dika*"[148] or that "a strong man puts an end to the former *dika*";[149] and of course Dike together with her sisters may be said to stand for the maintenance of the particular type of social order which Pindar himself approves. That is the order which entrusts power to ancient monarchies and to aristocracies; the rule of tyrants and of "the noisy crowd"[150] seems to be identified with the power of violence and disorder. But if Pindar's view of Justice is coloured by his own political sympathies, that does not mean that it is cynical, or that it lacks a moral element. Justice is contrasted by him, as by Simonides, with *kerdos*, the pursuit of gain;[151] the just man hates *hybris*;[152] time in the last resort protects the righteous.[153] Justice is mentioned in connection with the rights of strangers, as she has been in poetry since Homer.[154] As in Theognis, we find the importance of loyalty strongly stressed;[155] and though *areta* usually refers to some kind of skill or excellence, it is used also of the generosity of Croesus to the god of Delphi, of the self-sacrifice of Antilochus, of the hospitality of the Aeginetans and of the exertion for the common weal that Pindar holds to be the distinguishing feature of aristocracy.[156] Justice in Pindar does not simply mean justice in one's dealings with other men. When Bellerophontes tries to fly up to heaven on Pegasus, his action is contrary to justice. It is an infringement of the order maintained by Zeus within the universe, a failure to heed the warning so constantly repeated that mortals must remember that they are mortal.[157] As the gods maintain justice in the universe, so do kings like the mythical Rhadamanthys[158] or Eumolpus[159] or the living Hieron, Theron or Arcesilas maintain justice in the communities they govern; in other communities, like Thessaly or Pindar's own city, Thebes, power is vested in the nobles, whom Hesiod would have called *basileis*. That corresponds closely with the notion of justice that we found in Homer.

A recent papyrus discovery has increased our knowledge of the poem quoted by Callicles in Plato's *Gorgias* which opened with the words "Law is king over all, mortals and immortals; he governs all things, making just what is most violent with arm supreme." [160] From the initial mention of the triumph of Heracles over the three-bodied monster Geryones, Pindar goes on to narrate his expedition against Diomedes, the savage Thracian king who fed his mares on human flesh. Diomedes resisted him, Pindar says, "not in pride but in valour; for it is better to die in defence of possessions that are being seized from one than to be a coward." In his battles against Geryones and Diomedes, Heracles was according to the normal code of justice the aggressor; yet his actions were made just, says Pindar, by the power of Law. What is meant by Law in this connection? Geryones and Diomedes have placed themselves by their enormities beyond the pale, and every man's hand is against them; the obvious parallel is furnished by the Cyclopes in the *Odyssey* who have no Dike and no *themistes,* but live by violence, not caring for the disapproval of the gods. Their law is the law Zeus established, according to Hesiod, for fish, beasts and birds, that they should prey upon each other;[161] the law of Justice, which Zeus has given to men, does not apply to them.

For Pindar the gods, and Zeus above all, are the only source of power;[162] mortals can have no success without their favour. This does not mean that mortals who enjoy that favour can leave all to heaven and relax their efforts; only if they try their hardest will the divine favour be vouchsafed. Men and gods come ultimately from the same origin,[163] but the difference that separates them is infinite; gods are powerful and immortal, men feeble and ephemeral. Excellence in all things, in battle, in athletics and in the writing of poetry, comes only to those fitted for it by their nature, the special aptitude that descends to those sprung from divine ancestors; those who lack this may try hard to learn it, but will never attain success. Upon the privileged few, in whose veins a particle of their own blood flows, the gods may for a brief moment cause the divine radiance to shine.

The archaic age was in many respects a period of rapid change; but the preceding summary has shown that certain elements in religious and moral thinking remained constant to a degree which has not always been appreciated by scholars on the watch for new developments. The seventh century was the period in which the Delphic Oracle acquired its predominant position, and the outlook that is expressed in its utterances then and later is in close accord with that common to the early poets. Zeus and the gods are all-powerful, and human life is not worth much. Solon in Herodotus tells Croesus the story of Cleobis and Biton, whose mother prayed Apollo to reward them for their piety towards her with the highest gift that lay in his power.[164] Their reward was the same which the god gave to Trophonius and Agamedes, the builders of his first temple[165]—a painless and immediate death. That the best fortune for mortals is not to have been born, and the next best is to die as soon as possible is a common thought in early Greece; we find it in Theognis, in Pindar, and again in Sophocles.[166] The base of the statues of Cleobis and Biton has been found at Delphi, and the inscription on the base dates from the end of the seventh century, so that by that date their story must have been well known.[167] The insignificance of human life was indicated by the most famous of the three sayings inscribed on the temple rebuilt by the Alcmaeonids; "know thyself" means "remember that you are a human being." Delphi affirmed the justice of the gods. The best illustration is the story of Glaucus, which in Herodotus is told by the Spartan king Leotychidas in 490; since the person concerned is named, the story may well be true, and in any case it is indicative of the Delphic attitude.[168] When the sons of a man who had deposited money with the Spartan Glaucus asked for it back, Glaucus asked the god whether he might safely deny having received it; the Pythia replied with a warning of the consequences of breaking an oath, and by the time of the narrator the family of Glaucus had become extinct. The learned historians of the Delphic oracle find the oracle to Glaucus somewhat in contrast with the "unhelpful pessimism" expressed in the stories of Cleobis and Biton and of Trophonius and Agamedes.[169] But there is no reason why a belief in divine justice should not accompany a pessimistic view of human life, and we have seen that the combination of the two was in fact characteristic of the thinking of the archaic age.

Another of the sayings upon the temple—"nothing in excess" —illustrates the kind of mental attitude which this view of life tended to inculcate. Since human life is fragile and the gods all-powerful, it is all important to refrain from doing anything to provoke them. Prosperity itself is dangerous, for it may tempt one to actions that may offend the gods; excessive wealth and power are a danger to their possessors. Archilochus' carpenter does not envy the wealth of Gyges;[170] Solon covets no more wealth than suffices for his comfort;[171] and archaic literature is full of stories that exalt the moderation of wise men like Solon above the wealth of kings like Croesus. In Theognis the term *sophron,* rare in Homer and absent from early lyric, acquires importance;[172] its basic meaning is not "prudence" or "moderation" but "safe thinking," the kind of thinking that protects one from *hybris.* When one bears in mind the ineradicable tendency of the Greeks, once they have tasted wealth or success, to become intoxicated by it, the practical value of this moral concept becomes obvious.

Dodds argues that the archaic age was notable for its growing insistence on the importance of ritual purification, which was met by a large class of professional *kathartai.* "There is no trace in Homer," says Dodds, "of the belief that pollution was either infectious or hereditary";[173] and though the Homeric poems contain isolated references to cathartic practices, these are far less prominent there than they become during the Archaic Age. With the increased importance of pollution, Dodds associates that of the notion of divine envy, the primitive belief that human prosperity in itself can provoke the gods into destroying or harming its possessors. Such a belief, he says, is absent from the *Iliad* and comparatively rare in the *Odyssey,* but in the Late Archaic and Early Classical Ages he finds that it has become "an

oppressive menace, a souce—or expression—of religious anxiety." [174] A whole world seems to separate the archaic world, and
even the world of the early fifth century, from the world of
Homer. Since Rohde in his great book *Psyche* posed the problem, scholars have made one guess after another at the underly-
ing causes of that difference. Till something has been said about
this classic problem of the apparently radical cultural change in
this respect which separates the archaic age from that which
preceded it, any discussion of the religious and ethical history
of the period must remain incomplete.

III

Pollution and Purification: Herodotus

AT THE point of transition between what he considers to be the shame-culture described by Homer and the guilt-culture that came into being between the Archaic and Early Classical Ages, Dodds is struck by "the deepened awareness of human insecurity and human helplessness (*amechania*) which has its religious correlate in the feeling of divine hostility—not in the sense that Deity is thought of as evil, but in the sense that an overmastering Power and Wisdom forever hold man down, keeping him from rising above his station." [1] If the conclusions of my first chapter are correct, divine hostility in the sense in which Dodds here defines it is present even in the *Iliad*. From the beginning man has had only a humble place in the order of the universe, and if he claims more than the gods have allotted him, then divine justice requires that he be chastised. The gods do not punish men so long as men keep within their proper sphere. A man who commits an injustice against another man offends Zeus in his capacity as the protector of justice, so that if the victim of such an act appeals to Zeus, he will not go without redress. In the end, however late, Zeus will punish the offender, so that the victim is not *amechanos* in the sense in which

Dodds here uses the word. Whether "divine hostility" is an accurate rendering of the expression "divine *phthonos*" may be debated, at least when the meaning of the expression is explained as Dodds explains it in this place.

On the next page of his book Dodds seems to interpret the phrase "divine *phthonos*" somewhat differently, for he equates it with the notion that too much success incurs a supernatural danger, especially if one brags about it, a notion which as he says "appears in many different cultures and has deep roots in human nature." Divine *phthonos* in this sense, according to Dodds, is ignored by the *Iliad* and is not often touched on in the *Odyssey,* but in the Late Archaic and Early Classical Ages it "becomes an oppressive menace, a source—or expression—of religious anxiety." "Such it is," he continues, "in Solon, in Aeschylus, above all in Herodotus." Since the increasing prevalence of the notion of divine *phthonos* plays an important part in the transition from a shame-culture to a guilt-culture alleged to have occurred, the evidence bearing on the matter must be scrutinised.

Does the "uninhibited boasting"[2] in which the heroes of the *Iliad* indulge indicate, as Dodds believes, that the concept of divine hostility is not found in that poem? The heroes boast of their prowess, not of their prosperity; if a character boasts, as Niobe is said by Achilles to have boasted,[3] of being superior in any respect to one of the gods, that boast is fatal. If divine *phthonos* is taken to mean the unprovoked punishment of mortals by gods who are jealous of their wealth or happiness, then it is not found in the *Iliad;* but if it means the hostility of the gods to men who try to rise above the human sphere, it is. Dodds finds a clear instance of this in the *Odyssey* in the words of Calypso when she reproaches the gods for discouraging the unions of goddesses with mortals.[4] The gods might retort that they act not from common jealousy, but because such unions violate the order of the universe; this case is typical of many in which what the victims see as common jealousy appears differently to the gods who enforce the universal law.

When Menelaus says that a god has grudged him the pleasure of spending his declining years in the company of his friend Odysseus,[5] or when Penelope tells Odysseus that the gods have grudged that they should reach old age together,[6] the poet does not necessarily assign the god's motive to petty spite; when Poseidon grudges the Phaeacians the power to carry any man across the sea,[7] he is checking what he regards as an infringement of his own prerogative. In both epics I find many instances of divine *phthonos* in the sense of a divine checking of human encroachments beyond the human sphere, but none which can be explained simply in terms of the kind of primitive superstition which causes people to "touch wood." [8]

In Hesiod and in most of the poets discussed during my second chapter the position seems to be the same. Solon is said by Dodds to show a belief in divine *phthonos;*[9] can he be said to equate it with divine envy? His most famous elegy[10] starts with a prayer to the Muses for prosperity and fame, but only if they can be earned without injustice. If they are gained otherwise, he explains, they lead inevitably to disaster, for Zeus in the end inevitably punishes crime. Men delight in vain hopes, for each behaves as though skill and pertinacity in the exercise of his particular skill will automatically command success. But without good fortune given by the gods, even the most skilful mortal will not prosper; Fate gives evil and good to men, and what the gods give cannot be avoided. This whole argument is designed to show the folly of those rich men whose greed for more can never be satisfied, a favourite theme of Solon and one whose relevance to the political situation which he had to deal with is easily perceived.

When Solon says that no mortal effort can command success, but that success or failure depend upon the gods, he is not saying that the gods give good or evil indiscriminately. Indeed, he makes it clear that he is not of that opinion, for he say explicitly that Zeus punishes the guilty. That is in accord with his assertion elsewhere in his works that Zeus and Athene are protecting Athens,[11] but that the danger to her comes through the greed of her own citizens. So this poem yields no evidence that Solon believed that the gods are jealous of human success out of mere envy; like Aeschylus, he believed that the gods punish *hybris* or injustice.

The author in whose work "above all," according to Dodds, "the *phthonos* idea becomes an oppressive menace," [12] the author who has seemed to many to believe that the gods may destroy mortals simply for being rich or happy, is Herodotus. It is easy to assemble from his work a number of passages which if considered together and in isolation from their contexts seem to establish beyond question his belief in the malice of the higher powers. "In the fate which overtook great kings and generals—a Candaules or a Miltiades," writes Dodds,[13] "Herodotus sees neither external accident nor the consequence of character, but "what had to be"—Candaules was destined to come to a bad end."

However much or little Herodotus was affected by sophistic influence, he is usually thought to belong to the spiritual world of the Archaic Age.[14] In an early work, much influenced by nineteenth-century rationalism, Wilamowitz[15] found that he "had neither political understanding, historical sense nor a firm and clear world outlook, but wavered between rationalism and superstition, while Ionian science remained a closed book to him"; in his view "Herodotus as a man hardly deserved the fame his work has won him, which belongs rather to the genre in general." Writing just before the First World War, Jacoby[16] found Herodotus hopelessly handicapped by the religious outlook which he had inherited, and repeatedly precluded by his ethical and religious beliefs from making a correct assessment of historical motives and connections. But this attitude is no longer fashionable; for nearly forty years Herodotus has enjoyed far greater respect than he received from these two eminent authorities or from most of their contemporaries.[17] This is not simply because recent research has done much to confirm the accuracy of his facts, the precision of his chronology,[18] his freedom from prejudice;[19] it is also because Herodotus was not merely a great collector of facts but a great historian, one who saw history not simply as a mass of events and genealogies, but as a process whose meaning he made a sustained attempt to understand. He interpreted history in terms of the outlook upon human life common to educated persons of his place and time. His work is pervaded by all the characteristic features of the archaic Greek outlook; notably a conviction of the all-powerfulness of the gods and the insignificance of man, and a belief that the gods maintain the universal order of justice by chastising not only mortals who offend against each other but also mortals who infringe by word or action their own peculiar prerogatives.

The opening sentence of his work promises to explain the causes which have led Greeks and barbarians to make war upon one another; the word αἰτίη here is not easily rendered, but recent investigations[20] have shown that it carries a suggestion of guilt. First Herodotus gives a mythological motivation of the wars between the two sides by means of the abductions of four heroines; then he breaks off with the remark that he is uncertain of the truth of these early stories, but will now describe the man who to his knowledge was the first to begin unjust actions against the Greeks, Croesus the son of Alyattes.[21] If Herodotus doubts the truth of the ancient myths, why does he trouble to relate them? They supply him with a way of stating at the beginning of his work the principle of reciprocal justice which pervades the whole. This he must state with emphasis at the very start, as he must insist upon that notion of the mutability of human fortune which is fundamental to the outlook both of the early epic and of the early lyric poets. Further, by citing the stories told by the ancient *logioi* only to dismiss them and come straight to the first historical figure who occupies a key position in his narrative, Herodotus is able both to indicate the infinite length and complication of the causal chains formed by successive aggressions and revenges, and to draw the distinction between the remote past dealt with by the poets and the historical period which was to be his own

subject in a manner less sweeping but no less firm than that
adopted by his predecessor Hecataeus.

On Herodotus' own showing Croesus was not really the first
to commit aggression against the Greeks, for all the kings of
the Mermnad dynasty had done this before him; but the pattern of the history required that the narrative proper should
start with this great figure, whose career was so perfectly designed to illustrate the historian's own view of human life.
Some scholars speak of the so-called "Persian line," the narrative of Persian history, as the central thread of the fabric of the
work. But it makes better sense to talk of a "Lydo-Persian
line"; for the aggression against the Ionian Greek cities that
began the phase of the struggle between Greeks and barbarians
that Herodotus narrates was first launched by the Lydians,
from whom the Persians, after their conquest of Croesus, took
over the policy of subduing the Greek cities together with the
guilt that went with it. That in itself warrants the importance
given to Croesus in the narrative; but there is the further consideration that no story could be better calculated than that of
Croesus to serve as introduction to the part of the work that
forms the climax of the whole, the story of the campaign of
480–479 and the defeat of Xerxes. In the first volume of his
monumental study of Greek historiography,[22] Kurt von Fritz
has returned to the attempt, essayed by Jacoby in his important
Pauly-Wissowa article of 1913 but abandoned by most who
have worked in this field since, to trace in detail the historian's
development. Like Jacoby, and more recently Latte,[23] he believes that we can know that Herodotus was a geographer and
an ethnologist before becoming a historian; and he believes that
we can trace a development in Herodotus' thinking during the
writing of the part of the work that can strictly be considered
as historical. Von Fritz holds that a distinct difference can be
made out between the religious outlook shown in the Croesus-
logos and that shown in the Xerxes-*logos* of the last three
books.[24] In the Croesus-*logos* von Fritz sees exemplified the
working of retributive justice; Croesus, for all his piety, is

punished for the crime committed by his ancestor Gyges, and even the intercession of Apollo can only postpone for three years his inevitable catastrophe. Apollo cannot fairly be blamed for the ambiguity of the oracle that told Croesus that if he crossed the Halys a great empire would fall, but did not tell him whose; since Croesus was bound to pay for his ancestor's offence, it was inevitable that, to use the Homeric expression, a god should take away his wits. Xerxes on the other hand, von Fritz argues, makes no such error of judgment. First he announces his decision to invade Greece, but then he gives his advisers the opportunity of discussing his decision.[25] His uncle Artabanus speaks against it,[26] and at first the king is angry, but later he accepts his uncle's reasoning, and is about to cancel his decision when he is arrested by a warning given in a dream. When this dream has been repeated and has also been dreamt by Artabanus, Xerxes decides to launch his expedition after all.

Most scholars have taken this story to imply that although Xerxes himself has deliberated wisely the gods are determined that he shall suffer a disaster, and so force his hand; but von Fritz prefers to offer a political and psychological explanation of the dream of Xerxes.[27] The dream figure warns Xerxes that if he abandons the expedition he shall become as small as formerly he was great, and von Fritz takes this to mean that it is not possible for him at this stage to alter his decision without serious loss of prestige. This suggestion harmonises with von Fritz' view that in the Xerxes-*logos* we find a tone more realistic, more concrete and less metaphysical than in the preceding portions of the history. But in the history generally dreams, omens and portents are used, as a rule, much as they are used in early poetry; and it seems to me, as it has seemed to most scholars, that Herodotus supposed that this dream, like its obvious exemplar, the deceptive dream sent by Zeus to Agamemnon in the second book of the *Iliad*, was deliberately sent by the gods in order to deceive its victim. In fact the disastrous decision of Xerxes runs closely parallel to the disastrous decision of Croesus to cross the Halys and confront Cyrus.[28] Neither monarch decides hastily or rashly; each leaves nothing undone to ensure a right decision; but in each case the gods are resolved that a wrong decision shall be taken. The only difference is that Croesus, like Achilles and Agamemnon in the *Iliad,* makes his decision alone, doubtless with Ate working on his mind, but in the case of Xerxes the god directly intervenes to make him decide wrongly, as in the *Iliad* Aphrodite intervenes in person to stifle Helen's feelings of remorse and force her into bed with Paris.

So also in the later conference between Xerxes and Artabanus, the latter recommends caution and points out the danger and difficulty of the enterprise, but the king replies that if his ancestors had been cautious the empire would never have been won.[29] Every aspect of the issue is carefully gone into, but in the end Xerxes decides wrongly; he decides wrongly because the gods wish to punish him, as they wish to punish Croesus.

Other fateful decisions described in the history follow the same pattern. Cyrus is persuaded to fight the Massagetae in their own country and thus throw away his life through following, after the most careful weighing of the issues, the advice of Croesus[30]—Croesus who has gained wisdom from his sufferings and whom the reader is by now accustomed to regarding as the safest of counsellors. When Xerxes is deliberating as to whether he shall return home after Salamis,[31] the disastrous advice of Mardonius, who is throughout the counsellor of evil, receives the support of Artemisia, who the reader might well suppose would prove an entirely trustworthy adviser. For Herodotus, as for the other authors whom I have discussed, human deliberation, however wise and cautious, remains always fallible; in the last resort the outcome of all human ventures depends solely on the gods.

If the Xerxes-*logos* seems to us more concrete and objective, less mythical and paradeigmatic than the episode of Croesus, that is because it relates to more recent events and recounts them with more accuracy and in greater detail. The Croesus-*logos* is specially designed to have a paradeigmatic function, for it is an introduction to the story told in the last three books, which forms the climax of the whole history. The religious background of the two episodes is in all essentials one and the same.

Croesus, Cyrus, Cambyses, Darius, Xerxes—all the successive rulers of the east in Herodotus' narrative meet with a disaster. Why do they come to grief? Croesus, we are told, is punished for the crime of Gyges. But he loses his son Atys for a different reason; nemesis comes upon him for having thought himself— not for having been—the most fortunate of men.[32] Cyrus in the conference at which he decides to cross over into the kingdom of Tomyris and Darius in discussions with Atossa long before the expedition of Datis[33] show themselves the victims of Ate consequent upon Hybris; Cambyses is punished in the traditional manner, by the infliction of madness, for his impious arrogance towards the gods of Egypt.[34] What is the offence of Xerxes? Certainly he is forced by the gods themselves to persevere in his decision to invade Greece. But this happens because he is "presumptuous and impious";[35] once the invasion has been launched, he will flog the Hellespont, destroy temples in Athens and elsewhere and commit various barbarities. He can hardly, it is true, be punished for crimes he has not yet committed, even though in committing them he will reveal his own nature. The dream is sent to force him to invade because he has inherited from Cyrus and his successors, who have themselves inherited it from Croesus, the stigma of being an aggressor against the Greeks. In his description of the fatal decision, Herodotus resembles not the poet of the *Odyssey* but the poet of the *Iliad*. In the *Odyssey* the gods do not themselves put wrong ideas into men's minds, but men blame the gods for their own foolish actions.[36] In the *Iliad* once the gods have determined to destroy a man they see to it that he decides disastrously, and so also in Herodotus; but neither in the *Iliad* nor in Herodotus do they destroy him without just cause.

The part played by the gods in the action of the history indicates that the author's religious outlook resembled that of the early poets. That is what his remarks about religious matters would lead one to expect. If he mentions Persian criticisms of Greek anthropomorphism[37] or explains that the epithets, attributes and types of the gods were fixed by Homer and Hesiod,[38] that does not prove him to be a sceptic; the latter passage must be taken closely with the account of the Egyptian derivation of divine names which immediately precedes it. Nor does the frequency with which he refers to the divine power as a historical agent by such abstract terms as ὁ θεός, τὸ θεῖον, ὁ δαίμων, τὸ δαιμόνιον[39] prove him to be a disbeliever in the personal gods of legend. In one place Croesus says that "the god" has delivered him over to Cyrus,[40] in another he says that Zeus has done it.[41] In the epic the poet can tell his readers which god has caused a particular event, but in real life it is seldom possible to be so specific. Even in Homer the characters sometimes refer to the unknown supernatural agency behind an event by such a term as δαίμων. In later writers this becomes more frequent, as in Herodotus. Indeed, out of respect such terms came to be employed even when the god responsible for a happening was known, sometimes when it could only be, according to common notions, Zeus himself. If Herodotus says that whoever believes that Poseidon causes earthquakes will believe that Poseidon made for the Peneius its passage through the Vale of Tempe,[42] that does not prove that he himself did not believe it, for he attributes to Poseidon the tidal wave that prevented the Persians from taking Potidaea.[43] Both Plataea and Mycale, he tells us, were fought in the neighbourhood of a shrine of Eleusinian Demeter, at Plataea no Persian managed to take sanctuary, though many perished near the temple, and he connects this with the Persian destruction of the temple at Eleusis.[44] It was the Greek habit not to deny existence to the gods of other religions, but to identify them with the gods of Greece. The respect and tolerance for Persian and Egyptian religion shown by Herodotus and his belief that deity manifests itself in different ways to different peoples are in no way inconsistent with his belief in the traditional religion of his own people.

Throughout the history Herodotus, as much as any of the early poets, stresses the mutability of human fortune and the evanescence of human happiness. Men's only resource lies in avoiding the kind of action that provokes the anger of the gods; if this proves impossible, they must endure. The poetic words τλάω and its cognates, so important in the *Odyssey* and in Archilochus, do not occur in Herodotus except in verse quotations; but in his history the thing itself has great importance. We are often told that two leading antitheses of the history are those between Greek and barbarian and between liberty and despotism; this is true, but there is another antithesis that is far more fundamental. Herodotus well knows the weak points of Greeks and liberty and the strong points of barbarians and despotism; he does not even accept that the Persians are inevitably predisposed towards despotic government.[45] The most significant antithesis of all is that between softness and hardness, endurance, toughness.[46] The Persians at the start were hardy mountaineers whose toughness gave them victory first over the Medes and then over the Lydians. Soon after their conquest by Cyrus the Lydians revolt and Cyrus wishes to punish them severely, but is deterred by Croesus. Let him instead encourage them to grow soft, says Croesus, and this policy is executed with great success.[47] The Ionian Greeks, living in a perfect climate, are also soft; unwilling to submit to the hard discipline imposed by Dionysius of Phocaea, they are deprived of liberty.[48] Greece, like the mountains of Iran, is a hard country, whose inhabitants have always lived with poverty;[49] the Greeks of the mainland, and above all the Spartans, are correspondingly tough. By the time of Xerxes' invasion the Persians have lost much of their original hardness; that is brought home by the talks of Xerxes with the exiled Spartan king Demaratus and by the evidence of luxury found in the camp of Mardonius after Plataea.[50] The history concludes with a series of episodes that were once thought to provide obvious evidence of its unfinished state; their significance has only lately come to be appreciated. First comes the harem intrigue which leads to the barbarous mutilation of the wife of Xerxes' brother Masistes, ordered by Xerxes' queen Amestris but condoned by him, and later to the murder of Masistes and his sons.[51] That episode may well look forward to the murder of Xerxes fourteen years later by his son Darius, who was married to Masistes' daughter; in itself it confirms that Xerxes is "presumptuous and impious." Next Herodotus describes the sacrilege of the Persian Artayctes in the shrine of the hero Protesilaus near Sestos and his punishment by the Athenian commander Xanthippus, father of Pericles.[52] A forebear of that same Artayctes, Herodotus with seeming inconsequence continues, long before suggested to Cyrus that the Persians should leave their mountainous home country and occupy some of the rich land that they had conquered. "Very well," Cyrus replied, "but in that case you must be prepared to become subjects instead of being rulers, because soft countries produce soft men." [53] Herodotus nowhere implies that softness is necessarily an attribute of subjects of a despot or of Orientals. He may prefer Greeks to barbarians, but he impartially reveals the strengths and weaknesses of both, just as he may be partial to Athens, but is far from being an Athenian partisan.[54] His universe is not a whit less ruthless than that depicted by Thucydides; power is in the gift of the gods, but they give it only to the hardy, those who are able to endure. It is often suggested that Herodotus' work shows the influence of Attic tragedy, and they have much in common. But we are not compelled to suppose that it had influence upon him; Herodotus, Aeschylus and Sophocles alike owed a common debt to the Homeric epic, with which Herodotus must have been familiar during his formative years, before he came to Athens.

Do we find in Herodotus that "new accent of despair," that "new and bitter emphasis on the futility of human purposes" [55] which Dodds finds to be characteristic of the Archaic Age? Let us look first at the Croesus-*logos*, which offers near the start of the history such a complete epitome of the outlook that permeates the work. When Croesus asks Solon who in his view is the most fortunate of men,[56] Solon names first the Athenian Tellus, who after a happy life, during which he saw his sons grow to maturity, died in battle for his country and received a public funeral. In second place he puts Cleobis and Biton, the young Argives who, after their mother had prayed Hera to give them the best gift that lay in her power, fell peacefully asleep and woke no more. In Herodotus the strain of pessimism exemplified by the second story runs deep. When Xerxes sees his great army crossing the Hellespont, he weeps to think how soon none of them will be alive; few men, says Artabanus, do not often wish for death.[57] When Mimnermus expressed a wish for early death, Solon protested, insisting that a successful life was better;[58] and that is also the attitude of Herodotus, who makes Solon give first place to Tellus. No mortal can command success, for however carefully a man may plan, success or failure depend only on the gods, who may, perhaps because of chains of crime and punishment which he is unable to perceive, doom him to disappointment. Still, it is worth a man's while to make as much effort as he can, and to win honour by showing courage even in the face of hopeless odds.

Dodds finds evidence for Herodotus' belief in the hostility of the gods in those passages, not infrequent in the history, in which it is said that Candaules, Miltiades, or another "was bound to come to a bad end." [59] Nowhere is it implied that this was in virtue of a purely arbitrary decision; nowhere have we reason to suppose that the fate of the character in question was assigned to him unjustly. As Latte has remarked,[60] it often happens in Herodotus that part of a causal chain can be observed, but that its beginning is not there. That may be because the historian is not able to supply it or because he does not feel obliged to; but so many causal chains of crime and punishment are shown in their full extent that it is not safe to conclude that Herodotus thought that the beginning did not exist. For him, as for the early poets, the purposes of the gods are inscrutable to men; sometimes, especially to one looking back into the past and surveying a long period of time, each link in a chain of guilt and retribution may be perceptible, but often much of its extent must remain obscure to human understanding.

Is this belief not refuted, it will be asked, by the references to divine *phthonos* which appear in the history? Solon warns Croesus that "the divine" is always envious and prone to make trouble.[61] Amasis tells his friend Polycrates that he is alarmed by his excessive prosperity, "knowing that the divine is envious." [62] Artabanus warns Xerxes that the tallest creatures, buildings and plants are the likeliest to be struck by lightning, and that a large army is likelier than a small one to be punished by an envious god.[63] The god, Artabanus says later, lets us sample the sweetness of existence only to demonstrate his enviousness in our lives.[64] Themistocles attributes the Persian disaster not to the Greeks but to the gods and heroes, who have grudged that one man should rule over both Asia and Europe.[65]

Solon tells Croesus that man is all $\sigma\upsilon\mu\phi\sigma\rho\acute{\eta}$, [66] that word which basically means "a combination of circumstances," but often means "disaster," and the rich and powerful, in Herodotus, are more prone to sudden disaster than the others. Clearly this is not simply because they are rich and powerful, but because their wealth and power are in themselves a temptation not only to laziness and softness, but to pride and boastfulness. Nemesis comes upon Croesus and robs him of his son not because he is rich and powerful, but because he fancies himself the most fortunate of men;[67] the great king, the vast army are exposed to danger, Artabanus says to Xerxes, because "the god does not allow anyone but himself to think great thoughts." [68] The gods and heroes have grudged that one man should rule Asia and Europe, "being, as he is, presumptuous and impious." [69] As the gods punish Glaucus the Spartan for contemplating an injustice,[70] Cleomenes for plotting against Demaratus,[71] the Spartans through their chosen representatives for their murder of the Persian heralds,[72] so do they punish Xerxes for his hybris; "divine Justice shall quell mighty Koros, son of Hybris," says the second oracle given to the Athenians before Salamis.[73] Belief in divine *phthonos* originates from the ancient and undeniably primitive fear that some supernatural being may conceive a spite against one, the kind of belief that survives in the Mediterranean superstition of the evil eye or in the Anglo-Saxon practice of touching wood. But in such writers as Pindar and Herodotus, it has already developed into a concept of a comparatively advanced theology.

That is confirmed by its occurrence in other authors of the Archaic Age. Pindar prays that the good fortune of Hippocleas may encounter no envious reversal from the gods,[74] and that no *phthonos* from the gods may disturb the calm in which he celebrates the triumph of Strepsiadas.[75] Such language does not imply that the gods, if they were to "grudge" the victors in question their success, would be doing so from malice; to impute such a feeling to the gods would be unlike Pindar. When the messenger of the *Persians* tells how Xerxes sailed into the Bay of Salamis "not understanding the cunning scheme of the Greek nor the envy of the gods," Pohlenz suggests that as an ordinary man he is speaking in character in using the language of popular superstition.[76] Rather in Aeschylus, as in Herodotus and Pindar, the primitive concept of divine envy has undergone refinement. When his wife tempts him to make a triumphal entry into his palace over purple tapestries normally reserved for the service of the gods, Agamemnon fears that such an action may bring *phthonos* upon him.[77] His action in succumbing to the temptation is of course of small importance in the assessment of whatever guilt he bears, but still it is an act of *hybris,* and the scene of the tapestries effectively symbolises the reasons for his downfall.[78] The *phthonos* of the gods provoked by such an act is not unjust but just, as is the punishment which will soon fall upon the son of the giver of the Thyestean feast. Nor need we feel surprise when the chorus of Euripides' *Iphigenia in Aulis,* in lamenting the collapse of moral standards, find the culminating proof of that collapse in the fact that "it is no longer men's common purpose to escape the *phthonos* of the gods";[79] for according to Greek notions that *phthonos* actually formed part of justice.

Another general trait of the Archaic Age on which Dodds lays special stress is "the universal fear of pollution (*miasma*) and its correlate, the universal craving for ritual purification (*catharsis*)." [80] Since Rohde's great book *Psyche* appeared in 1893, scholars have been vexed by the problem of why pollution seems to play a minimal part in Homer but looms so large in early tragedy. Following Rohde, Dodds notes that after the plague at the beginning of the *Iliad* the Achaeans wash and throw the dirt into the sea, and that after the killing of the suitors in the *Odyssey* Eurycleia is told to bring brimstone and purify the hall;[81] otherwise, he finds no significant occurrences of purification in the epic. When the seer Theoclymenus asks Telemachus to take him to Ithaca on his ship, explaining that he has to leave his country because he has killed a man, Telemachus does not hesitate to take him; in the fifth century, however, a defendant in a murder trial can point as a proof of his innocence to the safe arrival in port of the ship that carried him.[82] "There is no trace in Homer," Dodds writes, "of the belief that pollution was either infectious or hereditary." [83] "The haunted, oppressive atmosphere," he says, "in which Aeschylus' characters move seems to us infinitely older than the clear air breathed by the men and gods of the *Iliad*." [84]

We should surely expect the belief in pollution to be something ancient, something far older than any extant literature, older perhaps than any literature whatever. Must we really suppose, as many scholars have done, that it came into existence, or at least acquired the passionate intensity with which it seems to be held by Aeschylus and Sophocles, during the period of transition that followed the epic age? Dodds[85] is rightly not content with the suggestion that the troubles caused by the Dorian Invasion, followed by the economic crisis of the seventh century and the political crisis of the sixth, "encouraged the reappearance of old culture-patterns which the common folk had never wholly forgotten," so strengthening the belief in daemons and the popularity of magic. He puts forward,[86] with all possible caution, a psychological explanation of the phenomenon, starting not from society at large but from the family. So long as the old sense of family solidarity lasted, he suggests, the old beliefs remained unshaken; but when the bond of family became relaxed, sons more and more came into conflict with their fathers and uneasy feelings of guilt came to be aroused. "The psychologists have taught us," he writes, "how potent a source of guilt-feelings is the pressure of unacknowledged desires . . . desires which are excluded from consciousness save in dreams or daydreams, yet are able to produce in the self a deep sense of moral uneasiness. Thus men came to project upon the heavenly father Zeus curious mixed feelings about the human one, so that Zeus appears as "the inscrutable source of good and evil gifts alike, as the jealous god, who grudges his children their heart's desire, and finally as the awful judge, just but stern, who punishes inexorably the capital sin of self-assertion, the sin of *hybris*." [87]

Even suppose one accepts without question the credentials of such a Freudian argument as this, one is bound to ask how often cultural changes of such magnitude occur within so brief a space of time; and if such changes do occur, how often they operate in a reactionary direction. Long before the bonds of family came to be relaxed, sons must have quarrelled with their fathers. This may well have affected the concept of Zeus which people formed; but why should this have happened at so late a stage in the evolution of the Greek people? This doubt may encourage us to consider an alternative line of explanation to the problem posed by Rohde, which seems so far not to have been much investigated.

Can it be that the notions of pollution and purification play a minor part in Homer not because they were unimportant in the early period, but because the epic poets did not choose to allow them any prominent place in the world depicted in their poems? This was suggested as long ago as 1833 by Karl Otfried Müller in his *Eumenides*;[88] but it was not then supported by any detailed argument, and has often been neglected.

Although Homer mentions only purifications of an elementary sort, from dirt, blood or sickness, there is much later evidence that indicates that purifications of other kinds also were known from very early times. In the *Iliad,* prophets, singers and doctors already form three distinct classes. Yet we have good reason to suppose that at first all three Apolline professions were combined by the same person, as in historical times they were combined by Epimenides and Empedocles[89] and that such a combination implied from the first, as it did for Aeschylus[90] the practice of ritual purification. Even in Homer, traces of the original unity of these professions linger in the methods adopted by their members. Machaon and Podalirius, the sons of Asclepius who are the Greek doctors before Troy, use both incantations and purifications; when they start by cleaning a wound, it would not be safe to assume that they distinguish sharply between sanitation and ritual cleansing. At Hector's funeral in the last book of the *Iliad,* he is lamented not only by the women of his family, but by professional mourners.[91] Walter Burkert, in the valuable paper[92] in which he has shown that those magicians or medicine-men whom it is now the fashion to call shamans were called by the Greeks first γόητες and later μάγοι, has pointed out that the "wailings" of the early medicine-men were often directed to the souls of the dead, and with proper caution has suggested that the Trojans who "began the laments" may have been persons of this kind. γόητες occur first in the early epic called *Phoronis*;[93] and Epimenides and those like him are not without predecessors in heroic legend. The *Odyssey* contains a mention of the seer Melampus,[94] whose curing of the daughters of the Argive king Proetus from madness, or from a loathsome affliction of the skin, or from both complaints, was later narrated in the Hesiodic *Catalogue* and in the epic poem called the *Melampodia*.[95] That does not prove that purifications were employed for such purposes as early as Homer; yet there is circumstantial evidence which will take us somewhat further.

In historic times divine anger against a community often had to be guarded against by means of purifications. During the Archaic Age the recognised authority on such matters was the Delphic Oracle, which would often prescribe the proper ritual or recommend an accredited expert to its consultants. In the Ionian cities an annual rite of diverting the guilt of the community upon scapegoats, known as *pharmakoi,* was practised from an early date; though we hear of this first from Hipponax in the sixth century, it may be very ancient.[96] The legal procedure used in murder trials in several places seems to presuppose the notion that if the community fails in its duty of securing atonement for the victim's next-of-kin it will be in danger from the victim's ghost.[97] In the Homeric society a killer was in danger of death, unless his atonement was accepted or he went into exile. Once out of his own country he became a suppliant, and, it would seem, had to be accepted. In later legend such a suppliant underwent a ceremony of purification, as we know from many myths. In the *Aethiopis,* Achilles was purified by Odysseus from the killing of Thersites;[98] in the Hesiodic *Catalogue,* Neleus refused to purify Heracles from the killing of Iphitus.[99] An early epic probably mentioned how Zeus himself purified Ixion from the killing of his father-in-law;[100] in the *Epigonoi* Cephalus was purified by the Cadmeans from the killing of his wife Procris.[101] Apollo himself was purified from the blood of the Python, which was commemorated in an annual rite at Delphi;[102] Apollo himself purified Orestes, Coroebus[103] and many others.

All this evidence, it will be objected, shows only that during the period after Homer purification for murder became a feature of epic poetry; none of it lends substance to the view of Nilsson[104] that in cases like that of Theoclymenus a purification ceremony must have been assumed to have taken place, although the poet does not mention it. Let us see if the text of the Homeric epics themselves yields any evidence in favour of such a supposition.

Soon after the beginning of the *Iliad*,[105] Agamemnon carries off the daughter of Chryses, a priest, or rather "cursing-man," in the service of Apollo. Chryses prays to his god, and Apollo hears him, takes his bow and comes down from Olympus to shoot into the Achaean camp his deadly, plague-carrying arrows. The Greeks do not know the cause of the plague, until Achilles calls an assembly and there questions the prophet Calchas. A similar situation obtains at the start of the *Oedipus Tyrannus* of Sophocles. There too the Thebans do not know what has caused the plague, until Creon returns from Delphi and is later seconded by Tiresias; but the audience does not learn till later the full causes of Apollo's anger. The laws of tragedy demand that the past history be only gradually revealed; but since the world of gods as well as that of men lies open to the epic poet, the origin of the plague is not surrounded with the same aura of mystery. But the belief behind both incidents is the same; an offence by one member of a community brings down a mysterious punishment upon all its members.[106] Measures of purification must of course be taken; but the trouble will vanish only when the proper measures are taken to appease the god by giving satisfaction to the victims of the outrage. No word for "pollution" occurs in the first book of the *Iliad*; the thing itself is there. In its most important aspect, its presence is obvious; and that even the less important, the technical notion of pollution, is also present is shown by Agamemnon's order to the Achaeans to cleanse themselves and dispose of the dirt into the sea.[107]

A still more notable instance of a community threatened with divine punishment for the action of one of its members is that of the Trojans, who must suffer for the crime of Paris. All know what the inevitable consequences of this must be; Troy and its inhabitants will be destroyed. Just so in the *Odyssey* the crew of Odysseus are doomed for their slaughter of the cattle of the sun, and the suitors for their flagrant *hybris*. The crimes of the

Trojans, of the crew of Odysseus and of the suitors are not spoken of, it is true, in terms of the concept of physical pollution, although the supernatural warnings which in the *Odyssey* herald the destruction of the guilty seem to show that their offences are conceived after this fashion. But this kind of concept must have existed at this time. Hector tells Paris that he deserves stoning,[108] a punishment specially designed to enable each member of a community to work off his own share of a collective guilt by taking part in the execution of the victim.[109] In the cyclic epic *Iliou Persis,* Odysseus wished the Achaeans to stone Ajax of Locri for his violation of Cassandra; had he persuaded them, the storm would not have struck their fleet as it sailed back across the Aegean.[110]

Aeschylus knows of very primitive methods employed by murderers to escape their victim's ghosts; how they sucked some of the victim's blood and then spat it out,[111] or how they performed upon the corpse the ghastly form of mutilation known as *maschalismos.*[112] Did these notions come into being only in post-Homeric times? Such measures presuppose a belief in the ghost dwelling in the tomb, from which it may emerge to take revenge upon the killer. In the *Choephori* the ghost of Agamemnon has in a sense become superfluous; Zeus and justice should be powerful enough to ensure that Orestes overcomes Aegisthus. But the belief in ghosts is so deeply rooted that Aeschylus cannot do without the great scene of conjuration. In Homer the belief in avenging ghosts has already been sublimated into the notion of the Erinyes. Aeschylus makes them say that in their home beneath the earth they are called Curses,[113] and I believe with Rohde that in origin they are the personified ghosts, or later curses, of the victims of injustice.[114] In Homer they have already become the protectors of justice in the sense of the universal order. Not only do they punish offences against a father,[115] a mother,[116] an elder brother,[117] but they pursue breakers of oaths,[118] and when the horse Xanthus violates the order of things by speaking, it is they who silence him.[119] Indeed, only once in the epic are they mentioned in connection with a violent death, and then they avenge an offence committed against a mother;[120] so far have they travelled from what must have been their original function.

With the Erinys as a minister of justice is associated Ate; it was the Erinys, together with Zeus and his portion, who caused Agamemnon to quarrel with Achilles by putting Ate into his mind.[121] Even the gods are not exempt from her operations; Poseidon must fear the Erinys of his elder brother Zeus,[122] Ares that of his mother Hera;[123] even beggars may have Erinyes, at least in the *Odyssey*.[124] The belief that certain persons may become accursed is closely linked with that in the Erinys and in Ate as a punishment which she inflicts. If an offender goes unpunished, she may strike against a whole community. It is often claimed that in Homer's world only the relations of the murdered man trouble about redress. The duty of prosecuting the murderer falls on them, and if they choose to accept blood-money, they have a right to; but if they are denied redress, then the whole community is in danger. "Often does the whole *polis* suffer because of an evil man," says Hesiod.[125]

Circumstantial evidence strongly indicates that the belief in pollution was strongly held long before Homer's time. This view is supported, for what that is worth, by comparative evidence from other Indo-European cultures;[126] and it is also supported by a number of indications in the Homeric epics themselves. The Archaic Age, which saw the rise of Delphi and Eleusis and the beginnings of "Orphic" poetry, was much concerned with purification;[127] yet I doubt greatly whether the belief was more strongly held in the Archaic Age than during the "epic" era that preceded it. The *Iliad* and *Odyssey* are not literal reproductions of life but works of poetic fiction, whose authors were at liberty to give or refuse prominence to any belief or practice according to their pleasure. The dark, the daemonic, the numinous side of religion is on any view surprisingly absent from the Homeric poems; when we meet it in the *Works and Days*—particularly the *Days*—or in the Demeter hymn, are we to suppose that it has suddenly sprung into being

since Homer's time? More than one reason for its absence may
be suggested. When the world of the gods, no less than that of
men, is directly presented by the poet, the actions of the gods
must to some degree seem less mysterious. Further, one can understand that the Homeric poets may have felt that certain manifestations of religion that existed before, during and after their
own time would ill cohere with the imaginative picture of reality which they present.[128] To the early tragedians, on the other
hand, it was artistically convenient to stress these darker aspects
of the higher powers.[129] For a writer of trilogies on a continuous
theme, for instance, the working out of a family curse made an
admirable subject; and in order to secure suspense, it might be
desirable that the origin of such a curse should not at the outset
be made known.[130] In tragedy the gods did not often appear in
person to explain their attitude to the human actors and their
fortunes. The chorus might be used to bring to mind the theological truths which were to be exemplified in the action of
the drama, but the exact way in which this happened was revealed only by the outcome of the plot itself. Even in early tragedy, it must be observed, the idea of physical pollution, though
utilised for some striking dramatic effects, is not often integral
to a play's action. In the *Choephori,* as I have remarked, the
ghost is not essential; in the *Eumenides* the physical pollution
of Orestes is rapidly removed by Apollo's ceremony of purification, but the really important business of placating the Erinyes
still remains. In the *Oedipus Tyrannus,* how much importance
attaches to the fact of ritual pollution and how much to the
curse which Oedipus himself has put upon the murderer of
Laius? [131]

The poets make a highly effective use of primitive beliefs, but
are careful not to let them interfere with the theology based
on Zeus' championship of justice which supplies the central
background. That theology was in all essentials already present
in the archetypal source of Attic tragedy, Homer's *Iliad.*[132] If
divine hostility and physical pollution seem to us to loom far
larger in early tragedy than in epic, if the late archaic age seems

far more haunted and oppressed with guilt than does the world of epic, that is in the main due to accident. The beliefs and attitudes held in Greece in the epic and archaic ages are in the main very much the same, and the emotional reactions to them during that long period vary, on the whole, astonishingly little. Still, the evidence indicates that, far from having grown stronger than it had been in the epic age, belief in pollution during the fifth century had become distinctly weaker. That happens to be very much the conclusion that a person starting this inquiry with an open mind might expect it would lead to.

IV

Presocratic Thinkers: Aeschylus

IT IS now usual to stress the continuity between the early cosmogonies of the poets and those of their first philosophical or quasi-philosophical successors.[1] Homer's reference to Oceanus as "the birth of the gods" now seems in all seriousness relevant to Thales' derivation of all things from water.[2] Still, Thales seems to have differed from the poets in postulating an initial creative act that was not conceived in mythological terms. The gods of which he thought everything was full were different from the gods of mythology. Having postulated a single originative process which could be called divine, Thales could find divine power everywhere;[3] in Homer, we remember, every event is both divinely and naturally determined. But presumably the divine power that set in motion Thales' universe must have had a single origin.

That was the case with his follower Anaximander, who made the impulse to creation come from the primal undifferentiated substance itself. "The *apeiron*" is itself immortal and undying —both standard epithets of the Olympian gods—and it itself is "the divine." [4] A cosmogony of this type meant a move towards monotheism, and towards monotheism of an impersonal kind.

Yet Anaximander still spoke of the order of the universe in terms of Dike. "Destruction comes to existing things," he wrote,[5] "from the same source from which existence comes to them in accordance with destiny; for they pay each other penalty and retribution for their injustice according to the assessment of time." We have seen that to a writer like Herodotus the doctrine that Zeus punishes men for their offences against each other implies that the successive crimes and punishments of men must form a pattern too complicated for humans, in most cases, to make out; indeed even for Homer the inscrutability of Zeus' purposes to men is already an established fact. Anaximander extends this intricate pattern of crimes and punishments from the fates of men to the fates of all things within the universe.[6] In time, Zeus punishes all injustices of men to men; that is the notion in the mind of Solon when he summons Earth herself to bear witness to his righteousness "before the court of time." [7] Just so for Anaximander Time is the judge who determines the penalties owed to one another by the constituents of the universe.[8]

The chief importance of Anaximander's implying that the universe was governed by Dike lay in the implication that all within it was subject to causal laws;[9] and in this belief he was followed by all presocratic thinkers. The belief in question was by no means universally accepted, even as late as the second half of the fifth century, when the author of the Hippocratic tract about the so-called "sacred disease" found it necessary to warn against all kinds of magical and thaumaturgical practitioners.[10] When he affirms that no disease is more or less sacred than any other, he is affirming the principle that the same Dike governs the whole universe.[11] That is confirmed by the terminology of other early Hippocratic works; the normal condition of a limb is "its just nature," [12] the operation that restores a twisted limb to normality is "a just operation," [13] the correct method of treatment "is established like a just law." [14] In maintaining this principle, so vital to the advance of medicine and all other sciences, against their wonder-working rivals, the doctors of the late fifth century were following a doctrine inherited from the sixth-century Ionian philosophers. But the origins of that doctrine can be traced in the Homeric epic itself. In the epic, it is true, magic is still practised, notably by physicians. But we have found operating there a kind of censorship[15] which avoids mentions of magic, pollution and other primitive beliefs that were widely held long after Homeric times. In as far as for Homer each event was determined in terms both of divine and of human action, Homer's is a unitary universe, governed by the same Dike under Zeus. The tendency of the epic poets to eliminate the miraculous shows a kind of awareness of this principle, which was later consciously grasped and made explicit by the philosophers and the doctors.

The monotheistic implications of early cosmological thinking were first pointed out by Xenophanes, apparently a younger contemporary of Anaximander. It has lately been suggested that Anaximander's system shows traces of Iranian influence;[16] and Xenophanes, who was brought up in Asia Minor under Persian rule, may have had the same favourable impression of Persian monotheism as Herodotus. He believed in "one great god . . . unlike mortals in form or thinking," one who "remains unmoved and governs all things by the thought of his mind." [17] Aristotle can hardly have been right in thinking that this god was imagined as being coextensive with the universe in the way later supposed by Parmenides and his followers;[18] once such cosmogonies as that of Anaximander had been put forward, it was natural for a god of this kind to be imagined. Xenophanes ridiculed the customary representations of the gods, pointing out that barbarian gods resembled barbarians and that the gods of animals, if animals had gods, would resemble animals.[19] Inevitably an abstract single god acquired the attribute of perfection,[20] and in doing so lost his individual character. The old belief that the gods lived a life governed by different rules from those of men was no longer understood;[21] and Xenophanes found a number of the myths related by Homer and Hesiod to be unfitting to the dignity of the gods, who he complained were made out as thieves, adulterers and deceivers.[22]

I have no wish to deny the possibility of Zoroastrian influence upon Xenophanes; but even if such influence existed, the characteristics of a theology like his are present in embryo even in Homer. There, it is true, the gods often affect the course of events on earth by direct physical action, or by giving an order to a mortal, though most often by putting an idea into a mortal's mind. Yet above the others, and in a position wholly superior to theirs, is Zeus. In battle he is more than a match for all the rest together;[23] though the others often try to thwart him, and even occasionally succeed, the general rule is that Zeus always prevails. What places him in a different category from all the other gods, even in the *Iliad*, is that in a general way he determines the course of events. His counsel, his plan, is fulfilled, as we are told at the very beginning of the poem;[24] after his reconciliation with Agamemnon, Achilles sees his hand in what has happened, rightly, for Zeus has told Hera beforehand how his purpose is to be accomplished. This preponderant power of Zeus does not consist merely in overwhelming physical strength; for though the poet does not directly express the comparatively sophisticated notion of omnipotence, he shows himself in effect aware of it. Of course many actions of Zeus conform to the ancient anthropomorphic pattern. But unlike the other gods he is able to control events without moving from his throne;[25] he could be said, like Xenophanes' god, to govern all things by the thought of his mind. With even more force this applies to the Zeus of the *Odyssey*, in whose name and through whose power Athene controls the whole course of the action presented in the poem. When Semonides begins a poem, "Boy, Zeus has power to decide all things and disposes them as he will," [26] he is in no way going beyond the Zeus of Homer.

Hesiod says that the eye of Zeus sees all things and notices all things, and also that thrice ten thousand watchers report to Zeus the evil deeds of men;[27] these are two different ways of ascribing to Zeus the power of observing all things that is a common property of omnipotence. In one place Hesiod can tell how Zeus was deceived by Prometheus, in another he can say that Zeus can never be deceived.[28] The apparent contradiction is not to be resolved by arguing that Zeus is differently conceived by the authors of two different strata of the poem. It is rather that the early Greek conception of Zeus attributed to him many human actions and qualities together with others beyond human range, and that in early times the apparent contradiction was only beginning to cause perplexity.

The immortal fire of Heraclitus, which is identical with "the one wise," [29] exists both in and outside the world; it is identical with the Logos which holds together the world's constituent parts,[30] but the fire that is immanent in the world is only a small part of the divine fire belonging to the aither. His conception of divinity is thus inconsistent with polytheism and anthropomorphism, and he is often critical of inherited beliefs associated with such attitudes; this tendency explains much of his contempt for earlier poets and thinkers.[31] He thinks it irrational to purify from deeds of blood by shedding more blood;[32] he says that the mysteries are conducted in an unholy manner;[33] he criticises accepted notions about the importance of burial,[34] the truth of dreams[35] and the cult of images.[36] He has little regard for the practitioners of magic,[37] or for the cult of Dionysus,[38] so popular during his century. To this extent he may be regarded as a contributor to what is called the Greek Enlightenment; but to call him that hardly does justice to all aspects of his attitude.

He seems to have made no protest against religious observances; "the one wise is unwilling and is willing to be called by the name of Zeus." [39] Like Zeus, his god is supreme over all and rules by violence; "every creature is herded by blows," [40] and all is steered by the thunder,[41] Zeus' traditional attribute. His one reference to the Delphic oracle seems to be respectful.[42] As in Anaximander, Dike stands for the world order, and as in Homer, she is protected by the Erinyes;[43] just as in the *Iliad* they check the utterance of the horse Xanthus, so in Heraclitus they will check the Sun if he outruns his course. Contradicting Hesiod, he identifies Dike with strife, Eris;[44] she is maintained by a perpetual conflict of opposites. We have met already the notion of the many complicated chains that link early injustices with late atonements; Heraclitus says that for men some things seem unjust and some just, but to the gods everything is fair and just.[45] Hybris must be quenched, even more than a conflagration;[46] Hybris is of course the antithesis of Dike. Human laws are nurtured by the divine law,[47] just as in Homer it is from Zeus that the *themistes* come to kings.

Like the early poets, Heraclitus often stresses the ignorance of men. Human character lacks *gnomai,* the knowledge of right and wrong that dictates right action, but divine character does not.[48] Men are blinded by their passions; it is hard to fight with one's *thymos,* for what it buys, it buys at the cost of vital power.[49] All this corresponds exactly with the *Iliad.* But was Heraclitus not a striking innovator when he wrote that character is for man a daimon—that is, a god or the dispenser of his fate?[50] Even in the *Iliad,* the daimon, the god who influences a man, acts through that man's own thoughts and feelings, and the man himself is held responsible for his decisions. Men go wrong, according to Heraclitus, because of their inability to comprehend the Logos,[51] which holds the key to that Dike which is at once justice and the order of the universe. That Logos is in a sense identical with Zeus.[52]

It is clear that the first philosopher to treat of ethics and politics takes a view of divine justice and of human error very close to that of Homer. His sense of values is correspondingly Homeric. The excellent (*aristoi*) choose one thing in preference to all others, eternal fame among mortals, but the many sate themselves like beasts;[53] one man for Heraclitus is equivalent to ten thousand, if he is excellent. Gods and men honour those who die in battle;[54] the many are bad, the few are good.[55] However critical his attitude to the traditional theology, Heraclitus adhered firmly to the traditional scheme of social values.

It was once a commonplace to say that the conception of Zeus found in the tragedies of Aeschylus was materially influenced by the monotheistic tendency of the early philosophers whom we have been discussing. Some scholars have supposed that once it is agreed that the presentation of Zeus in Aeschylus is not entirely anthropomorphic, that his Zeus is able to influence events without physical exertion, then it follows that his Zeus is substantially different from that of earlier writers.[56] I have already pointed out that these characteristics of Zeus are found as early as the *Iliad*. Zeus, it is claimed, is more predominant over the other gods in Aeschylus than in any earlier poet. Certainly Zeus in Aeschylus determines the general course of events; certainly Zeus as the protector of the law of justice has a special importance in this author. But Zeus determines the course of events as early as the *Iliad*. That Zeus is important as the guardian of justice in Hesiod is obvious; that this is so in the *Odyssey* is very nearly as obvious; that it is so in the *Iliad* is not quite as obvious, but is none the less certain. It is also clear enough that in Aeschylus other gods as well as Zeus play an effective part in the action; Aphrodite in the Danaid trilogy, Apollo in the Theban trilogy and the *Oresteia*, Athene in the *Eumenides*, Apollo and Dionysus in the *Lycurgeia* exercise no small influence upon the action.

So much for the two main arguments of the believers in a new kind of monotheism pioneered by Aeschylus; it remains to say a word or two about minor arguments. "Whoever Zeus is," says the Chorus in the Parodos of the *Agamemnon*,[57] "if he is pleased to be called by this name, by this name do I address him." We have long known that to make sure one does not offend a deity or fail to attract his attention by using the wrong name when we invoke him is an age-old religious practice, from which formulas of this kind originate.[58] In this context the use of this invocation has the further effect of laying stress upon the inscrutability of the all-powerful divinity whose aid is being implored, and thus striking a note of appropriate humility. Nothing compels us to suppose that we are intended to recall the famous words in which, perhaps echoing formulas of this kind, Heraclitus doubts whether Zeus is or is not an appropriate name for the one god of his own system;[59] nor does the way in which the Chorus goes on to recount the ancient succession myth of

Uranus, Kronos and Zeus as it is known from Hesiod suggest that any reference to modern speculations is intended. Much play has been made also with the famous "pantheistic" fragment quoted from Aeschylus' *Heliades* by Clement of Alexandria:[60] "Zeus is the aether, Zeus is the earth, Zeus is the heaven; Zeus, I say, is all things and whatever is higher than these." In Parmenides and later the supreme god is immanent in all things; but it would be rash to suppose that this doctrine is in question here. For Aeschylus, as for Homer, Zeus is supreme above all other gods; and it is hardly unnatural that he should express this by saying that Zeus is equivalent in his own person to upper air, earth and sky. Earth and sky are two of the three parts of the universe which according to Homer and Hesiod he and his two brothers divided. What is emphasized is the supremacy of Zeus, as the word "higher" ($\dot{\upsilon}\pi\acute{\epsilon}\rho\tau\epsilon\rho o\nu$) clearly indicates.

We need hardly trouble to take note of attempts to exploit trivial verbal similarities, such as that between Aeschylus' saying that "the wise man is he who has useful, not he who has much knowledge"[61] and the remark of Heraclitus that much learning does not teach sense.[62] Nor need we answer those who think it significant that both Aeschylus and Heraclitus were interested in contradictions and in etymologies; so were many of their contemporaries. If Aeschylus knew of modern thinkers like Xenophanes and Heraclitus, he refrained from obtruding his knowledge upon his audiences. The authors who are really important influences upon him, as they are for his countryman Solon, are Homer and Hesiod.

From Hesiod Aeschylus takes over a doctrine of Zeus and Dike fully sketched in that author, but visible in the *Iliad* and clearly present in the *Odyssey*;[63] it is also found in Solon whose works must have been known to Aeschylus. So little of Aeschylus has come down to us—of some ninety plays we have seven, two of them deplorably corrupt, together with a fair number of fragments—that one must always be careful not to generalise too confidently; but I believe that from these remains a more or less consistent theology can be made out. The chief obstacle to this belief is presented by the *Prometheus* trilogy, to which I shall devote most of the rest of this chapter.

The supreme god of the universe is Zeus; other gods are powerful, but he determines in a general way the pattern of events. He is the champion of Dike, the order of the universe. That means first that he defends his rule against any challenge from the other gods; when Prometheus says of Zeus that "he keeps Dike by him," [64] that has a different ring from Hesiod's saying that Dike sits beside his throne.[65] Secondly, it means that he preserves justice among men. If they challenge Zeus' ordinances, he will punish them. But he has bestowed upon them "a grace that comes by violence";[66] this consists in his punishment of their injustices against each other. If one man offends against another man, Zeus' daughter Dike records his offence in her father's tablets,[67] and sooner or later Zeus will be sure to punish him, either in his own person or through his descendants. Reference is made also to the punishment of the guilty in the underworld; before we suggest that this may be due to the influence of "Orphism," we should recall that the same belief is present in the *Iliad*.[68]

Aeschylus strongly maintains that Zeus does not punish the innocent.[69] Punishment falls oftener upon the rich and powerful than upon the poor and humble. But that is because the great are more prone to temptation, for power and riches in themselves do not arouse the envy of the gods. When in the *Niobe* a speaker says that Zeus occasions guilt in mortals, when he has decided utterly to destroy a family,[70] that does not mean that he makes such a decision for an arbitrary reason; rather, he destroys a family only when its members have been guilty of some grave crime.

From their observation of the working of the law of Zeus, men may learn to think safely—*sophronein*—or to think—*phronein*;[71] it is the observer rather than the victim who profits from the lesson. The likeness of this Aeschylean doctrine to Heraclitus' saying that "every beast is herded with blows" [72] seems to some people a piece of evidence for the Heraclitean

Aeschylus; rather it shows that both held a belief which Homer and Hesiod had held before them. The purposes of Zeus are inscrutable to mortals; only in the light of experience can men think over the past and trace out the working of the law of justice.

Let us now examine the manner in which Aeschylus accommodates the stories he narrates to the theology that has been described. The play that best shows Aeschylus' application of Zeus' law of justice to a given story is his earliest surviving tragedy, the *Persians;* not only is it our only self-contained tragedy of his, but despite our ignorance of Phrynichus' earlier treatment of the same material we are less handicapped than in other cases by our ignorance of previous treatments of the story. In this play the poet presents an event of recent history, seen through the spectrum given by his own outlook on the universe; and the distortions which are caused by the fitting of the material to the medium can illuminate that medium's nature.

Aeschylus, like Herodotus, regards the defeat of Xerxes as the punishment of Hybris by Zeus and Dike.[73] Herodotus may have known the *Persians,* and may conceivably have been influenced by it; but only those who will allow nothing to come into being without some "influence" will insist that the resemblance between their accounts must be due to imitation. It was natural for both to see the campaign of 480/79 in the light of the religious outlook which they shared with their contemporaries.

From the start Aeschylus lays stress on the vast power and wealth of Persia. This has been granted to the Persians by Zeus himself, and is held only at his pleasure;[74] should he decide to take it from them, no mortal man is strong enough to resist the deceit of the gods, to overleap the net which Ate will stretch across his path.[75] Persian valour, as well as Persian power, is given every emphasis; this serves to accentuate the consequences of Hybris. The scourging of the Hellespont and the destruction of the temples, though they are strongly stressed,[76] are not in themselves sufficient manifestations of Hybris to explain the consequences. Aeschylus feels obliged to make the very action

of invading Greece into a transgression of the bounds appointed
by the gods for mortals. In order to do so he makes the ghost of
the king's dead father expound a doctrine of Zeus-allotted
spheres of influence, which Darius himself has ordered Xerxes
to respect.[77] Some, at least, of Aeschylus' audience must have
known that this was unhistorical; Darius himself had sent the expedition that was checked at Marathon, and according to
Herodotus had never abandoned the desire for his revenge. But
for the purposes of the plot, Darius must be the bearer of the
wise counsel which the event justifies; his wisdom must be set
against his son's foolishness. The manner in which the defeat of
Xerxes comes about typifies the workings of Ate as we know them
from as early as the *Iliad*. Whether or not the poet wished to
praise Themistocles, the sending of Sicinnus with the disastrous
advice to Xerxes to sail into the bay of Salamis was an episode admirably calculated to serve Aeschylus' purpose. It could be regarded as the manifestation of an alastor, or an evil demon,[78]
much as in the *Oresteia* Helen and her sister Clytemnestra are
said to have been sent among mankind as instruments of Zeus'
destructive purpose. The plot also requires that the extent of the
Persian debacle must be enormously exaggerated.[79] Like the ex-
altation of the might of the defeated, this must be partly due
to patriotic sentiment; the veiled encomium of the Athenian
empire in the third stasimon surely confirms this;[80] but it is also
meant to heighten the effect of the drama and the lesson it
conveys.

Let us now consider the working of justice in the other
Aeschylean plays we are in a position to discuss. Aeschylus liked
to dramatise a conflict between persons, human or divine, or
between principles; he tended to choose subjects which involved
such conflicts.

In the trilogy about Achilles, Aeschylus was not afraid to
treat of the central subject of the *Iliad* and even, as it would appear, to present the moral issue in a way very like Homer's;[81]
even if Aeschylus did not, as Athenaeus asserts, call his tragedies
"slices of dried fish left over from Homer's great banquets," [82]

the story indicates the truth. In the trilogy that told how the Thracian king Lycurgus resisted the introduction of the cult of Dionysus and was punished by the god, Aeschylus seems to have dramatised a clash between the new worship of Dionysus and the established worship of Apollo; one can imagine that at the end an accommodation must have been reached between the cults devoted to the two brothers and sons of Zeus.[83] In the *Suppliants* the Danaids claim that they have justice on their side and are confident that Zeus, their ancestor, will grant their prayer. But it seems certain that in the end their aversion to their cousins the Aegyptiads was not held to justify the aversion they seem to have felt to marriage in general, and their murder of all their cousins except Lynceus had to be atoned. The Theban trilogy began with a play about Laius, father of Oedipus. In Aeschylus Zeus never punishes the guiltless, and as I shall argue later,[84] Laius must have acted criminally for Apollo to warn him that he could only preserve his city by dying without issue. The second play of the trilogy, the *Oedipus,* must have shown how Oedipus inherited the curse from his father and himself cursed his two sons. The third and surviving play exploits the contrast between Eteocles as the heroic defender of his city against the Argive enemies brought against her by his wicked brother and as a son of Oedipus, doomed no less than the wicked Polynices by their father's curse. At the end, both brothers perish; no ray of consolation illuminates the gloom which surrounds the extinction of the house of Oedipus.

The fate of Agamemnon is determined, long before the action of the play starts, by the curse laid upon his father Atreus.[85] Atreus has punished his brother Thyestes, who has disputed his possession of the Argive throne, by feasting him on the flesh of his own children. In the first two-thirds of the play this happening is not directly mentioned, but dark hints point continually to some sinister secret in the royal family's past; it is brought into the open only by the foreigner Cassandra, whom at first Clytemnestra supposes ignorant of Greek. At the start of his great expedition to punish the guilty Trojans, Agamemnon is confronted with a fearful dilemma. Artemis, one of the gods who take the Trojan side, is hostile to the army that is fated to sack Troy; she sends winds which will detain the fleet at Aulis, unless Agamemnon sacrifices his own daughter. Agamemnon can hardly refuse the sacrifice, since it is the will of Zeus that the expedition shall sail, and it can sail only when the sacrifice has been performed; but the sacrifice is none the less a dreadful crime. Why has Zeus allowed Agamemnon, the minister of his just revenge upon the Trojans, to be faced with such a choice? Because Agamemnon is the son of the guilty Atreus. The killing of his daughter brings upon Agamemnon the deadly hatred of his wife; she takes as her lover a surviving son of Thyestes, and when Agamemnon returns the two take their revenge on him.

Clytemnestra and Aegisthus are represented as unsympathetic characters. Agamemnon himself, like Eteocles, has two aspects; on the one hand he must be seen as the noble king and warrior, on the other as the son of the accursed Atreus. Because of the curse, Ate is liable to take away his judgment, as she does when he decides to sacrifice his daughter and when he allows the ruthless massacre of the Trojans and the destruction of their temple. Yet the case of his murderers against Agamemnon is not unjust; only they must expect that the curse upon the family will strike them down in their turn. At the end of the *Agamemnon* and throughout the *Choephori*, it is certain that Orestes will eventually treat his mother and her lover as they treated his father.

The analogy of the Theban trilogy might suggest that Orestes should be allowed to perish. But in this case the legend was that he survived; and the connection of Orestes with Athens encouraged Aeschylus to invest the last play of his trilogy with a special significance for his own city. Orestes has been confronted with an impossible dilemma no less perplexing than the paradoxes of Zeno. If he had failed to avenge his father, the Erinyes would have pursued him for his failure;[86] since he does avenge him, they pursue him for the killing of his mother. Here Aeschylus brings into play the Delphian connection of the story, which certainly existed before his time;[87] Orestes has consulted the oracle of Apollo, who has not only given him advice but has promised him protection. With Apollo's help, he makes his way to Athens, where the issue between him and the Erinyes is submitted to the judgment of Athene and the Areopagus. The votes are equal, and when Athene gives her casting vote, she does so for a reason that has nothing to do with the issue that is being judged; that is essential, for neither party is in the wrong and neither party must be defeated. The anger of the Erinyes at the verdict is terrible, and they threaten to avenge themselves on the Athenians; but by a dignified and tactful mixture of threats and bribery, Athene finally appeases them. At the conclusion of the play, the terrifying, sinister beings, who have dominated the action of the first two plays, though invisible except to Cassandra in the *Agamemnon* and to Orestes at the end of the *Choephori,* and who in the third have finally manifested themselves in horrifying fashion, so far change their tune that they sing a majestic hymn of benediction upon the city which a moment before they were threatening to destroy, and where they are now to enjoy unusual honours.

This startling change in the aspect of the Erinyes is intimately connected with the relevance of the third play of the trilogy to the poet's own community. Immediately before the trial, the Erinyes sing the second stasimon.[88] "Now is the end of the new ordinance," they begin, meaning the ordinance by which Athene has set up her new court, "if the plea and the evil-doing of this killer of his mother are to prevail." If Orestes is acquitted, mortals will feel free to offend against the divine interdiction of the shedding of kindred blood which the Erinyes protect. "There is a place," they insist, "where what is formidable is good and must remain seated to watch over men's minds. It is to men's advantage to learn good sense beneath constraint." [89] Here we see a clear allusion to the "grace that comes by violence" of the Zeus-hymn contained in the parodos of the *Agamemnon.* "Who," they ask,[90] "that fears nothing in his heart . . . , what mortal or what city would have the same

reverence for Dike? " Neither a life of anarchy nor one of despotism, they continue, deserves praise; "to all that lies between
the god has given power." It is true that all men, however extreme their views may seem to others, appear moderate to themselves; but here the Erinyes are surely praising a mean between
anarchy and despotism.[91]

There is no way of avoiding the connection between this ode
and the scene in which Athene pronounces judgment, for her
charge to the court of Areopagus before the vote contains obvious echoes of its language. In that court, she says,[92] "the reverence of the citizens and their inborn fear shall restrain them
from injustice by day and night alike." "I counsel the citizens,"
she says later,[93] "to respect what is neither anarchy nor despotism, and not to expel what is formidable from the city altogether; for who among mortals that fears nothing is just? "

Undoubtedly, these words echo those of the second stasimon.
In that ode, the Erinyes are speaking of themselves and of their
function; in her charge to the court of Areopagus, Athene is
speaking of that court. We can hardly avoid concluding that
an analogy between the Erinyes and the court of Areopagus is
being indicated; what the Erinyes, the helpers of justice, are
in the universe, that the court of Areopagus is in the Athenian
constitution. At the beginning of the play, the audience no less
than the priestess of the Delphian Apollo has been horrified
and disgusted by the dreadful appearance of these beings from
an age far earlier than that of the birth of Athene and Apollo,
these creatures whose home is beneath the ground, who rend
their victim with their talons and suck from his body the last
drop of blood. Yet at the end of the play these hideous and
sinister beings are extolled and honoured by Athene and, at her
order, by her citizens. Far from having their traditional functions taken from them, as they have feared they will be and as
some scholars, incautious in their liberalism, have supposed
they are, they are given a special place of honour in Athens,
which will benefit enormously from their proximity. Material
welfare follows from their presence in a place, just as in Hesiod

it attends the presence in a city of that goddess whom the Erinyes protect, Dike.

Whether Aeschylus was for or against the reform of the Areopagus which had been carried through by Ephialtes, or whether, as Wilamowitz thought,[94] he adhered to neither side is a desperately difficult question, but for the moment I am not concerned with it. What is important for the present purpose is that beyond all doubt Aeschylus insists strongly on the value of the punitive element in the government both of the universe in general and of the Athenian state. Without "the grace that comes by violence," without the element which Aeschylus calls "the formidable," both the universal order and the order of the state of Athens would dissolve in anarchy. For Aeschylus human law is nurtured by divine law, as it is for Heraclitus and indeed for Homer.

Aeschylus' politics are an extension of his theology. In the Homeric state the *themistes* by which the kings do justice among the people come to them from Zeus.[95] So in Aeschylus Zeus makes known his will to mortals through Agamemnon; Aegisthus is no suitable substitute, and apart from his duty to avenge his father, Orestes has a duty to the Argive people to assert his rights by supplanting the usurper.[96] In the state of Athens, justice comes through the court of Areopagus, invested with its rights by Zeus' daughter. The cliché we have heard repeated all our lives, that the *Eumenides* depicts the transition from the vendetta to the rule of law, is utterly misleading. Even in the *Iliad,* the blood feud is regulated by the justice of Zeus administered through kings; even in the law of the Athenian polis in the fifth century, the blood feud and the Erinyes have their allotted place.[97] When the Erinyes become Eumenides, there is not the least question of their giving up their function; we have been assured that if they did the government both of the state and of the universe would collapse. Law and the state, it is true, are not prominent in the first two plays of the *Oresteia.* For just as, in the quarrel between Achilles and Agamemnon in the *Iliad,* the king himself happens to be a party in the dispute, the legal machinery that exists cannot be invoked to settle it, and the responsibility for punishing Agamemnon's murderers therefore devolves upon his heir Orestes. When Euripides in his *Orestes*[98] makes Tyndareus ask Orestes why he did not prosecute his father's murderers in the courts, he is anachronistically envisaging a situation alien to the heroic age. If at this time Athene chooses to institute a new court of justice, this court is not to replace, but to assist the Erinyes.

We now come to the work which seems to present the most startling exception to the rule of consistency in theological matters usually observed by Aeschylus—the Prometheus trilogy. The extant play about Prometheus is in several ways markedly unlike Aeschylus' other work; but the difference in language, style and dramatic technique, appreciable though they are, would not, I believe, by themselves have caused the play's authenticity to be disputed. Most of the doubts expressed on this score have been occasioned by the play's theology.

What has so shocked and puzzled many readers has been the different light in which the *Prometheus Bound* presents the character of Zeus. The god who in Aeschylus' other works is the champion of justice appears here as a savage and remorseless tyrant, the persecutor of the defender and educator of mankind. Wilhelm Schmid, the most notable opponent of the play's authenticity, held that it must be the production of a sophist of the last quarter of the fifth century.[99]

It was to overcome this difficulty that the scholars of the end of the last century argued that the two lost plays of the *Prometheus* trilogy must have shown a moral development in the character of Zeus. From a youthful tyrant, they claimed, he must have become a mature and beneficent ruler, who of his own free will released his noble enemy. That view won a large measure of acceptance until not long after the Second World War, when it was challenged from more than one quarter.[100] In its extreme form it is a product of the modern liberal and progressive outlook, out of keeping with all that we know about the ancient world. But though Zeus cannot have developed, his attitude must certainly have altered.[101] We have some evidence bearing on the change, evidence which the believers in the development theory seem to have neglected.

We know from the extant play that Prometheus had learned from his mother a secret which one day was bound to place Zeus at his mercy.[102] Zeus desired countless females; one day he was destined to desire one who was fated to bear a son mightier than his father. If she bore a son to Zeus, he would inevitably serve Zeus as Zeus had served his own father, Kronos. Prometheus knows who this female person is, and unless he chooses to reveal the secret, Zeus is bound to fall. Zeus from far off hears Prometheus boast of this knowledge, and sends Hermes to prise it from him. When Prometheus refuses to give up the secret, he is swept down to Tartarus, there to endure thousands of years of torture.

In the event, Zeus was not dethroned; Prometheus revealed the secret, and Thetis was married to Peleus and became the mother of Achilles. We know something of the events which led to a settlement between Zeus and his arch-enemy. Heracles, a son of Zeus by a mortal and a descendant of that Io who visits Prometheus in the extant play, came upon the captive Prometheus on his journey to the west to bring back the cattle of Geryones. He shot the eagle which Zeus had sent to feast daily on the liver of Prometheus,[103] but was at first afraid to release Prometheus for fear of offending Zeus.[104] But in the end Heracles was able to negotiate a settlement.

Hermes in the extant play warns Prometheus that he can never be released until a god is willing to take on himself the pains of Prometheus and go to live in Hades and Tartarus.[105] It is as though Zeus had passed upon his enemy a sentence of death which the immortality of Prometheus made it impossible to carry out, so that Zeus was obliged to adopt the nearest possible equivalent. We are not told this explicitly; but Prometheus boasts that Zeus can never do him to death, using none of the common words for "kill" but the highly unusual verb θανατόω, "do to death," [106] and this passage seems to confirm the inference.

Who was the god who renounced immortality so that Prometheus could be released? Till lately it was believed to be the centaur Chiron. Accidentally wounded by one of Heracles' arrows, the Hydra's poisoned blood caused him such agony that he willingly gave up his immortality. That seemed to be explicitly stated by the mythographer Apollodorus,[107] who in all probability followed Aeschylus. But in another account of this transaction Apollodorus[108] seems to say that Chiron died "when Prometheus gave Zeus someone to become immortal in his place." D. S. Robertson in 1951 pointed out that if that translation is correct Chiron gave up his immortality not to Prometheus but to Heracles. But these words could just as easily be rendered "when Prometheus gave Zeus an immortal to take his, i.e. his own, place"; so that we do not have to abandon the traditional view that Chiron satisfied the condition laid down by Zeus by giving up his immortality so that Prometheus could be released.[109]

Clearly Zeus and Prometheus negotiated a settlement, just as at the end of the *Eumenides* Zeus' daughter, Athene, negotiates a settlement with the Erinyes. But did Prometheus obtain nothing in the settlement but his own release? In the extant play we hear much about the fate of mankind, for which Prometheus has done and suffered so much. Surely some account of mankind must have been taken in the settlement in question. Unfortunately our knowledge of the missing plays of the trilogy hardly takes us further; but the problem is of such fundamental importance for the subject under discussion that I wish to put forward, in the fullest awareness that it is nothing but a speculation, a guess about the missing parts of the trilogy and the decisions taken in respect of men.[110]

It has long been generally agreed that the *Prometheus Bound* must have been the first play of the trilogy,[111] as the recapitulations of past events which it contains must surely indicate.[112] It is also widely held that the next play in order was the *Pro-*

metheus Loosed. But what was the third play? Most scholars would probably say it was the *Prometheus Firebearer*. But that title is mentioned only in three places, a suspiciously small number, especially when it is remembered that we have many quotations from the *Prometheus Loosed*. One mention of the *Prometheus Firebearer* occurs in the catalogue of Aeschylean dramas found in the Medicean manuscript.[113] That catalogue omits the *Prometheus Firekindler,* a satyr-play which had nothing to do with the Prometheus trilogy. Clearly it is possible that *Prometheus Firebearer* may be only another way of referring to *Prometheus Firekindler;* and that possibility is somewhat strengthened by the difficulty of guessing what a play with that title, beginning apparently after the release of Prometheus, can have been about.

It has been suggested that the third play of the trilogy was never written; that Aeschylus, on this occasion only, composed a dilogy.[114] It seems that no one has suggested that the third play of the trilogy may not have had "Prometheus" in its name; and this seems to me a possibility worth considering. Analogy suggests that the prominence of Prometheus in the two first plays of a trilogy does not guarantee his prominence, or even his appearance, in the third.

Plato in his *Protagoras* puts into the mouth of that philosopher a myth about Prometheus.[115] Prometheus and his brother Epimetheus are given the task of assigning to the newly-created mortal creatures qualities according to their various species. Epimetheus makes the division, leaving his brother to criticise his performance. He distributes the qualities so as to ensure that each species will survive, but mankind's turn is left till last, and when it comes all the qualities have been used up. Prometheus therefore steals from the craftsmen among the gods, Hephaestus and Athene, their technical skill together with fire, and gives these to mankind. But though men are now able to get a living, they are still incapable of making cities, so that they are at the mercy of wild beasts; and later when they combine against them, they still quarrel among themselves.

Zeus therefore, in order to ensure that they survive, sends Hermes to bestow on them[116] Aidos and Dike.

This must be the story which was cynically adapted by a character in the satyr-play *Sisyphus,* composed probably by the Athenian politician Critias.[117] Men, says this person, tried to end the state of nature in which all were against all first by making laws and later, when they saw that some could break the law without detection, by inventing gods who were supposed to punish even crimes that remained secret. Later we seem to find another echo of the myth in the Hellenistic tragedian Moschion,[118] who describes a primitive state of nature in which "Law was humble and Violence shared the throne of Zeus." In the end, he says, Time put a stop to this, "whether a plan of Prometheus or with the lapse of days Necessity herself was men's teacher." Demeter taught men agriculture, Dionysus brought them wine, and they built houses and cities for themselves.

The myth of Protagoras has Prometheus as a character, but Aidos and Dike, together with the capacity to acquire them, come to mortals not from Prometheus but from Zeus. In the extant play Prometheus expresses the traditional connection between Zeus and Dike by saying that he keeps her by himself.[119] Did Zeus, as part of his settlement with Prometheus, give a share in her to men?

The Chorus of the *Agamemnon* expresses gratitude to Zeus for "the grace that comes by violence," that grace which it holds to be the greatest blessing he has given to mankind. It consists in the assurance that injustice committed by one man against another will in the end be avenged by Zeus, either upon the criminal himself or upon his descendants. Was the grace that comes by violence given by Zeus to men as part of his settlement with their great champion?

We possess certain fragments of a play by Aeschylus in which Dike in person makes a notable appearance. In a papyrus published by Lobel in 1952,[120] Dike herself is found conversing with the chorus of the play, which seems to consist of citizens

of a city to which she has been sent. Since Zeus overthrew
Kronos, she says, he has done her honour; for Kronos had been
the aggressor in their quarrel, so that she, Dike, had been on
Zeus' side. Zeus sends her, she continues, to those he desires to
benefit. In the stichomythia beginning at this point the goddess
gives her name and describes her special privileges; she does
good to the just and harm to the unjust, whose names she enters
in the book of Zeus. In another fragment that is probably from
the same play,[121] the speaker praises the goddess Eirene, Peace,
as bringing prosperity to a city. Eirene, like Eunomia, is Dike's
sister, and the three together make up the trinity of the Horai,
begotten by Zeus after having overcome Typhoeus.

Pindar in the *First Pythian Ode* sang the praises of the three
goddesses in question. He was celebrating Hieron's foundation
of the new city of Aetna, which took place not long after his
defeat of the Etruscans and the Carthaginians. Near that city,
under the volcano from which it took its name, was supposed
to lie Typhoeus, the mighty giant who had offered the last and
gravest challenge to the supremacy of Zeus. After his defeat,
Hesiod had said in his *Theogony*, Zeus had engendered Dike,
Eirene and Eunomia. Just so Pindar hopes that the defeat of the
barbarians will be followed by the prosperity which the Horai
traditionally bring.

Fifteen years ago Eduard Fraenkel [122] suggested that the fragments of Aeschylus we have been discussing might come from
a play written for the same occasion. Aeschylus, according to
the ancient life of him, wrote his play the *Women of Aetna* "as
an omen of a good life for the citizens," [123] and himself produced it in Sicily while visiting Hieron.

Droysen suggested as long ago as 1832[124] that the Prometheus
trilogy itself was written for production not in Athens, but in
Sicily. His suggestion was revived by Bergk in 1884,[125] and was
argued with learning and ingenuity by Focke in 1930.[126] Focke
contended that the difficulties of imagining how the extant
Prometheus may have been staged are greatly lessened if we are
not obliged to suppose that it was presented in the Theatre of

Dionysus; but since the play, wherever it was performed, can hardly have been produced with any approach to modern naturalism, there is little strength in this argument. It is notorious that the choral lyrics of the play are shorter than those of other Aeschylean tragedies, and differ from them in style and language.[127] Focke wished to account for this by suggesting that they were composed for production by a Sicilian chorus, unused to tragedy but accustomed to perform the choral lyrics of poets like Stesichorus and Ibycus. He thought that the comparative simplicity of the play's language might be explained by its having been written for a comparatively unsophisticated audience.

The explanations of these difficulties offered by Focke's theory would certainly be welcome, if they could be confirmed by other and more positive indications. He found one such piece of evidence in the long account of the punishment of Typhos, or Typhoeus, which Prometheus is made to give. This is known to present very close resemblances to the account of the eruption of Etna given in the First Pythian Ode.[128] If we could suppose that the third play of the *Prometheus* trilogy was the *Women of Aetna*, we should have no difficulty in guessing why Typhoeus and Etna should have found this mention.[129]

A summary of the plot of the *Women of Aetna*, unfortunately very mutilated, happens to occur in one of the fragments published by Lobel in the same volume as the fragments we have been discussing.[130] The first part of the play[131] took place at Aetna, the second at Xuthia, the third again at Aetna, the fourth at Leontini and the last at Syracuse. We know that the play contained a mention of the local deities called the Palici, who were sons of Zeus by the Sicilian nymph Thalia; she was a daughter of Hephaestus, who is said in the *Prometheus Bound* to have his forge inside Etna, and who has other connections with Prometheus.[132] How important in the play the Palici may have been there is no means of knowing; it would be rash to assume that they were the main subject of the play.

Can we guess at what this may have been? There was a tradition that in early times Sicily was the home of two savage races, the Cyclopes and the Laestrygones.[133] The Laestrygones were located in the fertile territory of Leontini.[134] Those who massacred the crew of Odysseus were a mere remnant; most of their race had perished years before, slaughtered by Heracles on his way back from the far west with the cattle of Geryones.[135]

Suppose that in the *Prometheus Loosed* Zeus as part of his settlement with Prometheus promised to send Dike among men. There could be no part of the world in more need of her attention than that inhabited by the most savage and inhospitable races of Greek legend. Men who declined to listen to the warning voice of Dike were chastised by Zeus, as Polyphemus is punished in the *Odyssey*. It was the journey to the west after the cattle of Geryones that brought Heracles face to face with Prometheus. Suppose Dike was sent by Zeus to the Laestrygones and was spurned by them, how natural it would have been for Zeus to see that Heracles, the great champion of law and justice and the great destroyer of savages and monsters, should pass through their territory! Heracles was much worshipped in Sicily, and Diodorus, a local man and a good authority, tells us that he received divine honours first at Agyrion, near Leontini.[136]

My suggestion that the third play of the *Prometheus* trilogy was the *Women of Etna,* and that the whole trilogy was written for performance in Sicily, is nothing but a speculation; without new evidence, we shall never know if it is true. But whether it is true or false, the Prometheus trilogy shows no inconsistency with the theology of Aeschylus' other works. Zeus did not change his nature, but he and Prometheus did a deal, and Zeus sent Dike, hitherto his own private property, to men. Men will have benefited, in that offenders will have been punished, so that crime will have been avoided and prosperity will have followed. But men will not have enjoyed a golden age, as they do in Hesiod under the rule of Kronos. In the universal order, man has only a minor place; if he tries to rise above it, he will be annihilated. Dike may secure man against anarchy and war;

she also holds him down in subjection to the immortal gods.[137] Prometheus may do what he can to extend the privileges of his protégés, but whatever the generous sympathies of liberals like Shelley may lead them to imagine, Prometheus is only a minor figure in the Greek pantheon. Not Prometheus but Zeus is the ruler of the universe.

V

Sophocles

In a short article published in *Greece and Rome* for April 1966,[1] Dodds gives the clearest statement known to me of one of the central problems of Sophoclean interpretation. The last time he examined in Greek literature at Oxford, the candidates were asked to explain "in what way, if any, does the *Oedipus Rex* justify the ways of god to man?" Most of the candidates adopted one of three views which Dodds calls heresies; and after describing each of these and explaining why he rejects it, he briefly sketches his own answer to the problem. I agree with Dodds in rejecting all three heresies, but there is a difference between his answer to the problem and my own.

The first and largest group of heretics held that Oedipus, or Iocaste, or both, are punished for some offences which they have committed. Upholders of this view can no longer claim to be supported by the authority of Aristotle, for modern scholarship[2] seems to have established that what Aristotle called the μεγάλη ἁμαρτία that involves the tragic hero in misfortune[3] is not a crime but a mistake. Still, their argument rests not only on authority, but on the alleged evidence of the text. Against Oedipus they have brought up his action in killing Laius and his followers at the crossroads, and also his conduct towards Tiresias and Creon in the play itself. It is only reasonable to retort that in both cases Oedipus' behaviour is not such as to incur guilt of a kind that would cause him to deserve the terrible fate which later overtakes him.[4] The lives of Heracles, Theseus and other benefactors of humanity were full of such incidents as the killing of Laius and his party, and neither law nor intelligent opinion would have considered Oedipus' action as a grave crime. The same is true of his conduct towards Tiresias and Creon. Provoked by the prophet's refusal to answer his important questions, Oedipus concludes that he is plotting to replace him on the throne by Creon, the man who has advised Oedipus to send for him. In fact Tiresias is reluctant to speak out because he is unwilling to expose Oedipus; only in the face of extreme provocation does he do so. In the same way Oedipus' indignation is natural enough in the circumstances. Not that the contentions of those who argue for Oedipus' guilt are totally devoid of reason. Like other heroic characters of Sophocles, Oedipus is impetuous and irascible; to use the Greek expression, his *thymos* is hard for him to govern. Such characters were particularly prone to the disastrous visitations of Ate, to which we will recur presently. None the less, it is out of the question that Oedipus' behaviour towards Tiresias and Creon, or even his killing of Laius in ignorance, could have been enough in itself to cause him to deserve his fate.

Many scholars have held that a large measure of guilt resides with Iocaste.[5] Finding that Oedipus is much affected by the accusation of Tiresias, Iocaste tries to comfort him[6] by proving from her own experience the fallibility of prophets and oracles. Apollo—or his servants—had predicted that the son she had by Laius would kill his father, but the prophecy had not come true. Later, when Oedipus has heard of the death of his supposed father, Polybus of Corinth, but is still afraid that he may come to marry Merope, Polybus' widow, Iocaste repeats her distrust of prophecy. "Why should a man be afraid," she asks,[7] "a man for whom the event is all-powerful, and no true foreknowledge of anything exists? It is best to live without guidance, as one may." Not long before these words are uttered, the Chorus at the end of the second stasimon[8] has solemnly averred that if the ancient oracles given to Laius prove false then all oracles are discredited and the gods have lost their power. Has Iocaste provoked divine justice by an impious scepticism?

That view also has now gone out of fashion. How, asks Karl Reinhardt in the best of all modern books about Sophocles,[9] would any person who had had Iocaste's experience retain a belief in oracles, and how in her eagerness to comfort Oedipus, could she help making use of this seemingly decisive piece of evidence to undermine their credit? In any case, it is hardly reasonable to imagine that Iocaste's conduct at that moment can have a share in determining events which have long since become inevitable.

So much for the first type of heresy, the moralising view. Even less defensible is the second, that which regards the Oedipus as a tragedy of destiny, showing a man in the grip of a predetermined fate. Dodds rightly says that for the Greeks of Sophocles' time, belief in divine foreknowledge did not imply that all actions were predetermined; indeed, the philosophical notion of determinism did not exist before the Hellenistic age.[10] The Greeks of the fifth century thought that the gods knew the future, and also that the gods, or at least Zeus, in a vague and general way determined what occurred; at the same time they believed that men were responsible for their actions. To call the *Oedipus* a tragedy of destiny is wrong, if by that we mean a tragedy based on a mechanistic notion of determinism. If we simply mean that in the play we see Oedipus meeting a fate which he cannot escape, the phrase is harmless enough; but then it tells us little.

Dodds' third kind of heresy[11] is that which claims that the play conveys no particular "meaning" or "message," but merely exploits the terror of coincidence; close to this, he says, is the view that Sophocles merely tells a traditional story and exploits it for dramatic purposes, without raising any religious issue. Dodds confesses to feeling more sympathy with this heresy than with the other two. He truly says that it is absurd to talk as though the essence of a tragedy can ever be boiled down to a banal "message," and it is natural to feel sympathy with even an exaggerated reaction against the cruder kind of moralising explanation. All the same, to go too far in this direction is a mistake. In early choral lyric the myth seems to have been narrated with the aim of illustrating a general truth about man's relations with the gods, and this notion may well have been taken over from lyric by the early tragic poets.[12] In early tragedy at least, the parenetic element has a real importance; the actions of men are viewed against a background supplied by a theology little different from that of popular belief. Aeschylus' religion is not necessarily less profound for being simple; that does not mean that Aeschylus was incapable of thought, or that his beliefs were conventional in the sense of being foolish and superstitious. Far from attempting to instil a personal or "original" theology of his own, he saw human life against the unchanging backcloth of the divine world, whose laws men had to keep if they and their descendants were to avoid disaster. Men had to render to the gods their due honour; if a mortal offended a particular god, as Niobe offended Leto or Cassandra Apollo, the god destroyed him, not unjustly. By an extension of this principle, Zeus, the supreme god, punished offenders against Dike, who sat beside his throne; whoever offended against Dike was held to have denied due honour to Zeus himself. Among men Zeus with the aid of Dike and the Erinyes upheld a stern reciprocal justice, recalling the Old Testament but not the New; those who broke his law were destroyed, they and their children after them.[13] From the modern point of view, this is monstrously unjust; but the viewpoint of the Greeks, and other peoples who had similar attitudes to kinship, was different.

Was the attitude of Sophocles to the gods different from that of Aeschylus? Dodds thinks it was different, and in a most important respect. For when at the end of his paper he comes to his own solution of the problem of the *Oedipus Rex*,[14] he starts by asserting two propositions about Sophocles. The second is that Sophocles always believed that the gods existed and that men should revere them. This is confirmed by the evidence of

the plays, and also by abundant biographical evidence. Sophocles held various priesthoods; he played a prominent part in
introducing into Athens the worship of Asclepius; after death
he received the rare honour of worship as a hero. These facts
not only help to establish Dodds' second proposition, but help
to give his first a startling air of paradox. For the first proposition is "that Sophocles did not believe, or did not always believe, that the gods are in any human sense 'just.' "

Dodds is far from being alone in this opinion, which has been
held by most of the best interpreters of Sophocles during the
present century. "Towards the great problems of dramatic philosophy," wrote Erwin Rohde in his great book *Psyche*,[15]—"the
problem of the freedom or compulsion of the will, the guilt and
destiny of man—Sophocles took up a position that differed essentially from that of his great predecessor. A maturer and
calmer self-abandonment to the observation of life and its difficulties made him less able to rest content with simple or sweeping solutions of the complexities; made him seek out other and
more various modes of understanding. . . . The suffering and
calamity that befalls the hero comes not from his own conscious
decision and exercise of will, but from obscure decrees of
fate. . . . The divine purpose brings to maturity a plan in
which the individual man and his destiny are mere instruments. . . . Simply because such is the will of heaven must
Oedipus, unknowing and blameless, slay his father, marry his
mother and plunge himself into the deepest depths of misery. . . . Sophocles abandoned all attempt to reconcile the
worth and actions of men with their fate upon earth." Writing
six years later, Wilamowitz took a similar view.[16] "Mortals in
their weakness," he said, "are surrounded by animate beings,
as such like themselves, but having infinitely greater power, able
to harm or help them according to their nature and inclination:
one must not import inappropriate concepts of human morality
by calling them good or bad." In the *Oedipus Rex,* according to
Reinhardt, "the question of who is responsible for what has
happened—the question which Euripides or Aeschylus could

not have helped asking—is not raised." [17] One scholar has even written that "in the light of the dramas themselves, it seems impossible that Sophocles' allegiance could have been to the gods of Olympus," [18] and can depict Sophocles as an "heroic humanist" whose atheism set off his idealisation of suffering humanity.[19] But this view of Sophocles' attitude to the gods gives rise to certain difficulties. Homer is named by Dodds as an author who did not believe the gods were just; in the first chapter I have contested this. In any case Hesiod believed passionately that they were, and so did Aeschylus. Further, from the time of Hesiod to the collapse of paganism, it is generally true that anyone who believed in the existence of the gods believed that they were just and righteous. If the pious Sophocles rejected this belief, that is a fact so extraordinary that it needs detailed explanation. The two plays adduced by Dodds as providing evidence for his view are the *Women of Trachis* and the *Oedipus Rex*. I shall come to the *Women of Trachis* later; for the moment, I shall concentrate on the *Oedipus*.

Those who reject the moralising interpretation of the play will agree that one reason for the feeling of horror, or even outrage, which it inspires is that the man who is overcome by such appalling catastrophe is in his own person wholly innocent of blame; he is brave, clever and generous, a great ruler and an unselfish protector of his people. And yet the play contains one choral ode, and that one which most hearers and readers find particularly impressive, in which on any interpretation the question of guilt looms large, the second stasimon.[20] During the scene with Iocaste which follows his quarrel with Creon, Oedipus, considering whether Tiresias may be right in his accusation, asks whether he is not "altogether unholy." [21] Taking up this word, the Chorus prays for holiness, which it explains as meaning freedom from guilt of the kind incurred by breaking the laws of the gods. These are the same as the unwritten laws defended by Antigone;[22] among them are the laws which the Eumenides in Aeschylus' play claim that they protect. Men must do no wrong to a god, or to a host or guest, or to their parents;

such a crime involves pollution, and brings down an awful penalty. Then, in the first antistrophe, they warn against *Hybris,* the insolence of pride; *Hybris,* when followed by *Koros,* satiety, leads to disaster.[23] We are reminded of how the Chorus of the *Agamemnon* described how old *Hybris* begets new *Hybris,* and the result is *Ate.* Aeschylus looked back, it seems, to Solon, who had said that *Koros* begat *Hybris;* Pindar and an oracle quoted by Herodotus reverse the relation and make *Hybris* the parent,[24] and so does Sophocles.

In the next stanza[25] the Chorus utters an imprecation against arrogance in deed and word, shown by the man who has no fear of *Dike* and no respect for the habitations of the gods, the man who will not win his advantage fairly and abstain from impious conduct, the man who violates the sanctity of holy things.[26] We are directly reminded of the language in which the Chorus of the *Agamemnon* denounce the evil-doer who "tramples upon the grace of holy things";[27] they seem to have in mind Paris and the Trojans, but we find their words more and more applicable to Troy's conquerors. How shall such a man, the Chorus of the *Oedipus* continues, still ward off from his soul "the shafts of anger?" [28] We remember the form taken in Aeschylus by the evil-doer's punishment; *Ate* takes away his wits, causing him to commit rash actions which lead to his destruction. "If such actions as this man's," the Chorus ask,[29] "are to be held in honour, why must I honour the gods with dances?" The honouring of the gods with dances, as the latest interpreter of the ode remarks,[30] was a part of Greek worship everywhere, so that the Chorus do not suddenly cease to be Theban elders and become Athenian *choreutai* in the disturbing fashion usually supposed. Still, the main point is clear; if the offender is to go scot-free, they say, this is fatal to religion, just as the Erinyes insist that if Orestes is to escape, this is the ruin of religion and morality.

Much of the interminable discussion of this ode has centred round the question of what persons the Chorus has in mind; Tiresias, Creon, Laius have all had their advocates, but most of all Oedipus, Iocaste, or both together.[31] I see no ground for assuming that any specific person is intended. The Chorus has portrayed the traditional unrighteous man, the traditional victim of *Hybris, Koros* and *Ate*. Such a man, they are saying, must be responsible for the death of Laius, and hence for the pollution now upon the city. The guilty man must be punished, or religion and the rule of law are at an end; and the oracle of Apollo, who is the spokesman of Zeus himself, must be proved right. Neither the words of the ode nor the surrounding context contain any suggestion as to who is the criminal; but the ode does prove that the notion of guilt, impurity, pollution plays an important part in the drama. Guilt that is described in this Aeschylean fashion, the guilt of the victim of *Hybris, Ate,* and *Koros,* of the man who has no fear of *Dike* and lays his hand on holy things, does not sound like the involuntary guilt of one who has acted in ignorance; it is not contracted by one who kills, in a brawl, wayfarers who have provoked him, nor by such threats as Oedipus has uttered against Tiresias and Creon. It is true, however, that the man on whom a curse lies will be especially prone to fits of passion that will cause him to commit actions that will have disastrous consequences. Oedipus is portrayed as being liable to such fits of passion; his acts have been of the kind we might expect from a man under a curse. May not a family curse inherited from the past have more importance for the plot of the *Oedipus Rex* than most scholars have allowed?

That was the view of Gennaro Perrotta, the author of one of the best modern books on Sophocles,[32] whose approach to this play is very similar to mine. But many recent critics have denied that family curses play any part in Sophoclean tragedy.[33] Dodds, it is true, is not among them, for he admits the importance of the curse both in the *Antigone* and in the second *Oedipus*.[34] But since I believe that the curse is important in the *Electra* also, and that in the *Antigone* its importance is considerable, I shall turn aside and try to show its significance in these three plays before coming back to the first *Oedipus*.[35]

The Sophoclean *Electra* presents a single episode in the history of the Atreidae, and in doing so focusses attention on a single figure. Any allusion to the pursuit and acquittal of Orestes that lie ahead would be damaging to the particular effect at which the poet aims, so that the persistence over three generations of the chain of murder and revenge is not here stressed. Still, Zeus and Justice have their place in this play, and so has the curse upon the house of Atreus. During the anapaests that precede the parodos, Electra invokes "the house of Hades and Persephone, Hermes of the Earth and the potent Curse, and the revered children of the gods, the Erinyes" to grant her prayer for revenge upon her father's murderers.[36] During the parodos the Chorus in trying to console Electra remind her that Zeus, who governs all things, still rules in heaven, and that he can be trusted one day to satisfy her longing.[37] In the last words of the parodos, Electra declares that if Agamemnon is to lie there dead, reduced to earth and nothingness, while his killers escape the killing they deserve, *Aidos* has vanished from the world, and so has the piety of all mankind.[38] We must note the markedly Aeschylean features of the short ode that follows the scene in which Electra forces Chrysothemis to suppress their mother's offering to the dead Agamemnon and replace it with one likelier to be acceptable.[39] "If I am no crazy prophet, lacking in wise judgment, prophetic Justice shall come, wielding in her hands power that is just; she shall come after them, my child, in no short space of time." Symmetrical with the mention of *Dike* in the strophe is that of the Erinyes in the antistrophe;[40] all prophecy in dreams and oracles is false, if the warning dream that has struck terror into Clytemnestra is not to be fulfilled.[41] Then follows an epode that traces back the sorrows of the Atreidae beyond even Atreus to the treachery of Pelops. Pelops overcame the terrible Oenomaus and won the bride whom thirteen suitors had died to win; according to the version preferred here, he did so not by reason of the matchless speed of the horses lent him by Poseidon, but because his enemy's charioteer had loosened the lynch-pins of his master's horses. Rather than pay Myrsilus his reward—according to one story, it was to have been the virtue of Pelops' bride—Pelops hurled him over a cliff into

the sea. Indeed, there is no explicit statement that this was the
origin of the curse, but only of the woes of the Atreidae; still,
there seems little doubt that Sophocles meant to imply what
Euripides in his *Orestes* expressly states.[42] When at the moment
of Clytemnestra's murder the Chorus exclaims "The curse is
accomplishing its work!", I doubt if they mean simply the curse
of the murdered Agamemnon. The dramatist's purpose does not
require that the framework of divine justice and human curse
should receive as much attention here as in the *Oresteia,* but it
is present none the less, and its significance is marked by several
Aeschylean echoes.

We come now to the *Antigone.* At the very start Antigone
reminds her sister of "the evils that come from Oedipus," and
soon afterwards[43] Ismene recalls the sad fate of their father,
mother and brothers, a fate which her sister, if she persists in
her present resolve, may come to share. When Antigone is
brought in as a prisoner, the Chorus greet her thus: "Unhappy
one, daughter of an unhappy father, Oedipus." [44] Then after
the condemnation of Antigone by Creon, the Chorus sing an
ode of great beauty in which they reflect on the history of the
house of Labdacus.[45] The leading metaphor of the opening pair
of stanzas, the comparison of the afflicted family to a beach
struck by successive waves, appears also in the great ode in
which, near the conclusion of Aeschylus' trilogy about the
Labdacids, the Chorus of the *Seven Against Thebes* looks back
upon their history;[46] the thought quite as much as the expression
of the opening passage recalls Aeschylus. Then at the end of the
first antistrophe[47] the Chorus applies the general statement it
has begun with to the present situation; even these last surviving members of the house of Oedipus are now to be cut down.
Their executioners will be the usual ministers of *Ate,* "foolishness in thought and the Erinyes in the mind." [48] We remember
Agamemnon's apology in the nineteenth book of the Iliad,[49]
and so we remember also Aeschylean accounts of the same destructive process, when Agamemnon made up his mind to sacrifice his daughter. "Mortals are made reckless," the Chorus says,

"by the evil counsels of rash Infatuation, initiator of ill." [50] *Ate*
is sent by Zeus, and it is to the glorification of Zeus' power that
the Chorus of the *Antigone* now proceeds;[51] as they assert his
matchless and everlasting supremacy, again Aeschylus is recalled. "This law," they say, "shall be valid for present, future
and past; to none among mortals shall vast wealth come without
Ate." [52] The textual uncertainty here does not affect the sense;[53]
the Chorus seems to be saying that great prosperity by itself
brings *Ate*. It is not, however, probable that Sophocles meant
them to deny that it is not prosperity by itself, but crime, that
brings down punishment. Even the ode that contains the classic
statement of the Aeschylean doctrine that only the unrighteous
and their children are punished by the gods goes on to tell how
"justice shines beneath smoky rafters, and honours the righteous life, but the gold-bespangled halls where men's hands are
dirty she abandons with averted eyes, having no respect for the
power of wealth made counterfeit with praise." [54] The rich and
mighty are more prone to incur the onslaughts of *Ate* than the
poor and humble.

This is confirmed by the next words;[55] for the Chorus go on
to explain their previous utterances by saying that prosperity is
a danger because it encourages hope, and hope, though it brings
advantage to some, deceives others by instilling wild longings;
the victim know nothing of his danger till suddenly he treads
on fire. "It is wisdom," say the Chorus, "that has revealed to us
through one unknown a famous saying—that evil seems good
to him whose mind the god is leading towards *Ate*." [56] In the
last line, the text is again uncertain, but luckily this makes little difference to the sense; if my own suggestion[57] is right, the
Chorus looks back to the end of the preceding stanza by saying
that the poor and humble man is free from danger. In saying
that evil seems good to the victim of *Ate*, Sophocles is again
describing its working in a way closely resembling that of Aeschylus.[58]

The Chorus have analysed the situation of the Theban royal
house in Aeschylean terms; must that analysis be taken seri-

ously? In the first stasimon of the play,[59] they have described the act of burying Polyneices as something "formidable," an instance of that human courage and resource which may accomplish great good or great evil. In the third stasimon[60] they will dismiss Haemon's advice to his father as due to the distorting power of love, yet soon the audience will see his claim to have given Creon sound and disinterested counsel amply vindicated. This has encouraged some critics to write off the second stasimon as a beautiful ode written to fill an interval, with no dramatic function but that of giving expression to a wrong opinion of the deluded Theban elders. There could be no better illustration of the grave dangers that result from the too prevalent habit of treating the choral lyrics as an unimportant element in Sophoclean drama;[61] for in this case a later episode in the play supplies the answer to the question we are asking.

During their last scene with Antigone, not long before she is led off to be buried alive, the Chorus recur once more to the subject of the hereditary curse.[62] "You have advanced to the extreme of rashness," they tell her, "and have run against the high pedestal of Justice with your foot. You are making atonement, I think, with an ordeal come to you by inheritance." If my interpretation of the phrase about "the high pedestal of Justice" is correct,[63] Antigone is being spoken of in terms of a metaphor twice applied by Aeschylus to the conduct of the unrighteous. What matters more is the last line. The Chorus tell Antigone that she is making atonement for her ancestors, and she does not deny this but accepts it. "You have touched upon a thought most grievous to me," she replies, "that of my father—ever new is the sorrow of which you speak—and of the whole destiny that has come to us, the renowned offspring of Labdacus." [64]

From the evidence that has been cited, it seems to result that Antigone must be accounted a victim of the family curse. If we do not believe that in Sophocles the gods were always just, we shall not be troubled by the thought that, unlike Creon, she has done nothing to deserve her fate. But if we think that the gods seemed just to Sophocles as they did to Aeschylus, we may feel that this suggestion makes the play easier to understand. Certain general considerations about Antigone may be adduced in its support.

The attitude of those who contend that Antigone is hardly, if at all, less to blame than Creon makes me even angrier than the attitude of those who contend that Oedipus is punished for his own crimes;[65] but there are certain features of Antigone, as there are certain features of Oedipus, that help us to understand why such an attitude has been expressed. Antigone is a figure of heroic stature, braver and more resolute than the common run of women typified by Ismene, but also more passionate and more obstinate. "That terrible heroine," writes Perrotta, "is by no means the woman of love that some have wished to see in her; she is an indomitable character who can be admired and loved only by those who have a sense of the heroic." [66] The best key to understanding her is furnished by the Sophoclean Electra, who like her is contrasted with a sister in no way cowardly or contemptible, but not cast in the same heroic mould. Like Electra, like Ajax, like Oedipus in both plays, Antigone has the defects of her heroic qualities. From the beginning of her dealings with Creon, she gives way to her natural indignation, with no regard for tact or caution. This in itself might signify little, for it may be argued that Creon is too headstrong for any attempt to reason with him to be worth while. But an unmistakable indication is given by Antigone's behaviour to her foil, Ismene. During the opening dialogue, Antigone becomes angry the moment Ismene shows herself reluctant to assist her in her scheme. First she accuses her sister of "dishonouring what the gods hold in honour";[67] then when Ismene urges her to keep her plan secret and promises herself to do so, she urges her to proclaim it to all;[68] finally she tells Ismene that if she persists in calling the plan impossible, she will become an enemy both to her and to their dead brother.[69] Later, when Ismene has heard of her condemnation, and with great courage tries to support her by claiming to have been her accomplice, Antigone indignantly, and even brutally repulses her:[70] "I do not care for a dear one who shows her love with words." True to her heroic nature, she sacrifices all for Polyneices not out of personal affection, but in loyalty to a male member of her own family; there is the answer to the problem of the speech so many misguided persons have wanted to expunge, an answer which Perrotta clearly and concisely gave.[71] To the last moment, when instead of waiting to starve to death—or rather, as it turns out, to be released—Antigone hangs herself, she remains rash and impetuous. To a believer in inherited curses which cause Zeus to send *Ate* to take away men's wits, her behaviour, like that of Oedipus, might indeed seem to show the working of "foolishness in speech and the Erinys in the mind." [72] After admitting that she has shown piety—that quality specially characteristic of Electra—the Chorus tell her that she has been brought to ruin by her self-willed passion.[73] They concede also, and they cannot now be mocking her, that her death will be glorious, as she herself has claimed [74] and Haemon has said the citizens think it will.[75] That is no comfort for Antigone, any more than it is for the Aeschylean Cassandra,[76] but to the Greek way of thinking it does not count for nothing.[77]

The third play in which a family curse has real importance is the second *Oedipus*. After the blind wanderer with his daughter has reached Colonus, prologue and parodos attain a climax at the moment at which the Chorus of local inhabitants become aware of his identity.[78] At once they order him to leave;[79] but Antigone in the lyrics that conclude the parodos[80] pleads for him to be allowed to stay. The Coryphaeus gives a courteous answer, but insists that Oedipus must leave, since he and his companions fear that the presence of a polluted person may bring upon them the anger of the gods.[81] At this Oedipus protests that it is his name only, not his actions, which the men of Colonus are afraid of; his actions have consisted in suffering rather than doing.[82] His parricide and incest were performed in ignorance; and though in the first *Oedipus* it is nowhere suggested that the fact of ignorance mitigates pollution, in the second play Oedipus insists throughout that his ignorance makes a difference to his guilt. After Ismene has departed to offer sacrifice, the Chorus again questions Oedipus about his past;[83] the scene is included, it seems, to give Oedipus the opportunity to insist upon his ignorance with the strongest possible emphasis.[84] He even claims that he is "pure according to the law." [85]

Does this indicate a marked change in the Athenian attitude to pollution since the production of the first Oedipus, which is usually guessed to have taken place during the thirties or twenties of the fifth century?[86] I wonder whether the difference is not to be accounted for by the comprehensive curse which in the first play Oedipus lays upon the killer of Laius.[87] Apollo has said that the murderer must be killed or banished,[88] and the curse itself condemns him to be an outcast.[89] In the second play we hear nothing of such a curse, and the form of the story used is not consistent with its having been pronounced, for here Sophocles, like Homer and Euripides, makes Oedipus remain at Thebes after the discovery of his involuntary crimes.

Theseus, who as the men of Colonus recognise is the person best qualified to pronounce upon religious matters, has no hesitation in admitting Oedipus to his country, and when they meet makes no mention of his visitor's parricide and incest until Oedipus himself appears to raise the subject.[90] Later, after Theseus has rebuked Creon for his violent attempt to force Oedipus to go away with him, Creon tries to justify himself by protesting that he has felt sure that Athens would never harbour a man guilty of such crimes.[91] Again Oedipus insists on the involuntary nature of his actions. They happened, he says, because it was the will of the gods that they should happen; perhaps they nursed an ancient wrath against his family.[92] The origin of the curse upon the Labdacids is no part of the subject-matter of the second *Oedipus,* and to go into it in detail would distract attention from the main issues. But the curse has by no means ceased to be effective, as we see not only from the conduct of Eteocles and Polyneices, but from that of Oedipus. Even the intercession of Antigone can do nothing to mitigate the fierce hatred of Oedipus for his sons, which is even greater than the love he bears his daughters. Like the earlier Oedipus, like Antigone, like Electra, the aged Oedipus has all the pride, anger and stubbornness which go with a heroic nature. Against him the curse has done its worst, and can no longer cause him suffering, but it can still affect his attitude towards the next generation of its victims. Not only the end of Eteocles and Polyneices, but that of Antigone and perhaps Ismene, is foreshadowed; what else can be the meaning of Antigone's final request to Theseus that he convey her and her sister to Thebes?

That the importance of hereditary curses in Sophoclean drama is so little recognised is due, I suggest, to the poet's abandonment of the practise of composing the three tragedies of a tetralogy on a continuous theme; but there is still abundant evidence to prove the fact. Now we must inquire whether the curse incurred by Laius can have any bearing on the plot of the first *Oedipus.*

According to the Chorus of the *Seven Against Thebes*,[93] Apollo forbade Laius to have issue, warning him that if he disobeyed his son would kill him and marry Iocaste. "In Aeschylus," says Dodds, echoing Wilamowitz and others, "the disaster could have been avoided, but Laius sinfully disobeyed, and his sin brought ruin to his descendants. In Aeschylus the story was, like the *Oresteia,* a tale of crime and punishment; but Sophocles chose otherwise—that is why he altered the form of the oracle." [94] Did Sophocles alter the form of the oracle? In his play[95] Iocaste tells Oedipus how the oracle once warned Laius that he would die at his son's hands. She does not add that the oracle also told him that the son in question would marry his own mother. Her reason for omitting this detail is presumably that it was not at that moment relevant; because it is not omitted from Oedipus' later account of the oracle given to himself,[96] and it can hardly have been conceived as absent from the earlier oracle given to Laius. Since Iocaste in telling Oedipus of the oracle to Laius omits this detail, it is hardly surprising that she should omit another which is not important for her purpose, that Apollo did not merely predict that Laius would perish at his son's hands, but warned him not to beget a son who would be sure to kill him. In any case, it makes no difference which thing Apollo did, since the effect would be the same. As Perrotta has already shown, it is not true that Sophocles altered the form of the oracle.[97]

Even in Aeschylus, the story of Oedipus was not strictly a tale of crime and punishment; but what of the story of Laius? All that we know of Aeschylus indicates that he strongly believed that the gods did not punish men without a reason.[98] If in Aeschylus' trilogy Apollo told Laius not to have children, we cannot help wondering what Laius had done to cause Apollo to do this.

Several ancient commentaries and mythographic works contain a story which might explain the guilt of Laius; its substance is as follows.[99] Laius was hospitably entertained by Pelops, who had a young son, Chrysippus, famous for his beauty; he is said to have fascinated Zeus and Theseus, as well as Laius. Under pretext of teaching the boy how to drive a chariot, Laius kidnapped him and carried him to Thebes. Chrysippus killed himself, and his father Pelops cursed Laius.

That story, perhaps with some variations, formed the plot of the *Chrysippus* of Euripides. Welcker[100] believed that it was told in the early epic called the *Oedipodeia,* which must have been written not later than the sixth century; and it formed part of the bold attempt to reconstruct the plot of the *Oedipodeia* published by Erich Bethe in 1891.[101] Bethe's reconstruction was severely criticised by Carl Robert in his learned book *Oidipus,* published in 1915.[102] Robert showed that Bethe had not proved that the *Oedipodeia* used the Chrysippus story, but he did not show that it cannot have used it; despite much discussion, the point remains in doubt.[103] Was the Chrysippus story used by Aeschylus, as not only Welcker but his great adversary Hermann believed? [104] The evidence is purely circumstantial. First, it is most unlikely that Euripides invented this legend; either he found it in an early epic, or in Aeschylus, or in both. Secondly, all that we know of Aeschylus indicates that Laius cannot have been punished for nothing; at the beginning of his trilogy about the Labdacids must have come the initial act of *hybris*, the ἀρχὴ κακῶν His three plays were called *Laius, Oedipus, Seven Against Thebes;* in the first, Laius spoke the prologue.[105] What was the Laius about? The one suitable legend that involves Laius is the Chrysippus story.[106]

It is impossible to rule out this suggestion, as one learned scholar wished to, on the ground that Aeschylus would not have made use of the "erotisch-pathologische Stoff" of this legend.[107] Two fragments of his trilogy about Achilles prove beyond all doubt that Aeschylus made the love of Achilles and Patroclus into one of the homosexual relationships that in his own day so frequently existed between young Greek noblemen.[108] Laius was according to one tradition the first mortal to adopt this practice. If reproached with it, he would have been able to quote the precedent of Zeus' dealings with Ganymedes and Poseidon's with the aggrieved father of his victim.[109] If Aeschylus told the story, he doubtless made more of Laius' rape in violation of hospitality than of the abnormal character of his passion; the crime of Laius would amount to neither more nor less than that of Paris.

I think it probable that Aeschylus did use the Chrysippus story. I think also that Sophocles took it for granted that his audience would realise that a curse inherited from Laius rested upon Oedipus. Why, then, I shall be asked, is this not made explicit in the text? My answer is firstly that the text does contain several passages that are not easy to explain except in terms of this suggestion,[110] and secondly that this is not the only case in which Sophocles has made an allusive and almost enigmatic use of a story whose existence is essential to his purpose, but which for artistic reasons must not be allowed to loom too large.

Let us first consider certain places in the text. After the Theban slave has at last removed all doubts about his real identity, Oedipus prays that he may prove now to be looking for the last time upon the light of day—"I who am sprung," he says, "from those who should not have begotten me, who am living with those I should not be living with, who have killed those whom I should not have killed." [111] Why should Laius and Iocaste not have begotten Oedipus? The words have far more point if we recognise that Laius was warned beforehand. Next, during the kommos that follows his self-blinding, Oedipus tells the Chorus that the daimon who put into his head the idea of tearing out his own eyes was none other than Apollo.[112] Apollo's prediction had by that time been accomplished; why should he take delight in still continuing to persecute the wretched Oedipus? In the Aeschylean trilogy he nourishes a special animosity against the Labdacids. When Eteocles sees his inevitable end approaching, he cries out, "Let the whole race of Laius, loathed by Phoebus, vanish in the wind, having the wave of Cocytus for its inheritance." [113] When the messenger comes to announce the death of the two sons of Oedipus at each other's hands, he declares that the seventh and last gate of the city has been taken by Apollo himself, "bringing to its conclusion for the race of Oedipus the ancient rashness of Laius." [114] Earlier in the *Oedipus,* Apollo's answer to the prayer and sacrifice of Iocaste[115] has been the coming of the Corinthian messenger, who thinks he brings good news, but brings in fact the final proof of Oedipus' origin. In this play, as in Aeschylus, Apollo loathes the race of Laius. Later in the kommos, Oedipus exclaims, "But now I am wretched and the child of parents unholy." [116] That is most easily explained if we assume that the words mean what they say. In the long speech following that kommos, in which Oedipus tries once more to justify his self-blinding, he tells how he himself by uttering his curse has commanded all men to cast out "the impious one, him whom the gods have shown to be impure and of the race of Laius." Membership of the race of Laius was not, of course, specified in the curse, but that is not a sufficient reason for doubting the soundness of the text. "Oedipus' thought passes," in Jebb's words, "from the unknown person of the edict to himself." [117] For him, the strongest possible proof of his impurity is his belonging to the race of Laius.

One may still ask why the poet has not taken care to insert

into the text a passage that would make it quite obvious that Oedipus is punished for his father's crime. For such a passage to occur before the point at which it is established that Oedipus killed Laius would of course be impossible.[118] For it to occur afterwards would be almost as undesirable; for this would mean removing attention from Oedipus to direct it upon his long-dead father. Thoughout the play, but above all towards the end, Oedipus remains the centre of the action; what matters now is not whether the crime was vcluntary or not, but the mere fact of crime. His story is not primarily a story of guilt and punishment. It is told to illustrate the fragility of mankind, even the strongest and cleverest of whom may in a moment be struck down.[119] After the climax of Oedipus' exposure, the Chorus do not sing, "The gods have punished the guilty family"; they sing, "Ah, the generations of men, how I esteem you in your life equal to nothing." [120] The main burden of the stasimon is the feebleness of men, and only towards its end does the Chorus mention that Time the all-seeing has long since pronounced judgment on the evil marriage. Just the same sentiment is voiced by Aeschylus' Chorus a moment before the death of Agamemnon,[121] who like Oedipus does not himself incur, but has inherited, a family curse. At the conclusion of the *Oedipus,* it is repeated in the final utterance of the Chorus, whose ascription has been so wrongly doubted.[122]

The view of the *Oedipus Rex* which I have expressed was put forward, in all essentials, by Perrotta in 1935;[123] no one who has written on the subject since appears to have taken any notice. Why is this? It is natural for a modern audience to resist the suggestion that a tragedian may presuppose in his audience a knowledge of a myth which he indicates only by a hint. Our attitude to the delights of mythological narration, so richly savoured by the ancients, is somewhat puritanical. Brought up as most of us have been to suppose that the moral, the religious, the parenetic content of a tragedy is in every way by far its most important part, we are apt to treat the legends as if they were nothing but a collection of independent stories which served the tragedians as pegs on which to hang their warning tales. We have rightly been instructed that the play itself contains all that is relevant to its explanation, and this may make us slow to realise what slight indications may serve to show that something in a play is relevant to its understanding.

But for the tragedians heroic legend did not exist simply to provide dramatists with plots. It was known to them for the most part from the many epics then extant; and though they were free to choose between varying stories, and even to invent new features, in the main they respected epic tradition. The gods and heroes of the epic were to them not simply fictions, or figures of the distant past with no importance for the present; they were real beings, many of whom had power to influence events on earth, and they were able to inspire genuine terror or devotion. The tragedians made use of vast numbers of mythic personalities and legends; the apparent predominance of certain families may well be due largely to the makers of the selections of tragedies that have survived, who liked to compare tragedies by different authors about identical or similar subjects. Legend for them resembled a vast, intricate and loosely coherent web, any one of whose parts was ultimately connected with all other parts. We are sometimes told that the audience did not know the myths on the authority of Aristotle; he uses the present tense and refers presumably to his own time. A generation earlier, the comic poet Antiphanes says that the audience does know the myths. The best way of knowing whether the fifth-century audience knew the myths is to study the use made of them by fifth-century poets, and that suggests that the fifth-century audience, or at any rate the most discriminating part of it, knew the myths well.[124] They had an enormous relish in hearing the myths narrated, as the popularity of the epic recitation would lead us to expect; one feature of tragedy in particular, the messenger speech together with such narrative speeches as the false account of the chariot race given by the Paidagogos in the *Electra,* makes this affinity particularly clear. The close connection of tragedy with epic was in the ancient world a commonplace; that we need to be reminded of it results partly from our obsession with the development of Greek civilization to the neglect of its more static elements, and partly from the preoccupation with the religion and morality implicit in a work of art which leads us to view this part out of proportion to the whole.

Let us in illustration briefly glance at the place of the legend in each of the complete plays of Sophocles. Each not only describes what happens to its characters during the space of time covered by the action, but tells a good deal about the events that precede and follow it; each contains allusions to several different characters and legends outside the main action, some of which would be obscure to those ignorant of myth and not all of which are unimportant for the plot.

Take first the *Ajax*. During its course we learn that Ajax was son of Telamon by Eriboea, Teucer by the Trojan captive Hesione,[125] and that Telamon took part in the earlier sack of Troy and expected Ajax to equal his achievement.[126] We learn of the great deeds performed by Ajax before Troy, of the duel with Hector and the defence of the ships, and of the award of the arms of Achilles to Odysseus. As in the *Philoctetes*, Odysseus is taunted with being the bastard son of Sisyphus;[127] similarly the Atreidae are taunted with the Phrygian origin of their ancestor Pelops and the adultery of their mother Aerope.[128] Afterwards Teucer was to be driven from home by the angry Telamon[129] and Ajax' line was to be continued by his son Eurysaces; both facts are clearly indicated.

In the *Electra*, the curse of the Atreidae is taken back to the crime of Pelops;[130] as I have already indicated, knowledge of the story of Pelops and Hippodamia, Myrtilus and Oenomaus is presupposed. The sad fate of Electra is illustrated by comparison with Niobe and Procne, [131] the supposed life of Agamemnon in the grave with that of Amphiaraus.[132] Clytemnestra and Electra debate the justice of Iphigeneia's sacrifice; the night of Agamemnon's murder is recalled.[133] If nothing is said about the future troubles of Orestes, that is because any mention of them would damage the effect of the conclusion.

I have already mentioned the part played in the *Antigone* by the fate of Oedipus and Iocaste; that of their sons also finds a place. Antigone's fate is compared with those of other illustrious persons who have suffered incarceration, Danae, Lycurgus, Cleopatra;[134] like Electra, she compares herself with Niobe.[135] Tiresias' speech glances at the story that Creon's exposure of the bodies of his enemies led to foreign intervention;[136] the legend of an attack on Creon by Theseus was of course well known at Athens. Eurydice, lamenting for the death of Haemon, speaks of the earlier loss of another son, Menoeceus, who in the *Phoenissae* of Euripides plunges into the dragon's lair to save the city by sacrificing his own life.[137]

The *Philoctetes* presupposes a considerable acquaintance with the whole range of legends about Troy. Philoctetes is the son of Poeas and a native of the region about Mount Oeta,[138] a district which receives almost as much notice as Lemnos itself. He has acquired the bow of Heracles by lighting, after the hero's son Hyllus has refused, the pyre containing his agonised but still living body.[139] Like the fates of Electra and Antigone, that of Philoctetes is illustrated by a mythological parallel, that of Ixion on his wheel.[140] Earlier events in the siege of Troy have their importance; the deaths of Achilles, Patroclus, Ajax and Antilochus, the survival of Odysseus, Diomedes and Thersites find a mention;[141] so do even such figures as Phoenix and the sons of Theseus. The capture of the Trojan prophet Helenus has importance for the plot;[142] after the play ends, Philoctetes will kill Paris[143] and with Neoptolemus will share in the Achaean triumph.

Still more extensive knowledge of the sagas is required for the full understanding of the story of the *Women of Trachis*; that is why in place of an hypothesis we find a long extract from the mythographer Apollodorus.[144] Long ago, Heracles won Deianeira, daughter of the Aetolian king Oeneus, in battle with the great river that flows through her father's dominions; carrying her away, he met and killed the centaur Nessus. Six of the labours done for Eurystheus by command of Hera are recalled

by Heracles. Most important is the killing of the hydra, whose
blood poisoned his arrows; Deianeira knows how Chiron, accidentally pricked by one, gave up his immortality in order to
escape the agony it caused.[145] Finally I come to the instance
which supplies the closest parallel to the allusion in the *Oedipus
Rex* to the curse on Laius. Once Heracles realises that his last
hour is come, he orders his son Hyllus to prove his paternity
by helping him in a matter of supreme importance;[146] before he
will tell Hyllus what it is, he makes him swear by Zeus that
he will perform it. When he hears, Hyllus is much distressed;
he is to heap up a great pyre upon the summit of Mount Oeta,
place the living Heracles upon it and then set light to it. In the
end Hyllus is forced to do all that is required, except that he de-
clines in person to apply the torch.

We know well, though not from Sophocles, why Heracles
ordered the pyre to be lit and who finally lit it. According to a
legend which was beyond all question universally known in
Sophocles' time, the fire extinguished only the mortal part of
Heracles; Zeus caught the spirit in his arms and took it to
Olympus to become a god. Bowra has observed that Sophocles
means to allude to this story, and has explained the reason for
his oblique way of doing so.[147] Direct reference to the apotheosis
would spoil the tragic effect of the story just enacted; yet sup-
pression would be impossible. Hyllus, left alone upon the earth,
can see nothing but the tragedy of the terrible end of both his
parents, brought upon them by the crime of Heracles in destroying Eurytus and Oechalia to win Iole; he breaks out into
what Professor Dodds has called "a violent protest against
divine injustice." [148] Telling Iole to remain in the house, the
Chorus says she has witnessed "terrible and sudden deaths, and
many fresh disasters, and none of these is not Zeus." [149]

The evidence of this passage is the only evidence outside the
Oedipus Rex that Dodds has cited in favour of his view that
Sophocles "did not believe, or did not always believe, that the
gods were in any human sense 'just.'" Before we admit its
value, we must consider the whole context. Hyllus and the

other survivors know nothing of the real purpose of the pyre; yet it is certain that Sophocles intends that the audience shall know it, for a poet who chose to recall the detail that not Hyllus but Philoctetes or his father Poeas lit the pyre[150] certainly meant his hearers to remember all the rest. For the audience, Sophocles has made it possible to transcend for a moment the limited view of happenings in the world normally possible to mortals and to see, for once, into the purposes of Zeus. In the *Philoctetes,* this purpose is effected by the speech of the now divine Heracles from the machine; in the *Women of Trachis* a subtler method is employed.

The conclusion of the *Women of Trachis* affords a specially clear insight into the attitude to divine justice which a careful study of Sophocles reveals. The justice of the gods is not, in his view, easy for mortals to perceive; yet had he ceased to believe in it, Sophocles would have asked, "why must I dance?"; in Electra's words, "Aidos would be gone, and so would the piety of all mortals." Since it is far removed from Christian or other modern notions of justice, Sophoclean justice is even harder for us to understand than it was for Sophocles' contemporaries. *Dike* means not only "justice," but "the order of the universe," and from the human point of view that order often seems to impose a natural rather than a moral law. Yet Sophocles believed that the gods were just, and just in a sense in which the word was in his day applied to men.[151] What made it hard, he thought, for men to understand the justice of the gods was the immense extent of time which may separate cause from punishment, and the complex interweaving within human history of different causal chains of injustice followed by chastisement.

VI

The Sophists:
Thucydides:
Euripides

THE SCEPTICISM regarding the gods expressed by
Xenophanes seems not to be echoed by any of his contemporaries, nor by any writer before the middle of the fifth century.
But from that time on scepticism and atheism became forces to
be reckoned with. Political life was such as to provide a market
for those able to teach rhetoric and politics, so that the theories
of such persons became widely known. Euripides and Thucydides lived in a world conditioned by the methods and the
opinions of the great sophists, and many have supposed that
they themselves shared and wished to propagate many of those
opinions. The influence upon them of sophistic methods may
be thought to be confirmed; but how far such opinions actually
formed part of the background against which these authors see
the world remains a complicated question.

Unbelief, says Plato in the tenth book of the *Laws*, results
from a combination of the scepticism engendered by such cosmological speculations as the materialistic theory of Anaxagoras
about the heavenly bodies with the relativism in ethics promoted by such thinkers as Protagoras.[1] The increasing familiarity of educated persons with views about the cosmos not at

first sight easily reconcilable with traditional beliefs, or with the worship of the heavenly bodies which Plato so warmly recommended, was no doubt a factor in the growth of scepticism. Aristophanes ridicules Euripides for his occasional exploitation of theories of this kind, especially those of Diogenes of Apollonia, to strike out effective paradoxes about the gods and the nature of the universe.[2] Anaxagoras was actually prosecuted for atheism on account of what he said about the heavenly bodies.[3] But this was a political move, directed against Pericles; and what seems to me notable is how little persecution the expression of such views attracted. The thinking of the early cosmologists was in general far from irreligious. Virtually all their systems could with a modicum of ingenuity be made consistent at least with a belief in Zeus, "the one wise who is unwilling and willing" to be called by that name. Even Xenophanes seems to have respected cult and belief in ordinary life,[4] and the same is true of his fifth-century followers.

A more important factor in the growth of atheism is relativism. The comparative study of institutions, going back at least to Hecataeus,[5] encouraged people to doubt whether the traditional Greek account of the gods was necessarily truer than those given by other peoples. The story of Protagoras' early training by the Magi[6] may symbolise a true fact in that the study of Persian religion may have influenced his outlook, as it did that of Herodotus. But was Protagoras an atheist? His famous declaration that he did not know whether the gods did or did not exist is not a statement of unbelief but a confession of ignorance. The key word in the sentence is surely the word "know," which must be viewed in the light of the distinction between knowledge and opinion fashionable at the time.[7] Von Fritz seems to me right in maintaining that when Protagoras wrote that "man is the measure of all things, indicating of those that exist that they exist and of those that do not that they do not," he had in mind not the judgment of the individual man, but the collective opinion of mankind in general.[8] He had therefore to take into account the empirical fact that all human communities known to him held some kind of theistic belief, and that he did so is confirmed by the myth put by Plato into his mouth and widely held to reflect his actual doctrines.[9] Zeus is there said to have sent Aidos and Dike to men, or rather to have given them the capacity to acquire these attributes, provided they are rightly educated. Men alone among animals believe in the gods, because they are akin to them. For Protagoras, the concept of justice was not a given empirical fact based on sensation, like, say, the notion of a rhinoceros, but a norm, a concept created by the human mind.[10] To call such a norm man-made is not to call it arbitrary, nor is such an opinion necessarily irreligious; indeed, Protagoras in Plato maintains that the power to establish such a norm is implanted in men by Zeus himself.[11] For Protagoras, the existence of Zeus was a matter not of knowledge, but of belief; but that does not make Protagoras an unbeliever.[12] It is of prime importance to distinguish the real position of Protagoras, with which Plato nowhere comes to grips, from that of the immoralists whom Plato so vividly portrays.

Democritus found some difficulty in accommodating to his atomic theory the existence of immortal gods; yet like Protagoras he was not an atheist. He too reckoned with the objective fact that most men believed in gods. They got their notions of divinity, he thought, partly from contemplating the wonders of nature, in particular the heavenly bodies and their regular movements.[13] He describes how in early times a few wise men held up their hands towards what the Greeks now call the air and said, "All things are words of Zeus and he knows all things and gives and takes away all things and is the king of all." [14] Like Protagoras he held that our evidence for the existence of gods is uncertain; but he was impressed by the appearance in dreams and visions of what he called *eidola,* which he held must correspond with some empirical reality.[15]

In ethics, Democritus shows no sympathy with immoralism but strongly insists on the paramount importance of *Dike,* which he couples with *Arete.* He explicitly denies that the just

man will act differently whether he is observed or not; the just
man, he says, will feel *Aidos* before himself, which will restrain
him from wrong action, whether he is observed or not.[16] *Aidos,*
in the myth of Protagoras, accompanied Dike when she was sent
by Zeus to men. All too many classical scholars, lacking philosophical training and imbued with reverence for Plato, have
taken his word that his was the only serious philosophical attempt made at this time to fill the gap left by the old literal
belief that just conduct was enjoined by Zeus;[17] and we must lay
special emphasis on the empirical theory of justice of Protagoras
and Democritus and its likeness to those held by modern empirical philosophers.[18]

Certainly Protagorean relativism could be abused. After
Gorgias, Protagoras was the first rhetorician, the first to claim the
ability to make the weaker case appear the stronger. The carica-
ture of Aristophanes in the debate of the two Logoi in the
Clouds shows how easily this could be confused with making
the worse case appear the better.[19] But were immoralist theories
of justice openly advocated at this time? The largest papyrus
fragment of the sophist Antiphon[20] has often been cited as an
instance, but there is not enough preserved to make this any
thing like certain; if we had more of the surrounding context,
we might well learn that this writer was no more an immoralist
than Protagoras, but the piece certainly indicates that such
theories of justice were in the air. How an immoralist theory
could be developed out of Protagorean relativism is shown by
the famous speech preserved from the satyr-play *Sisyphus,*
ascribed by some to Euripides and by others to Plato's relative,
the notorious politician Critias.[21] The speech gives an account
of early human progress very like those of the Platonic Protagoras or Theseus in Euripides' play *The Suppliant Women;*[22]
only here the gods do not send Aidos and Dike to men. Instead,
men make laws, so as to set up Dike as a tyrant, and since these
laws cannot control men whose actions cannot be observed, a
cunning man invents the gods, who are supposed to punish
crime.[23] We have to remember that this speech was spoken by a

character in a play, probably by that Sisyphus whose punishment by Zeus was a notorious example of divine justice; and however well the theory may have accorded with Critias' personal practice, he cannot have put it forward as his personal opinion.

Such theories were certainly in the air towards the end of the fifth century, however cautious we are in handling the evidence of Plato, which we shall presently consider. Even more than new opinions about the heavenly bodies, they were held by conservative persons to have a corrupting tendency. But the conservatives were overwhelmingly in the majority, and on the whole they found it necessary to take very little action against the sceptics and immoralists. The occasional fun poked at the gods in comedy is no evidence against the religious conservatism of the ordinary man; it is when a religion is sure of itself that such amusement is permitted.[24] Pericles might be a friend of Anaxagoras, but he was also on good terms with the diviner Lampon.[25] The scare over the mutilation of the Hermae deprived the Athenian force in Sicily of its best commander, and the refusal of Nicias to order a retreat before the moon had suffered eclipse cost it its last chance of escape. Clearly the great mass of Athenians shared the complacent piety and the superstitious reverence for signs and omens that are attested everywhere in the works of Xenophon, an author who supplies far better evidence for the beliefs and attitudes of the common man than Thucydides, Euripides or Plato. There were people like Socrates' sceptical acquaintance Aristodemus[26] or the poet Cinesias with his ancient form of Hellfire Club;[27] but every mention of such people shows that they incurred overwhelming social disapproval. Such sporadic and unsystematic action as was taken against atheism contrasts sharply with the inquisitorial methods recommended by Plato[28] and later put into practice by churches and parties based upon dogmatic monism. The prosecution of Anaxagoras was a political move against Pericles. The evidence for a prosecution of Protagoras is, as von Fritz has pointed out,[29] unimpressive; he may have been confused with the less celebrated person but more notorious atheist, Diagoras of Melos. He actually wrote a book, the *Apopyrgizontes Logoi*, denying the existence of the gods and mocking various cults; it would be highly interesting to know what arguments he used and whether the Athenians had any special reasons for not allowing his atheism to go unpunished.[30] In the more famous case of Socrates, we happen to know that there were such special reasons, and that the charge of atheism was unjust.

Those who have written on this subject have usually failed to point out, perhaps because they are, whether consciously or not, confused by apparent modern analogies, that being an atheist in late fifth-century Athens was very different from being one in any Christian country while the church was still strong enough to persecute. The absence of anything like a clergy—I know that some scholars have done their best with prophets, diviners and exegetes, but it is a miserable best—or of any systematic body of religious doctrine supported by a church, made it hard for the ancient atheist to find anything to protest about, and if he could, it was hardly worth protesting. Indeed throughout the period we have been discussing the educated classes were gradually coming to dismiss much of the traditional mythology, as Xenophanes had done, as untrue and unedifying. But they realised, as Heraclitus had done, that the traditional beliefs and observances were by no means incompatible with a more sophisticated kind of theism; belief in a god or gods that had been refined by the doctrines of philosophy could easily go together with the maintenance of the ancient worship. Further, the world outlook of many modern thinkers did not radically conflict with that of the established religion; Heraclitus, Protagoras and Democritus are all cases in point. Among the lower classes the traditional religion was more persistent; from time to time it was supplemented by the importation of a new oriental cult or the emergence of a new mystery religion.[31] Until the rise of Christianity, atheism in the ancient world was to present no social problem.

Let us now return to Plato. He strongly maintains that the atheism and immoralism of the sophists and their pupils were in a large measure responsible for the immoral policies adopted by the Greek states, particularly the Athenian democracy, and for the catastrophes to which they led. But the people responsible for these policies were not the sophists or their pupils, whatever share of guilt may be assigned to Critias or Alcibiades, but the entire governing bodies of the states concerned, consisting for the most part of conservative and pious persons. In the Callicles of the *Gorgias* and the Thrasymachus of the *Republic,* Plato draws two brilliant portraits of immoralists, one a politician and the other a rhetorician, and allows Socrates to refute their doctrines. But nowhere, not even in those passages in the *Protagoras* and the *Theaetetus* in which the views of Protagoras are discussed, does Plato deal systematically with the empirical conception of justice as it was developed by Protagoras and by Democritus.

According to the traditional religion, injustice was punished by the gods, and Plato set himself to replace this primitive religious sanction with a metaphysical and theological construction. His contention that justice in itself is good, injustice bad, depends ultimately on the soul's intuition of the form, the essence, the hypostatised ideal concept of justice. But as if this metaphysical guarantee were not enough, Plato clings to the ancient belief that injustice is punished in another world, using his eschatological myths to lend it the strongest possible dramatic emphasis. Human destiny is regulated according to moral law, he argues in his last work, for the universe is so contrived that the place of everything depends upon its quality, but the quality of everything depends upon the human will.[32]

In the traditional Greek belief knowledge of justice came to men from Zeus, and Zeus punished men who failed to act on it. If according to Protagoras the notion of justice exists only in the human mind, that is not to say that it is not Zeus who has implanted it. In a sense, therefore, Protagoras' theory is close to the traditional Greek view. Plato's, on the other hand, rests upon a metaphysical and theological dogmatism having more in common with the religions of the east, and also with the monistic and dogmatic systems, both religious and secular, of the modern world. Many contributors to the discussion of the reasons for the Greek decline have used J. B. Bury's phrase "the failure of nerve." [33] The first important failure of nerve was that of Plato.

But supposing it is granted that the chauvinism of the Athenian imperialists cannot be assigned to the evil influence of the sophists, what can be said of the sister theory that it can be traced directly to the imperfect concept of morality inherited from the Homeric age? [34] Was such behaviour inevitable in a people whose basic terms of ethical commendation had been designed to describe not moral but physical or intellectual excellence? We can look back, as Plato could not, upon many centuries of history in which the whole population of great nations has been educated in terms of a religion which inculcates an elevated conception of righteousness, supported by a solemn supernatural sanction, centuries during which belief was hardly questioned. Yet can we truthfully maintain that the standard of morality observed by the people of these nations either in public or in private life has on the whole been notably higher than that attained by the Athenian democracy and other Greek communities during the fifth century? I doubt if any serious student of history would reply with an unhesitating Yes.

In most periods of history and among most peoples that have risen above the state of savages we find a double standard of virtue. First comes the original notion of *arete* or *virtus* as the quality of manliness or courage, and later of all kinds of competitive excellence; soon afterwards emerges the standard of virtue seen as the quality of righteousness or justice. Without some measure of both kinds of virtue not even a gang of thieves, much less a civic community, can for long maintain existence. Like many religions Christianity places most emphasis on virtue as goodness, and has sometimes given to this alone the name of virtue; but not all Christians have subordinated one kind of virtue to the other. The early Greek civilisation, on the other hand, used the word *arete* to denote virtue as valour or excellence, and spoke of virtue as righteousness in terms of a different concept, that of Dike. As time went on, the second concept became more prominent, and the word *arete* itself acquired more and more ethical overtones.

Among the philosophies of the Hellenistic world the influence of Plato was paramount; only in the system of Epicurus did the views of Protagoras and Democritus, remaining faithful as they did to some essential features of the early Greek world outlook, find an echo. Only when the Middle Ages were at an end could the thread of this undogmatic strain in Greek philosophy be taken up. But my present purpose is not to go further with the history of Greek ethics, but to consider the standpoint with regard to Zeus and justice of two great writers of the period I have been discussing, Thucydides and Euripides.

In the history of Thucydides the gods are conspicuous by their absence; the divine motivation which Herodotus took over from the epic has been totally abandoned. Oracles and prophecies may find a mention, but never in a way that suggests that we should believe them. Those who in moments of desperation put their trust in the gods are pitilessly dealt with. The Plataeans appeal for mercy in the name of heaven and get none;[35] the Melians hope the gods will help them and are disappointed;[36] Nicias tries to encourage his defeated troops by arguing that the gods cannot allow their fortune to be bad from start to finish, and he proves mistaken.[37] The world depicted by Thucydides is a ruthless world, in which the strong openly assert and pitilessly exercise their right to rule over the weak.[38] Some historians draw from this the inference that the historian himself held the same values which obtain in the world which he portrays; that under sophistic influence he had come to believe in the right of the stronger; that he regarded Athenian imperialism with wholehearted approval, and deplored only the tactical mistakes which after the death of Pericles led to its collapse. Such a view has most often been taken by those who have most strongly insisted on the "scientific" nature of his way of writing history, on his exemption from the superstitions and prejudices of his time, and on the modernity of his views and methods. Some writers have assumed that the admiration for Pericles shown in his work, and particularly in the famous chapter following the mention of his death, proves him to have been an adherent of that statesman, and to be concerned to justify his policy. Thucydides has made it clear that he felt no admiration for Pericles' successors, but it is argued that he deplored only their incompetence, not their inhumanity, or that if he deplored their inhumanity, he did so only because it was bad policy.

The notion of Thucydides as a *Realpolitiker* has lately been challenged in a series of brilliant articles by Hermann Strasburger.[39] He has drawn attention[40] to the marked difference between the presentation of the Athenian empire by Thucydides and the line regularly taken by its apologists during the fourth century and later. Thucydides in his brief summary of events between the Persian and the Archidamian Wars remarks that Naxos was the first allied city which Athens "enslaved contrary to custom";[41] this is a powerful emotive expression of a kind found throughout the history in the mouths of the enemies of Athens. At Sparta in 431 the Athenians justify their empire by tracing its history from its origins; in the beginning it was forced upon them, and now honour, fear and profit forbid them to relinquish it.[42] They claim that they have earned it by their services to the common weal; they openly assert the right of the stronger to rule over the weaker. If the Spartans think it unjust, that is because it is in conflict with their interest; but no one has ever been restrained by the thought that he is acting unjustly from acquiring what his strength permits him to acquire. They claim special credit for using their strength more humanely than they might use it; if others took over their empire, they say, their own moderation would be appreciated. All this is said by an Athenian envoy in 431, while policy was still under the control of Pericles.

Pericles himself does not say that the Athenians have acquired their empire only for the benefit of others; nor does he assure the Athenians that their allies are only too willing to be their subjects, as Athenian apologists were to maintain during the fourth century and indeed later. There is indeed something to be said for this view, as recent controversy has shown;[43] there is also, as the same controversy has shown, something to be said against it; what matters at the moment is that it was certainly not the opinion of Thucydides. Pericles tells the Athenians that their empire is like a tyranny, which it is thought wicked to acquire, but which it is not safe to let go.[44] But more than with fear or profit, he is concerned with honour. He is proud that the Athenians have ruled over more Greeks than any other Greeks;[45] for him the empire is something that an inactive man may find fault with, but which anyone who has the ambition to achieve anything must admire.[46] At present it incurs hatred and envy, but in the future it will bring renown. Most modern critics have been too intent on seeing Pericles' speeches as evidence of his belief in democracy, free speech and enlightenment to notice that he is scarcely less concerned with honour, fame, renown than is Alcibiades or indeed Achilles.

The striking saying of Pericles that the empire is like a tyranny is echoed unmistakably enough, like other Periclean phrases, by Cleon.[47] Even those who are persuaded that Cleon was an admirable person, unfairly traduced by a hostile tradition, must agree that Thucydides did not share this opinion. Why are the echoes there? Are they simply to underline the absurdity of Cleon's claim to be Pericles' successor, or are they there to indicate that there was indeed a significant measure of continuity between their policies? In different ways Cleon, Nicias and Alcibiades might each have claimed to be the heir of Pericles, but none of these claims would have been justified, and all would have been rejected by Thucydides. Cleon is not blamed for giving up the Periclean policy of not trying to make new conquests in time of war; that reproach falls rather upon Alcibiades. Cleon is severely blamed for rejecting, for corrupt motives, the chance to make peace after the victory at Pylos; it may also be argued, though the point might be disputed, that he is blamed for being the first Athenian politician to punish a revolted ally by a general massacre. Is the echo meant to suggest that the policy of Pericles was likely to lead, in different circumstances, to the policy of Cleon?

The once generally held opinion that according to Thucydides Athenian imperialism took a moderate form under Pericles, but became violent and ruthless under his successors has been powerfully disputed by Strasburger. Thucydides, he argues, aims not at showing how Athenian imperialism developed over a period of time, but rather at revealing the various aspects which it assumed under different leadership and under different political and military conditions. He remarks that the whole question deserves re-examination in detail.[48] As a prelude to such re-examination, one may offer certain observations regarding the historian's personality, his intellectual background and his historical technique.

Given the intellectual atmosphere of the nineteenth century, it was inevitable that the severity of Thucydides' style by comparison with that of Herodotus, together with his strong emphasis upon factual accuracy, should lure its historians into treating him as one of themselves. An historian so painstaking in the establishment of fact and who dispensed, moreover, with the apparatus of divine motivation which Herodotus had taken over from the epic must surely be in every sense a rationalist, a kind of Ranke or Mommsen born before his time. Some went further, and inferred that such an historian must have approved heartily of the attempt made by the one progressive and enlightened power in fifth-century Greece to instil order and discipline into the mass of conflicting petty states, many of them lost in tribalism and superstition.

That view of Thucydides is by no means dead; but in modern

times we have gone some way to redress the balance. Momigliano has pointed out[49] that in many ways Herodotus is a more "scientific" historian than Thucydides; his interests, embracing as they do geography, ethnology and anthropology, are immensely wider, and his practice of offering more than one version of a story in some ways preferable to Thucydides' habit of giving only that version which he himself preferred. Strasburger has pointed out[50] that Thucydides, just as much as Herodotus, is indebted to the epic, a proposition to which many have paid lip service but on which few have acted. He owes to the epic, for example, his view of war and diplomacy as the main subject-matter of history and also his decision to restrict himself to the description of a single war which seemed to him the greatest known to him. In depreciating the importance of the Persian War—it was over in no time, in two land and two sea battles[51]—he is announcing himself as the rival of Herodotus; in depreciating the importance of the Trojan War,[52] he is announcing himself as the rival of Homer. One could draw attention to various allusions and features of technique in Thucydides which recall the epic;[53] but my present concern is not with features of technique, but with ways of thought.

If Thucydides dispenses with the divine motivation of events, that in itself does not show him to have been an unbeliever, or even an agnostic after the fashion of Protagoras. He might simply have abstained from speculations about the divine purpose that could in the nature of things be no more than guesswork. But even if Thucydides was a confirmed atheist, it would hardly be safe to assume that with the act of denying the existence of the gods he at once threw off the beliefs and attitudes of his own time and became a rationalist in any modern sense. A close examination of the pattern of his history reveals the working of a view of human life far easier to relate to other fifth-century attitudes than has often been supposed.

Thucydides believed that if the Athenians had not disregarded Pericles' warning not to try to extend their empire in time of war nor to run risks with the city as the stake they would have emerged from the war successful. The decision that proved fatal was the assembly's resolution to dispatch the Sicilian expedition.[54] It has long been realised by most scholars that the stress on this event, coming just after the Melian Dialogue and the massacre that follows it, can hardly be without significance.[55] The affair at Melos was not in itself an event of major significance in the fortunes of the war, and yet the special emphasis laid upon it by Thucydides must show that it played an important part in his view of the sequence of events. Earlier, after the revolt of Mytilene, the Athenians had narrowly escaped making themselves responsible for such a massacre, and they had been prevented from doing so not by any moral considerations but by arguments based solely on expediency.[56] That episode also was not in itself of vital military importance, and must have been chosen for emphasis for some special reason. During the debate over the proposal to massacre the inhabitants of Mytilene, Cleon's opponent, Diodotus, explains why even the most fearsome deterrents do not restrain men from taking the most deadly risks. Poverty, he says,[57] lends daring to necessity, power adds to insolence and pride the greed for gain, and other human dispositions, as though by the agency of some irresistible power not to be got rid of, lead men into danger. Everywhere are hope and desire, desire leading the way and hope following, desire thinking out the plan and hope furnishing the assumption that good fortune will attend it. Both are infinitely harmful; invisible, as they are, they are more potent than any seen evils. Further, fortune does no less to raise men above themselves; its unexpected appearance can lead even humble persons into danger, still more whole communities, in so far as they can endanger what matters most, freedom or empire, and the individual judges all more wildly because he is one among many.

Diodotus' picture of human motivation is drawn in order to explain why even the most dire deterrents are not effective, but it is relevant not only to the case of the Mytileneans, but to all human action. Men may know well the dangers involved in any enterprise, he says, but still their passions will lead them to take risks; they will give way to the love of gain, spurred on by insolence and pride, for desire and hope together will encourage them to take the plunge. What is said about hope irresistibly recalls the great elegy of Solon; "each mortal is confident until he suffers; then he laments; until that time we gape foolishly in the delight furnished by vain hopes." [58] Men know what is right, says the Euripidean Phaedra, but do not act on this knowledge, because their passions are too strong for them.[59] Achilles when he receives the embassy knows that Ajax is right, but cannot bring himself to yield, because his *thymos* swells with anger.[60] In his case, we are told that Zeus has put it there;[61] in the case of Phaedra, we are not; but how much difference does this make? [62]

When the Athenian assembly takes its most important decision of the war, whether to invade Sicily or not, it ignores the testament of Pericles and chooses wrongly. Homer or Aeschylus would have said that Zeus had sent Ate to take away its wits. They would have asked why he should have done so, and they would surely have found their answer in the brutal imperialist policy which Thucydides has chosen to exemplify in the Melian massacre.[63]

Some believers in Thucydides the *Realpolitiker* have argued that he thought extreme ruthlessness should be avoided simply because it was inexpedient. The way in which the massacre at Melos is followed by the decision to invade Sicily, closely fitting as it does the pattern of Hybris and Ate which a study of the historians's predecessors might have led us to expect, makes it no easier to defend that thesis. Yet we should equally distort the balance of his tragic history if we were to argue that his whole presentation of Athenian imperialism was subtly hostile, and that the story of the war was told as a cautionary tale to warn against imperialism. Those who point to Thucydides' obvious admiration of the magnificence of the empire and the greatness of Pericles are not mistaken; it is only at the moment that they claim that this must show him to be a Periclean partisan[64] that they fling away their chance of perceiving the delicate ambiguity of the historian's attitude.

Thucydides sees the history of the empire in tragic terms, not necessarily because he has been influenced by tragedy,[65] but more probably because like the tragedians, like Herodotus, like most of his contemporaries his mind was profoundly conditioned by the epic and the whole attitude to human life which it expresses. In his presentation of the main action of the history, he gives weight with the impartiality of a great poet both to the empire's splendours and to its miseries; most modern commentators incline the balance one way or the other, and so distort the picture.[66] Individual persons come in only in so far as this cannot be avoided; this is not the tragedy of Pericles, or of Alcibiades, or of any man or men, but the tragedy of Athens. Athens at first judges events rightly, but later is betrayed by hybris into injustice, and loses the faculty of correct judgment. How far this can be put down to divine agencies is a matter for speculation, and the historian does not commit himself. But Greeks who believed in such agencies held, from Homer's time on, that they worked upon the world not from outside but from inside, through human passions acting upon human minds. For all we know, Thucydides may have been a Protagorean agnostic, but we cannot be certain. In the last resort, the question as to whether he believed in the gods or not is not one of any great significance; for if he did reject them, it was the Greek gods, not any other gods whom he rejected.[67] The world as he presents it, like the world presented by Herodotus, is a hard and ruthless world; it is the world of the traditional Greek religion.[68]

Now we come to Euripides. At first sight his world seems radically different from the world of Aeschylus or even Sophocles. Both the older poets present events against the permanent backcloth furnished by the divine world; the human actors, and still more the choruses, constantly reflect upon the question of how the gods may view the current situation. In Euripides the gods are sometimes characters in the plays and often descend from the machine to wind up the action at the end. But for most of the time the divine will remain obscure to the human actors in the drama; the earlier belief that the gods directly motivate human action appears to find no place; and Zeus and his justice either find no mention or are given only perfunctory notice.

These differences are usually accounted for by pointing out that the second half of the fifth century was an age of enlightenment at Athens, and that Euripides was the poet of the enlightenment. His plays abound, as those of Sophocles do not, with echoes of the debates and speculations of the sophists. Speakers in the *agones,* the debates between characters in dialogue metre, which are so frequent in his works use many devices of the new rhetoric; such devices are not absent from Sophocles, but Euripides sometimes echoes the very tone of the sophists in a way Sophocles is careful to avoid. Choral lyrics and monologues, as well as debating speeches, abound with general reflections that echo or repeat the metaphysical or ethical speculations of contemporary philosophers. This poet, it is easily inferred, is a product of the enlightenment whose attitudes he so often mirrors, and must secretly, if not openly, aim to convert his audience to its beliefs and attitudes.

Those scholars who late in the last century revived the study of Euripides with so much enthusiasm themselves wrote in the aftermath of an enlightenment which originated in the seventeenth century, triumphed in the eighteenth and reached its acme, after the reaction against it was already under way, about the middle of the nineteenth. Euripides appealed to them because his situation seemed to them like their own, and they too easily assumed that the enlightenment of his time resembled the enlightenment during theirs. Their Euripides was what would be called in modern jargon a "committed" poet, an enemy of traditional religion, a pioneer of female emancipation and a protester against the brutalities of his own country's imperialism. That portrait was made popular in English-speaking countries by Gilbert Murray,[69] but its creator was Wilamowitz;[70] Karl Reinhardt[71] has amusingly pointed out the resemblance of Phaedra, as sketched by Wilamowitz in the year after the première of *Hedda Gabler,* to an Ibsenian heroine. Murray's Shavian Euripides derives from the Ibsenian Euripides of Wilamowitz.

That conception of Euripides is now no longer popular. It now seems harder to extract from the many different opinions and attitudes voiced by Euripidean characters and choruses those which can safely be regarded as the poet's own. The inscrutability of the divine purpose is often stressed by referring to it in terms borrowed from the vocabulary of presocratic speculation, and the actions attributed to the gods by the familiar myths are often criticised. But the inscrutability of the divine purpose is an ancient commonplace of Greek religion, whose content is not altered by describing it in modern terms; and the expurgation of the myths has a long history, in which Pindar and Aeschylus play an important part. The case for women is sometimes argued with all the resources of the poet's eloquence, but so is the case against them; the same is true of almost every other regularly controversial subject. That Euripides was patriotic and wrote several plays designed to glorify his city, not without allusions to the contemporary situation, is beyond dispute; that in describing the cruelties of the Greeks towards the Trojans he wished to protest against the cruelties of the Athenians towards their subjects remains a matter of conjecture.[72]

Like all true tragedians, Euripides wrote not to advocate reforms or to advance theories, but to present under its tragic aspect an incident from human life.[73] He was a master of the rhetorical techniques which in his own time were developed with such intensive application, but he does not use them to advocate from the stage a particular point of view; rather, he places at the service of each speaker in his debates the entire resources of his expert advocacy.[74] General reflections that echo contemporary speculation are abundant in his works; but they coexist with others of a more traditional kind, and in virtually every instance can be shown to express a mood or an attitude closely related to a character, to a chorus, to a particular and perhaps momentary situation, which it is unsafe to assume to be the poet's own.

This is now so generally recognised that we are now chary of trying to extract a general world outlook from the poet's works. Critical attention has shifted from his supposed views and attitudes to his dramatic technique and methods of construction, often with valuable results. But the present investigation demands that we examine his work in the light of the old belief in Zeus and his world order and the relation between divine justice and human action. This must be carried out not merely by scrutinising individual passages, but by considering the action of complete works as a whole.

Two plays belonging to the earliest period of the poet's work of which we have any real knowledge describe with special clarity and fullness what since the Iliad had been a central topic of Greek poetry, the process of decision. Medea is torn between maternal love and her passionate desire to be revenged on Jason, Phaedra between the claims of honour and her violent longing for Hippolytus. In neither case, it is argued, is any importance assigned to that prompting by a god which plays a part in the motivation of the wrong decision taken by Achilles when he rejects Agamemnon's embassy. Medea's deliberations are powerless in the face of her *thymos,* the pride which will not allow her to risk being laughed at by her enemies. There is no mention, as there is in Homer, of a god who has placed an angry *thymos* in Medea's breast; "Medea," writes Dodds,[75] "knows that she is at grips, not with an *alastor,* but with her own irrational self." Just so Phaedra in the great monologue in which she analyses the factors that cause human beings to make wrong decisions makes no mention of divine intervention as an obstacle to right action. Mortals are prevented, she says,[76] from acting on the knowledge of what is right which they possess by "other pleasures" which they may place before honour. One such "pleasure" is having too much time for conversation; another is *aidos,* which in this context means paying too much respect, out of consideration for other people, to the advice they give. These "pleasures" may undermine a person's will to decide rightly in the face of passion; they are distinct from the passion itself, which in Phaedra's case is not wounded pride, but love.[77] Love for Euripides, as for other Greek poets, is a disease, a violent irrational force which not even Zeus himself is always able to resist.

According to traditional mythology love is engendered by a goddess, and the audience of the *Hippolytus* has seen that goddess openly proclaim her determination to destroy Hippolytus by means of the passion which she will inspire in Phaedra. We have been warned innumerable times against taking the two goddesses in the *Hippolytus* at all seriously; for the poet of the enlightenment, people say, they are mere symbols, whose presence in no way interferes with his purpose of presenting the determination of human action not by the external intervention of the gods, but by the ruin of good intentions by purely human passions.

This way of speaking has persisted since the great revival of Euripidean studies during the last quarter of the nineteenth century. It arises directly from the unconscious identification by the scholars of that time of the enlightenment of fifth-century Athens with the enlightenment of modern Europe. For them the belief that human action might in any sense be motivated by gods or spirits is a crude superstition, to be rejected by any rationalism that deserves the name. They therefore argue that Euripides as a thorough-going rationalist must have conserved the use of mythological themes and methods merely because it was the custom to employ them, while making in effect a complete break with the old religious view of moral action.

This view fails to reckon with the truth that the Greek gods were never thought to intervene externally in moral action; they acted not from outside but from inside mortal minds. In Homer Athene may tug Achilles by the hair to restrain him from drawing upon Agamemnon in open council,[78] but her warning corresponds exactly with the second thoughts which might in such circumstances restrain a man from action. More often the god's action is formally, as well as practically, internal; he works upon the man through his own thoughts and feelings. Achilles is prevented from accepting the offer brought by the ambassadors by the swelling *thymos* in his breast. Achilles himself has put it there, but Zeus too has put it there; we find here no inconsistency, but two different ways of considering the matter which for Homer are equally reasonable.[79]

Indeed Euripides employs far less frequently than Aeschylus, or even Sophocles, the ancient terminology in which Zeus is said to send Ate to take away a person's wits. When he does use it, Dodds thinks it "has now only the force of a traditional symbolism."[80] This way of speaking is justified in so far as the poet prefers to concentrate upon the natural rather than upon the supernatural or "demonic" aspect of wrong decision, on the struggle of the human being who knows what is right against the blinding force of his own passion. None the less, Euripides does sometimes employ the ancient terminology, and it is instructive to see how he does so. In the last scene of the *Medea*, Jason suggests that he has been the victim of an *alastor* who has avenged the murder of Medea's brother Apsyrtus; so also Hippolytus during his last minutes suggests that he may have paid the penalty for the offences of his ancestors.[81] In the parodos of the *Hippolytus* the Chorus wonders which god has sent Phaedra's sickness, but without naming the right name;[82] Phaedra herself says she has been driven mad by Ate sent by a *daimon*. Nothing in either play suggests that these statements are to be thought false, or dismiss as mere "symbolism"; it is simply that the poet has chosen not for the most part to present events under this aspect. When modern critics have instructed me to write off the Aphrodite and Artemis of the *Hippolytus*, so memorable in performance, as mere bloodless symbols, I have never been able to restrain a movement of angry protest; and this instinct is right, since their way of speaking dangerously oversimplifies the truth. Aphrodite has power only so far as she works through human passions; but does that make her power less real? The change of atmosphere that set in during the fifth century cannot be denied; if we had the whole of Aeschylus' trilogy about the Danaids, we might find that by comparison with its Aphrodite that of the *Hippolytus* lacked something of archaic dignity.[83] But the gods of the *Hippolytus* and the *Trojan Women* seem scarcely less vivid and less awe-inspiring than the Athene of Sophocles' *Ajax*; seen in modern Greek performance, they give the same impression of the supernatural which otherwise a modern audience can derive only from the superhuman characters of Japanese dramatic art. In the *Trojan Women*[84] Helen, captured in Troy and arraigned by Menelaus as having caused the war, pleads that she was helpless against the power of Aphrodite; Hecuba urges Menelaus to condemn her. Before the trial,[85] Hecuba invokes Zeus, who in his silent motions brings justice to mortals, Zeus who supports the earth and who has his seat upon it. It is difficult, says Hecuba, with an echo of earlier poetry, to know Zeus' nature; is he the necessity of nature or the mind of man? Anaxagoras conceived *nous* so differently that he is better not remembered here; more relevant is Heraclitus' saying that for man character was a *daimon*.[86] The echoes of fifth century speculation that we recognise here should not prevent us from remembering that even in Homer Zeus works through human passion and human reason. Helen pleads that she was forced to act as she did by Aphrodite; Hecuba answers that she was moved only by her own vanity and lust. By Homeric canons, both are right; Helen was helpless against the goddess, but she was moved by vanity and lust, because it is through human passions that the goddess works. Homer's Helen shows an acute consciousness of guilt; not she but Priam blames the gods for her behaviour. She is aware that though the gods have caused her actions, she is still responsible for her behaviour. So too in the Euripidean agon both sides are right; how much more powerful is its tragic effect if this is realised! But Hecuba is justified in brushing away Helen's excuses, not because Helen has spoken untruthfully when she has blamed the gods, but because here as in Homer mortals cannot evade responsibility for an action on the ground that it has been prompted by a god.[87]

I have argued [88] that Sophocles does not represent the gods as unjust, but that in his surviving works the pattern formed by the successive crimes and punishments is often so complicated that the working of divine justice is not easy to perceive. It is a commonplace in Greek thought that mortals cannot easily find out the will of Zeus, and Sophocles by giving up the practice of composing tetralogies on a single theme has made it harder to trace out the chain of crimes and atonements than it is in Aeschylus. Let us now consider the part played by the gods in Euripides, and examine their relation to the concept of universal Dike administered by Zeus.

On the face of it, the various lesser gods show in Euripides, as they do in earlier tragedy, much independent activity. Apollo in the *Alcestis* turns aside the course of fate to help a favourite, and Heracles assists him to go still further;[89] Helios protects his grand-daughter Medea; Artemis, though she cannot save Hippolytus, can avenge him. The gods still punish enemies who have denied them proper honour; Aphrodite punishes Hippolytus, Apollo in the *Andromache* punishes Neoptolemus, Dionysus punishes Pentheus; we may compare the Apollo of the *Agamemnon* or the Athene of the *Ajax*. Two gods may clash, as do Aphrodite and Artemis in the *Hippolytus* or Hera and Artemis in the *Helen*; in such instances, the will of Zeus resolved the conflict. In certain plays Zeus and Dike are appealed to in conventional fashion, and the appeal is answered. The *Cyclops* as a satyr-play may not be a significant example, but here the Cyclops is punished for his inhospitality and for the blasphemies he utters against Zeus.[90] In the *Heraclidae* the Chorus make supplication at Zeus' altar and invoke the name of Dike;[91] Demophon, like Pelasgus in Aeschylus, admits that Zeus will not allow him to reject them;[92] the Chorus declare their confidence in victory, since Zeus is on their side,[93] and are duly justified by the miraculous rejuvenation of Iolaus and the defeat of Eurystheus, for which they and Alcmene render thanks to Zeus.[94] The *Suppliant Women* follows the same pattern; Aethra persuades her son to support the Argive suppliants by reminding him of his religious duty to the gods and justice.[95] In plays with happy endings, justice and the will of heaven are said to prevail. In plays about the house of Oedipus and the house of Atreus, the family curses are traced back to their earliest origins,[96] as in Aeschylus and Sophocles; nor is their importance anywhere decried, even if the poet, who like Sophocles does not compose in connected tetralogies, has not chosen to dwell on the succession of crime following crime in Aeschylean fashion.

Other plays present greater complications. In the opening part of the *Medea,* the solemn invocation of Zeus and Dike can hardly fail to be remarked. The Nurse in the prologue says that Medea is calling on the gods to observe how Jason has repaid her kindness,[97] and after the sympathetic Chorus has appealed to Zeus, Earth and Light on her behalf,[98] and has assured her that Zeus will in the end see justice done,[99] she herself invokes Themis. When she declares that she will punish Jason, the Chorus replies that such punishment will be just;[100] justice itself, they impressively declare, has been subverted by Jason's action.[101] The moment Medea has found a protector in Aegeus, she appeals to Zeus, to Zeus' Justice and to her ancestor the Sun to grant her victory.[102] Like Clytemnestra, Medea goes too far in her revenge, Jason calls on the Erinys and on Dike to destroy her;[103] but Medea can still ask him what god will hear the prayer of a breaker of oaths and deceiver of his friends.[104] In the *Medea* justice, in the ancient sense, is done; as often, justice is terrible.

The *Hecuba* and *Trojan Women,* with their grim depiction of the sufferings of the female captives after the fall of Troy, have seemed to modern readers to indict the gods for unspeakable injustices. In the *Trojan Women* Hecuba and Andromache know that the gods have caused their ruin,[105] and at the climax of the play solemnly invoke Zeus and protest that that ruin is undeserved. But according to ancient notions of justice the fall of Troy was not unjust; the rape of Helen, the refusal of Priam to make amends, the breaking of the truce are relevant in this connection, and it is not for nothing that Euripides so often dwells upon the beginning of evil, the fatal judgment of Paris.[106] Like Medea, the Greeks go too far in their revenge; in the *Trojan Women* we know from the start that they will presently meet with disaster, as they do according to the epic tradition. The justice of Zeus is from the beginning harsh; Dike means not simply justice, but the order of the universe; yet the justice of Zeus is at all times recognisable as a kind of justice.

Let us now consider the plays in which a god punishes a mortal who has refused him honour—the *Hippolytus,* the *Andromache,* the *Bacchae.* A modern audience will feel that though the gods in these plays may have just complaints against Hippolytus, Neoptolemus and Pentheus, they go too far in their revenges. That is a natural human reaction, which is voiced by the old man of the *Hippolytus* when he says that gods ought to be wiser than mortals, and by Cadmus in the *Bacchae* when he calls the revenge of Dionysus just but excessive.[107] But from the standpoint of ancient Dike, each god is perfectly within his rights; for a mortal to refuse a god his due honour is dangerous. Is the Greek attitude necessarily nonsensical? Modern theories about the consequences of repression may throw some light upon the behaviour of Pentheus and Hippolytus; and like them Neoptolemus has shown a dangerous ignorance of the laws of nature.

The *Heracles* is another play which has appeared to many modern scholars as a protest against divine injustice. When at the start the family of Heracles is on the point of being massacred by the tyrant Lycus, Amphitryon's reproaches against Zeus[108] seem to be fully justified; then at the last moment Heracles returns to overwhelm the tyrant, and the Chorus sings an ode of triumph. Then Hera strikes; the maddened Heracles kills with his own hands the wife and children he has lately rescued; and the despair of Heracles after his recovery has seemed to some readers to express the poet's indignation at the injustice of the universe. But the play does not end upon this note; Theseus appears to persuade Heracles that he must resume his career of glory and of service to humanity. It is unfortunate that much of the principal speech of Theseus in this scene[109] is lost. He concludes it by reminding Heracles that no human life is without misfortune; ancient religion demanded that a man should bear misfortune, however crushing, with resignation. Heracles gives up his plan of suicide, and goes on, as the audience knew, to his final conquest of immortality.

The *Orestes* and *Electra* have often been considered to embody Euripides' criticism of the older poets' approval of the matricide committed by Orestes; do not even the Dioscuri, descending from the machine after the killing of Clytemnestra, echo the human characters' criticisms of Apollo's oracle? That view has been admirably dealt with by Kurt von Fritz,[110] who has shown that the new moral attitude towards Orestes' action expressed in these two plays results directly from new features of the situation in which the matricide here takes place; in Euripides it is not the moral standards but the circumstances which are different. In Euripides' *Electra,* Clytemnestra is made less guilty and her killing is less necessary than in the *Choephori* or in the Sophoclean *Electra*; in the *Orestes,*[111] Tyndareus says that Orestes might have won redress by launching a criminal prosecution in the courts, an action wholly inconceivable in the circumstances envisaged by the two older tragedians. Still, even in these two Euripidean plays, justice of a kind is done; Apollo's command in the *Orestes* was "just, but not honourable." [112] In each case the gods ordain that Orestes shall stand trial at Athens, where he will be acquitted; the new turn given to the situation has complicated the tragic issue, but has not altered the result.

In Euripides, as in Sophocles, Zeus rules the universe in terms of his own justice; this is not easily comprehensible to men, and may appear at variance with human justice. Occasionally the audience is granted a direct inspection of its working; this may be given through the medium of a character who, like Theonoe in the *Helen,*[113] is a mouthpiece of the gods, but it comes more often from a god descending from the machine. Since ancient times it has been customary to hold that the god from the machine is a mere device for finishing a plot that has reached an impasse, and that his utterances have little serious bearing on the play which they conclude. The superficiality of this opinion has lately been exposed in the admirable dissertation of Andreas Spira,[114] one of the most valuable contributions to Euripidean studies of the last decade. By careful analysis of the texts, Spira has shown how the god's appearance rescues the human characters from the situation into which their mortal limitations have brought them by leading them to recognise the wider purpose of the gods. Lineally descended as they are from the divine epiphanies in epic and in early tragedy, these descents from the machine continue the Greek tradition of a divine participation in the affairs of men. The god's command helps to bring about a restoration of the order of the universe, whose accomplishment is closely linked with that purification in which Aristotle saw the most significant effect of tragedy. The power that maintains that universal order is Zeus' justice; as the one wise is unwilling and willing to be called Zeus, so Dike is unwilling and willing to be called Justice.

VII

Conclusions

ONE OF the best reasons for studying the past is to protect oneself against that insularity in time which restricts the uneducated and those who write to please them. The ordinary man feels superior to the men of past ages, whose technology was inferior to what he is used to and whose ethical and political beliefs were not those which he has been taught to consider as the only right ones. When he condescends to pay any attention to the past, he looks at once for a resemblance to the present. If he believes that he has found any he may be willing to concede to the past some measure of patronising tolerance; but if he can find none, he will dismiss it with impatience. The educated man, however, will observe with interest both the resemblances and the differences between past and present.

Until some thirty or forty years ago, scholars on the whole tended to exaggerate the resemblance between classical antiquity and our own time, and that tendency was reflected in the comparatively high degree of approval which the ancient world was then accorded. Since then a reaction has taken place, and the past is taken to have been even more unlike the present than it really was. In consequence, it is often brushed aside as "irrelevant" to the privileged age in which we live.

This is nowhere truer than in the field of Greek religion. Once it appeared so unlike modern religions that scholars could hardly think it a religion at all. But a turning-point was marked by the publication, just a century ago, of Nietzsche's *Birth of*

Tragedy, a book which despite its deficiencies as a work of scholarship profoundly influenced scholars as well as many others. The importance of the numinous, the daemonic, the irrational side of Greek religion became recognised, and many important discoveries followed. Instead of starting with the assumption that the early Greeks were rational men whose processes of thought were like their own, scholars began to approach them as anthropologists may approach the primitive peoples whom they study, tending to consider them as beings whose feelings and thoughts were radically different from those of modern men. Both kinds of approach obviously carry certain dangers. The new movement has had notable successes, but in some respects it has now begun to go too far.

First, encouraged by the successes gained through the recognition that early Greek culture contained many primitive survivals, scholars have begun to treat that culture as having been itself primitive. That is a mistake. Recent research has confirmed that the Homeric poems, our first important document of Greek thought, were the product of a long tradition, and when they came into existence the society that produced them had in most respects evolved far beyond the primitive stage. The thought world of the early Greeks was indeed different from our own; but like ourselves they were reasonable human beings, and were able to take account of the basic factors that determine the condition of human life in a way different from, but not necessarily in every way less rational than ours.

Once a new movement in scholarship has begun to evolve methods and principles of its own, many scholars feel a strong unconscious urge to fashion these into a mechanical system, which has only to be applied to the material for guaranteed results to be turned out with a minimum of further intellectual exertion; it is at this stage that new movements usually begin to flag. One branch of the followers of the movement we are discussing has invented a mechanical system that works by means of lexicography. By analysing the vocabulary of Homer and of later writers, they try to show that Homer had no cognisance of several concepts now held to be essential for understanding the processes of reflection and decision, and can thus credit those later authors in whose works the concepts in question seem to make their first appearance with notable discoveries. I have suggested that a study of Homer's account of thought and moral action that pays regard not only to words but to things shows that his way of regarding them was different from ours, but not altogether less effective for describing them.

Scholars have underrated the early Greeks' comprehension not only of intellectual but of moral processes. Lexical analysis has shown that the most general Greek term of ethical commendation, the word *agathos,* generally translated "good," originally connoted being good at something, at first usually being good at fighting, and scholars have inferred that the Greek concept of goodness was from the first seriously deficient. In fact even the earliest documents known to us indicate, at least to those whose attention is not centred too exclusively upon words, a concept of goodness different, indeed, from our own, but less defective than has been contended. Much of the work done in our language by the term "good" was done in Greek by words other than *agathos,* particularly by the word *dikaios,* "just" or "righteous," and *agathos* itself and its corresponding noun *arete* acquired at an early date some ethical flavour. But the proof depends not simply on the examination of vocabulary, important as that is, but on an examination of ethical concepts at work in early literature that will attend not merely to words, but also to processes and actions.

Since the early nineteenth century, historians of Greek thought have concentrated on presenting its development, taking it from primitive beginnings to a climax. For some that climax comes with the imposing constructions of the fourth- and third-century philosophers; for others, with the incorporation of much of their achievement into the doctrines of the Church; for others, with the rationalistic doctrines of the fifth century. Both the first two groups have naturally associated the early Greek religion with primitive superstition, for they contrast it unfavourably with the monotheistic systems of the dogmatic philosophers and of the Christians. Not quite so naturally, the third group has tended to treat the early religion simply as a dogmatic obstacle to the advance of rationalism. They speak of it with disapproval, denoting it by such pejorative terms as "the Inherited Conglomerate"; many seem unconsciously to identify it with religion as they have experienced it in modern times.

There were, it seems to me, profound differences between early Greek religion and most other kinds, and these may be best perceived by abstaining, for the time being, from considering it simply in the light of historical development. The point may be illustrated by an analogy taken from the history of aesthetics.[1] Adapting Plato's theory of forms in the light of his own favourite science of biology, Aristotle held that each species had its proper nature, to which its whole development must tend; thus in his *Poetics* the *Oedipus Tyrannus* was the ideal drama and Aeschylus an imperfect struggler towards Sophoclean perfection. But Aeschylean tragedy has a form and principles of its own, and is better understood by trying to find these and judging the surviving specimens accordingly than by treating them as so many ineffective attempts to write a play in the manner of Sophocles, or of any other chosen dramatist. Just so early Greek religion has its own form and principles, which need not necessarily be considered only in the light of how Greek thought was to develop later. When Nilsson complained that Walter F. Otto in his portrayal of the early Greek religion took no account of the factor of development,[2] he betrayed his total failure to understand Otto's purpose. Development is an important and interesting topic, but there are times when it is more rewarding to direct attention to what has remained static over a long period. By doing so, we may end by throwing fresh light even upon the development of Greek thinking. We may not only disembarrass ourselves of the false notions about development generated by the mechanical application of the lexical method, but may advance further by considering the relation of the early Greek world outlook to the rationalism of the fifth-century enlightenment. That outlook deserves to be given credit for the fact that its own nature made it likely from the start that the Greeks would attain to a level of rational thinking about the great problems of life beyond the range of their oriental neighbours.

Three important differences mark off the early religion of the Greeks from those of the surrounding peoples, and also from those that are familiar to us in modern times. First, it is neither monotheism nor, in the strict sense, polytheism, but something between the two; it has many gods, but from the earliest times of which we have knowledge one of these is preponderant over the rest. Secondly, it is not anthropocentric; men are the creation only of a minor god, and have only a minor status in the universe and a minor place in the attention of the gods. Thirdly, these gods are not transcendent but immanent; they do not interfere from outside with the course of nature, but govern the inanimate world through natural processes and the animate through human passions.

Let us examine the consequences of these differences, and in particular their effect upon the Greek attitude to wrong or irrational human behaviour. First, this religion recognises not one higher power only, but a plurality of such powers. The justice of Zeus requires that men pay proper honour to the gods, and not all these gods can be honoured equally by all human beings. Artemis and Aphrodite, for example, cannot easily be given equal honour by the same human individual, and one who honours either exclusively may be in danger from the other. It follows that it is often difficult to determine whether a particular desire is wrong, a proposition which is suggested to most human beings by one or other of the experiences of life, but to which dogmatic monotheism does not always lend a hearing. Whether or not a belief in a plurality of higher powers is reasonable, it may be thought to have some practical advantages; it might be said, for instance, in psychological terms, to tend to minimise the dangerous consequences of the undue repression of powerful emotions.

If mortals are to render proper honour to the gods, they must abstain from any word or action that may suggest an attempt to pass beyond mortal limitations. Again and again Greek popular wisdom reiterates that men must not try to become gods, that they must adapt themselves to the laws of the existing universe, hard as these may be to comprehend, and to the realities of the actual situation.

Part of the honour due to Zeus from mortals is the duty to abstain from crime against each other; his greatest gift to them is that "violent grace" by virtue of which he punishes, late or soon, a man who has done injustice to another, either in his own person or in that of his descendants. Men, or at least all men who have been properly instructed, know Zeus' law of justice, but often their passions blind them and prevent them from acting on their knowledge. In the *Iliad* and sometimes in later literature, men may blame a god for prompting them to wrong action, but they may never disclaim responsibility for their decisions. Wrong action is due to the actor's perverse preference for self-interest over justice; even if the passions that caused it came from a higher power, that can never be effectively pleaded as an excuse.

Zeus has granted mortals a share in his own justice, and by a special favour condescends to punish crime. But he is not their creator, nor their benevolent father in heaven. The gods govern the universe not in men's interest but in their own, and have no primary concern for human welfare. When Epicurus, like Aristotle before him,[3] denied that the gods cared what happened in the world, these two philosophers were, as in other ways, closer to early thinking than either Plato or the Stoics. Even those who reject this view about the gods as false can hardly call it quite irrational; on the surface, at any rate, the view has the advantage of avoiding problems about the existence of sin and misery in the world which those who hold different opinions have been put to some trouble to explain.

Dike means basically the order of the universe, and in this religion the gods maintain a cosmic order. This they do by working through nature and the human mind, and not by means of extraneous interventions. The notion of a cosmos, of a universe regulated by causal laws, was a prerequisite of rational speculation about cosmology, science and metaphysics.[4] Any attempt to answer the inevitable but difficult question as to why modern science and philosophy began with the Greeks and not with any other people would surely start with the remark that the concept of an ordered universe was peculiar to the Greeks, who in this matter differed sharply from their oriental neighbours. Making an exception in regard to the initial postulates which it derived from revelation, Christianity took over this concept, and from an early date, as the Fourth Gospel plainly shows.[5] It was not derived from Judaism, nor from any other oriental source.

It is a gross misconception to suppose that the inherited religious thinking of the Greeks placed any barrier in the way of a rational explanation either of factual or of moral error. What happened in the world depended ultimately upon the gods, and their purpose was usually inscrutable to human minds; that did not mean that it was irrational, but that the reasons that governed it usually remained mysterious. *Tyche* acquired the sense of blind chance only with the advance of superstition during the Hellenistic age. Pindar called *Tyche* daughter of Zeus, and a Sophoclean character invokes "divine *Tyche* and you, guiding *daimon*";[6] they well express the fifth-century conception. Wrong moral decisions might be prompted by a god, but even in the *Iliad* the divine motivation of an act might be abstracted and the human motivation—and the human responsibility— remain unaltered; since these gods worked through human passions, the notion of divine causation might be abandoned and the human emotion responsible for wrong decision be the same. That made it possible even in the late fifth century for a tragedian to present moral error in a way which common sense has in all ages found more convincing than the paradoxical ingenuities of Socratic intellectualism.

Zeus had originally acquired his functions on the analogy of those of human kings, whose main duty was to protect justice. If the divine sanction for justice was removed, it could easily and naturally be replaced by an empirical theory of justice, such as that of Protagoras or Democritus. Such an empirical theory stands far closer to the early Greek belief than either does to an idealistic theory of justice, such as that of Plato.

Early Greek belief led easily and naturally to the empiricism of the fifth-century philosophers; then came the reaction. At a high cultural level it was promoted by dogmatic metaphysics, at a low by the growth of mystery cults and superstitions. That reaction cannot plausibly be presented as a return to the traditional Greek beliefs and practices. The question of how far Plato may have been influenced by oriental religion and philosophy remains obscure, but most scholars would agree with Dodds that Plato "cross-fertilised the tradition of Greek rationalism with magico-religious ideas" [7] derived from Pythagoreanism and emanating, in all probability, from remote cultures. Plato's crucial step beyond earlier Greek thinkers lay, as Dodds clearly shows,[8] in his adoption of a magico-religious view of the human psyche, and in the dichotomy between soul and body which resulted. Platonic puritanism has an obvious affinity with the Pythagorean and "Orphic" notions which had been current in restricted circles since the sixth century, and also with oriental cults which became increasingly popular with the Greeks from the fourth century on; the failure of nerve at a high cultural level is thus closely linked with the failure at a low. But though the reaction strongly enjoined belief in gods, it had little in common with the traditional Greek religious outlook. Plato may have wished to discipline the common man by reestablishing the official cults, but Plato's real theological beliefs had little in common with the ancient religion, as his criticisms of the poets help to show.

Reason helps us to make deductions from original postulates, but cannot guide us in their choice, and it is not easy to contend that any one set of arbitrary assumptions about the nature of divinity or the government of the universe is more "rational" than any other. Still, the set of assumptions made by the early Greeks must be acknowledged to account for the observed phenomena not noticeably worse than those made by most other peoples. I have not dilated on the beauty of their constructions, and have done no more than hint at the psychological truths which they express, but have chosen instead to point out certain practical advantages which the Greeks derived from them, both in science and in ethics. Human kind, says the bird in Eliot, cannot bear very much reality. The early Greeks were capable of their unique achievements largely because they could bear, as their religion shows, very much more reality than most human beings. It may be objected that I use the word "reality" in a mundane and superficial sense. From the sixth century on, and with increasing intensity from the fourth, many of the Greeks demanded a closer link with higher powers than the old religion could offer them. Plato and the other destroyers of the earlier culture would claim, and many of their modern followers would agree, that they achieved contact with a higher reality than their forbears; but it was not reality in *this* world that was their chief concern.

Notes

NOTES TO CHAPTER I
(Pages 1–27)

1. This was the theory of E. B. Tylor, *Primitive Culture* (1871; 3d ed., 1889), II 360 f.; it was accepted by most classical scholars, e.g., by Wilamowitz, *Glaube,* I 44 and by Eduard Schwartz, *Die Ethik der Griechen* (1951), 1f.

2. See, e.g., J. M. Yingen, *Religion, Society, and the Individual* (1957), 23 f.; G. E. Swanson, *The Birth of the Gods: The Origin of Primitive Beliefs* (1960), 153 f.; E. Norbeck, *Religion in Primitive Society* (1961), 169 f.; E. Evans-Pritchard, *Theories of Primitive Religion* (1962), *passim.* None of these scholars would agree with Tylor that in *all* cases the origins of religion and morality are separate. See Lesky, "Homeros," 40–41.

3. Dodds, *GI,* 32 with n. 18 on p. 52.

4. Chantraine, "Le divin dans Homère," *Entretiens de la Fondation Hardt* I (1952), 75–76, 81.

5. Adkins, *MR,* 62; he does not except even Zeus.

6. *Dikaiosyne* does not occur before Theognis; it denotes the quality of being δίκαιος. For its history, see E. A. Havelock, *Phoenix,* 23 (1969), 49 f., though I think he separates it off too sharply from *dike* and δίκαιος.

7. Dodds, *GI,* 17.

8. Hesiod, fr. 234 Merkelbach-West. Later Prometheus is said to have created them from mud. L. Séchan, *Le Mythe de Prométhée* (1951), 33 is surely right in arguing that the story that Prometheus created men must have existed before Aeschylus, but it is not found in Homer.

9. 2, 462 f.

10. 17, 446–447. See Wilamowitz, *Glaube,* I 351.

11. 5, 441–442.

12. See Eduard Fraenkel, *Proceedings of the British Academy* 28 (1942), 22–23; cf. his *Aeschylus, Agamemnon* (1950), II 372–374.

13. 24, 602 f.

14. 9, 533 f.

15. See K. Latte, *RGAG*, 63 f. = *Kl. Schr*, 233 f. Although Zeus punishes the injustices of men, the gods are not bound by human morality; see Walter F. Otto, *Die Gestalt und das Sein* (1955), 124.

16. See n. 28 below.

17. 8, 18 f.

18. 16, 439 f.

19. On the idea of fate in Homer, see Otto, *GG*[3], 257 f. (Eng. tr., 261 f.) and Dodds, *GI*, 21 n. 43. The articles of E. Wüst, *Rh. Mus.*, 101 (1958), 75 f. and W. Pötscher, *Wiener Studien*, 73 (1960), 5 f. reveal the difficulties in which Homer was involved by "the problem of free will," which he was not equipped to deal with; Chantraine, *op. cit.* (n. 4 above), 69–73 brings out the essential point that in the last resort what Zeus wishes to happen happens. As Eustathius remarks in his commentary on the *Iliad* (1686), the plan of Zeus is the same as the *moira* of the gods.

20. Dodds, *GI*, 52 n. 18.

21. A stranger had no legal rights, so that religion had to step in and protect him; see R. Köstler, Die homerische Rechts- und Staatsordnung (1950), 17 f. = *Griechische Rechtsgeschichte*, ed. E. Berneker (*Wege der Forschung* 45, 1968), 185 f. (first pub. in *Zeitschrift für die öffentliche Recht*, 23, 1944, Heft 4/5).

22. 4, 158 f.

23. The noun *dike* occurs seven times in the *Iliad* (see Erik Wolf, *Griechisches Rechtsdenken* (1950), I 85 f.). It means in these places either a judgment given by a judge or an assertion of his right by a party to a dispute. Both senses accord with the commonly received derivation of the word from the root of the verb *deiknumi*, "I show" or "indicate"; the German rendering of the basic sense is "Weisung." The sense "right" or "custom" first occurs in the *Odyssey;* and only once in each epic do we find *dike* used in a general or abstract sense (*Il.* 16, 387 and *Od.* 14, 84).

Dike originally meant the "indication" of the requirement of the divine law, *themis. Themis* derives from *tithemi*, "I place" or "lay down." R. Hirzel, *Themis und Verwandtes* (1907), 18 f. takes its basic meaning to be "counsel"; V. Ehrenberg, *Die Rechtsideeim frühgriechischen Altertum* (1921), 6 (cf. pp. 12, 16) takes it to be "advice" or "command"; both senses occur, but the best definition is Köstler's (*op. cit.*, 9 = 174): "Kundgebungen eines göttlichen oder von der Gottheit beratenen Willes." Cf. B. W. Leist, *Gräco-italische Rechtsgeschichte* (1884), 209 f. and E. Weiss, *Griechisches Privatrecht auf rechtsvergleichende Grundlage* (1923) I 19 f.

"Themis ist das himmlische Recht, Dike das ihm nachgebildete irdische, ersteres beruht auf göttlicher Satzung (*themis* von *tithemi*), letzteres auf Weisung (Aufzeigung) des gesetzten Rechts (*dike* von *deiknumi*), ist also abgeleitetes Recht und kommt im Richterspruch zur Geltung": Köstler, *op. cit.*, 13 = 180. A *dike* may be straight or crooked; kings by *dike* sort the *themistes* (*Il.* 16, 387; Hesiod, *Theog.* 85) which Zeus has given them to guard (*Il.* 1, 542).

On the etymology of *dike,* see H. Frisk, *Etymologisches Wörterbuch der griechischen Sprache,* s.v., 393–394; P. Chantraine, *Dictionnaire étymologique de la langue grecque* (1968), I 283–284. L. R. Palmer, *Transactions of the Philological Society* (1950), 149 f. accepts this etymology, but argues for a basic sense "boundary, mark"; he draws attention to the use of *dike* in the same contexts as *kairos,* but this is easily explained even on the usual view. See D. Loenen, "Dike: een histor.-semant. Analyse," *Mededel. Nederl. Acad. van Wetensch., Letterk.,* n. r. 2, 6, Amsterdam, 1948.

On the etymology of *themis,* see H. Frisk, *Eranos* 48 (1950), 1 f. and *op. cit.,* s.v., 660–661. On *themis* in general see K. Latte, R.-E. V A, 1934, 1626–30, 1641, 1642 = *Kl. Schr.* 140 f.; *idem, RGAG* 63 f. = *Kl. Schr.* 233 f.; Wilamowitz, *Glaube* I, 206 f.; Otto, *GG*³, 151 f. (same pag. in Eng. tr.); Erik Wolf, *op. cit.,* 22 f.; Köstler, *op. cit.,* 7–25 = 172–195; H. Vos, "Themis," Diss. Univ. Rheno-Traj, 1956; W. Pötscher, *Wiener Studien,* 73 (1960), 31 f.

24. 16. 384 f.

25. 220 f.; cf. 256 f.

26. E.g., P. von der Mühll, *Kritisches Hypomnema zur Ilias* (1952), 247; this view is stated at great length and with much conviction by H. Munding, *Philologus,* 105 (1961), 161 f. and 106 (1962), 60 f. Dodds, *GI,* 52 n. 16 would not go so far as to speak of interpolation, but evidently agrees with Wilamowitz, *Hesiodos, Erga* (1928), 66 that the Hesiodic passage must be earlier. Latte, *ARW,* 20 (1920/1), 259 = *Kl. Schr.* 6 (with n. 8) finds the passage "unique, but certainly genuine." Chantraine, *loc. cit.,* finds in it the sole exception to his rule that Zeus nowhere in the *Iliad* acts to enforce distributive justice, by which he presumably means the justice that assigns to each what he deserves.

27. See Lesky, "Homeros," 40.

28. See M. P. Nilsson, *Homer and Mycenae* (1933), 267–272; cf. Köstler, *op. cit.,* 10 f. = 178. f. See also G. E. R. Lloyd, *Polarity and Analogy: Two Types of Argumentation in Early Greek Thought* (1966), 193 f.

29. On *themis* and the *themistes,* see n. 23 above.

30. 9, 98 f.

31. 1, 238.

32. 16, 542. See Latte, *RGAG*, 65 f. = *Kl. Schr.* 236 f.; W. Jaeger, *Scripta Minora*, II 321 (pub. first in *Interpretation of Modern Legal Philosophies: Essays in Honour of Roscoe Pound*, 1947, 352 f.); Lesky, "Homeros," 41–42.

33. *Od.* 11, 568 f.

34. Hesiod fr. 286 Merkelbach-West.

35. Adkins, *MR*, 62.

36. 24, 27 f.; see K. Reinhardt, *Das Parisurteil* (1938) = *Tradition und Geist*, 16 f.

37. A notable exception is furnished by C. M. Bowra, *Tradition and Design in the Iliad* (1930); see in particular the first chapter.

38. H. Fränkel, *Dichtung und Philosophie des frühen Griechentums*,2 (1962), 83 f. Snell has discussed the problem at considerable length, first in *Aischylos und das Handeln im Drama, Philologus* Suppl. 20/1 (1928); see the review of that work by Erwin Wolff, *Gnomon*, 5 (1929), 386, whose criticisms are by no means invalidated by Snell's reply in *Philologus*, 85 (1930), 141 f. = *Ges. Schr.* 18 f.; later in *Die Entdeckung des Geistes* (3d ed., 1955; Eng. tr. by T. G. Rosenmeyer, 1953), chaps. i and ii. Snell has replied to Lesky's criticisms (*GGM, passim*) in *Argumentationen: Festschrift für Josef König* (1964), 249 f. = *Ges. Schr.* 55 f.

A particularly paradoxical result of Snell's belief may be seen in his *Scenes from Greek Drama* (1964), 1 f., where he argues that in choosing to avenge Patroclus and die young Achilles did not really make a choice, or a decision. Such an opinion is inconsistent with a proper understanding of an important, and by no means difficult, factor in the plot of the *Iliad*. See G. S. Kirk, *The Songs of Homer* (1962), 405 (note on text at p. 377) for sensible remarks about this question.

39. *Die Entdeckung des Geistes*, 42. Devereux points out that men at a "primitive" stage of development do not feel themselves to be mere puppets in the hands of gods or spirits.

40. Dodds, *GI*, 20 n. 31; Lesky GGM, 13.

41. GGM, *passim;* see also "Homeros," 50 f. and literature there cited, especially K. Lanig, *Der handelnde Mensch in der Ilias*, Diss. Erlangen, 1953 and H. Schwabl, *Wiener Studien*, 67 (1954), 46 f. Further relevant literature is cited by A. Skiadas, Ἀνθρωπίνη εὐθύνη καὶ θεία ἐπέμβασις εἰς τὴν πρώϊμον Ἑλληνικὴν ποίησιν (Ἑλληνικὴ Ἀνθρωπιστικὴ Ἑταιρία, Κεντρον Ἀνθρωπιστικῶν Σπουδῶν, σειρὰ πρώτη, Ἀρχαιότης καὶ συλχρονα προβλήματα, 39, 1967).

42. 11, 402 f. "Once Odysseus says 'I,' " Professor G. Devereux writes, "this establishes at least a general sense of psychic coherence."

43. Devereux points out that this amounts to what could be called in C. K. Ogden's terminology a "dual language" explanation of behaviour.

44. Nilsson, *GGR* I2, 371; Mazon, *Introduction à l'Iliade* (1948), 294.

Cf. L. Gernet and A. Boulanger, *Le Génie grec dans la religion* (1932), 108: "il n'y a pas de religion homérique."

45. "Die neuere Forschung hat bei ihren Versuchen, die Anschauungen und Gebräuche alter Völker zu deuten, eine seltsame Vorliebe für die gröbsten Motive, und dabei macht sie wenig Unterschied zwischen den Völkern und Begabungen. Die vorgeschichtliche Religion der Griechen wird uns gemeiniglich ganz so vorgetragen wie die einer beliebigen primitiven Gemeinschaft, als ob die geistvollen Vorstellungen, die wir alle bewundern, unvermittelt aus einem Wust von Plumpheit und Zauberei aufgetaucht wären": Otto, *GG*[3], 139 (p. 140 f., Eng. tr.). Without for a moment denying the great increase in our knowledge and stimulus to our studies that we owe to those who have drawn attention to the primitive elements surviving in Homer and in the early Greek world in general, we must admit that these words of Otto need, at the present time in particular, to be very seriously pondered.

46. Thus W. Kullmann, *Philologus*, 99 (1955), 167 f., corrected by Lesky, "Homeros," 76; Bowra, *op. cit.*, 12–13 had already warned against the error.

47. A similar pattern of events occurs in Aeschylus' *Agamemnon*. Artemis sends the winds to detain the fleet at Aulis; Iphigenia is sacrificed to appease her, and the fleet sails. But the sacrifice has set in train events that lead finally to the destruction of Agamemnon. By sending the plague Apollo has not only ensured the return of Chryseis, but has struck a damaging blow at the Achaean cause.

48. 1, 130 f.

49. 1, 172 f.

50. 3, 65.

51. 1, 233 f.

52. 1, 247 f.

53. Adkins, *MR*, 51.

54. W. Schadewaldt, *Iliasstudien* (1938), 152 with n. 2.

55. 2, 370 f.

56. 9, 17 f.

57. Adkins, *MR*, 51.

58. 9, 115 f.

59. 9, 158 f.

60. Adkins, *MR*, 56.

61. Thus D. L. Page, *History and the Homeric Iliad* (1959), 300 f.; against, see G. S. Kirk, *op. cit.*, 214 f. and Lesky, "Homeros," 103 f.

62. See Adam Parry, "Have We Homer's Iliad?" *Yale Classical Studies*, 20 (1966), 175 f.

63. 9, 225 f.

64. 9, 300–303.
65. 9, 496 f.
66. 9, 529 f.
67. 9, 624–642.
68. 9, 636–637.
69. 9, 628–629.
70. Pindar fr. 222 Snell; Euripides, *Hipp.* 534.
71. 258 f.
72. See M. L. West, *Hesiod, The Theogony* (1966), 40 f.; cf. the important article of H. Strasburger, "Der soziologische Aspekt der Homerischen Epen," *Gymnasium,* 6 (1953), 97 f.
73. 9, 696 f.
74. 9, 643 f.
75. See above, p. 9.
76. 11, 597 f.
77. 11, 656–658, 762–764.
78. 16, 29 f.
79. 16, 48 f.
80. 8, 473 f.
81. 15, 54 f.
82. Fr. 231 Mette.
83. 3, 365; cf. 2, 110 f. and *Od.* 20, 201 f.
84. 18, 98.
85. 18, 101 f.
86. See Schadewaldt, *op. cit.,* 103 f.; cf. *idem, Von Homers Welt und Werk* (1959), 234 f.
87. 22, 395; 23, 24; cf. 24, 22.
88. 24, 39 f.
89. 24, 112 f., 134 f.
90. 24, 186–187.
91. 19, 56 f.
92. 19, 78 f.
93. 19, 270 f.
94. 9, 636–637.
95. 9, 628–629.
96. 11, 191–194, 206–209.
97. 18, 310–311.
98. 22, 99 f.
99. 3, 386 f.
100. Cf. Wilamowitz, *Glaube,* I 352, 357; G. de Sanctis, *Storia dei Greci* (1939), I 263.
101. See Joseph Russo and Bennett Simon, "Homeric Psychology and

the Oral Epic Tradition," *Journal of the History of Ideas*, 29 (1968), 483 f.

102. *GI*, 17; cf. 28 f. Dodds took the expression from Ruth Benedict; see *The Chrysanthemum and the Sword* (1947), 222 f. Geoffrey Gorer, *The Dangers of Equality* (1966), 24 f. writes that societies have been classified by Erik Erikson and others "according to the predominance of one or other mechanism of internal or social control, the mechanism by which people regulate their own conduct, and which others can invoke to obviate or punish conduct which transgresses the norm prevalent in a given society in a given period."

103. *Honour, Family and Patronage; A Study of Institutions and Moral Values in a Greek Mountain Community* (1964), 327–328.

104. See the symposium *Honour and Shame: The Values of Mediterranean Society*, ed. by J. G. Peristiany (1965); cf. Gorer, *op. cit.*, 4 and G. Devereux, "Psychoanalysis as Anthropological Fieldwork," *Transactions of the New York Academy of Sciences* (1956).

105. I once heard someone observe that the modern Greeks are exceptionally free from the sense of guilt, "so different from their guilt-ridden ancestors." Perhaps the difference is not, after all, so very great.

106. Peristiany, *op. cit.*, 190. G. M. Calhoun *in* Wace and Stubbings, *Companion to Homer* (1963), 450 finds in Homer "clear recognition of what may be called the social virtues. Calhoun speaks of "the mistaken belief that there is in Homer no morality." "There is much," he continues, "but it is different from that of moderns."

107. 24, 527 f.

108. See K. Deichgräber, *Der listensinnende Trug des Gottes* (1952), 108 f., especially 114 f.

109. It is not surprising that the notion of cosmic justice should in Greece have become attached to a primitive conception of family solidarity (see Dodds, *GI*, 34); for that notion must have existed from a very early date, certainly much earlier than the *Iliad*.

NOTES TO CHAPTER II
(Pages 28–54)

1. 1, 32 f.

2. See Dodds, *GI*, 32 and nn. on p. 52; cf. Lesky, "Homeros," 42.

3. The significance of the episode was pointed out by W. Jaeger, *S. B. Berlin* (1926), 73 f. = *Scripta Minora* (1960), I 322 f. = *Five Essays* (1966), 83 f. See K. Rüter, "Odysseeinterpretationen," *Hypomnemata*, 19 (1969), 64–82.

4. *GI*, 32.

5. 11, 104 f.

6. 2, 157 f.

7. 20, 350 f. I am less sure than Page (*The Homeric Odyssey*, 83 f.) or Kirk (*The Songs of Homer*, 241 f.) that the final solemn warning given by Theoclymenus supplies an inadequate reason for the introduction of this character into the poem.

8. 4, 261; cf. 23, 223.

9. 12, 371.

10. 9, 112, 215, 266, 475 f.

11. 1, 48, 64 f.; 4, 690 f.; 5, 7 f.; 19, 385 f.

12. 1, 225, 368; 22, 39–40, 422; 23, 282.

13. 4, 103–104 = 137–138.

14. 3, 152, 160; 8, 81–82; 9, 262; 18, 411.

15. 6, 188–190; 9, 410–411; 18, 130 f.

16. 14, 283 f.

17. 6, 207–208 = 14, 57–58.

18. 17, 475.

19. 5, 447 f.

20. 8, 544–545.

21. 9, 266 f., 475 f.

22. 19, 134–135; 22, 39–40, 412; 23, 62, 351, 456.

23. 19, 328 f.; 21, 331.

24. 1, 255 f.; 19, 394–396. On these passages, see F. Dirlmeier, "Die Giftpfeile des Odysseus," *S. B. Heid., phil.-hist. Kl.* (1966), 2.

25. Von der Mühll, Irmscher and Schadewaldt, for instance, take this kind of view; see Lesky, "Homeros," 118–119.

26. See H. Strasburger, "Der soziologische Aspekt der Homerischen Epen," *Gymnasium*, 60 (1953), 97 f.

27. "Tradition und Geist in Homerischen Epos," *Studium Generale*, 4 (1951), 334 f. = *Tradition und Geist* (1960), 5 f. Cf. F. Jacoby, "Die geistige Physiognomie des Odyssee," *Die Antike*, 9 (1933), 159 f. = *Kl. Phil. Schr.*, I 107 f. well describes certain differences of atmosphere. Of course W. Jaeger, *Paideia*, I 19, finds that "by seeing and portraying as a living whole the culture of an entire social class . . . the *Odyssey* makes a decided advance in artistic observation of life and its problems." He says (*op. cit.*, p. 24) that "the morality of the *Odyssey* is universally on a much higher plane" than that of the *Iliad*.

28. Jaeger, *loc. cit.* seems to me to exaggerate its significance a good deal.

29. *Theogony*, 1 f.

30. *Works and Days*, 27 f.

31. See Wilamowitz, *Glaube*, I 332–333.

32. *Works and Days*, 42 f.; cf. *Theogony*, 535 f.

33. When the chorus of Euripides' *Hippolytus* (1146) says "I am angry with the gods," its utterance is in the highest degree exceptional.

34. Dodds (*GI*, 35) quotes Aristotle's remark that it would be eccentric for anyone to say he loved Zeus; that is the view of a sophisticated city-dweller of the late fourth century. Ordinary people felt affection for the gods whose cults were familiar to them, and particularly for their own tutelary deities, Athena at Athens, Hera at Argos, and so on. See Latte, *Kl. Schr.*, 51.

35. *Works and Days*, 109 f.

36. See V. Goldschmidt, *REG*, 73 (1950), 33 f. I am not satisfied by J. P. Vernant's reply (*Rev. Phil.*, 40, 1966, 247 f.) to the criticisms directed by J. Defradas (*L'information litteraire*, 4, 1965, 152 f.) against his ingenious interpretation of this myth (*Mythe et Pensée chez les Grecs*, 19 f.).

37. Fr. 234 Merkelbach-West.

38. See Hecataeus 1 *FGH* fr. 13; Acusilaus 2 *FGH* frs. 34–35 with Jacoby, *ad loc.*; Pindar, *Ol.* 9, 43 f. with scholia; Callimachus frs. 533 and 496, which have been shown by J. Irigoin, *REG*, 73 (1960), 439 f. to form a single elegiac couplet.

39. See L. Séchan, *Le Mythe de Promethée*, 33; F. Stoessl, *R.-E.*, 23, 1 (1957), 696 f.

40. Fr. 530 Mette = fr. 282 in my supplement to the Loeb edition of Aeschylus.

41. For instance by W. Jaeger, *Paideia*, I 60; cf. Wilamowitz, *Glaube*, I 346; "daher ist ein grosser Fortschritt über Homer getan."

42. 901 f.

43. See V. Ehrenberg, *Aspects of the Ancient World* (1946), 70 f.; M. Ostwald, *Nomos and the Beginnings of the Athenian Democracy* (1969), 63 f.

44. On the chronological relation between Homer and Hesiod, see M. L. West's commentary on the *Theogony*, p. 46 f.; his opinion may be contested, but will not be easily refuted.

45. Pfeiffer, "Gottheit und Individuum in der frühgriechischen Lyrik," *Philologus*, 84 (1929), 137 f. = *Ausgewählte Schriften*, 42 f.; Snell, *Die Entdeckung des Geistes*, ch. 4, 83 f.

46. Dodds, *GI*, 30.

47. *Ibid.*, 29.

48. *Ibid.*, 29; cf. Wilamowitz, *Glaube*, I 351.

49. The specimens of the poetry of "primitive" races offered by Bowra, in his book *Primitive Song* (1962) do not rule out this supposition.

50. *Loc. cit.*, 139–141 = 43–45.

51. *Il.* 24, 49.

52. Fr. 7, 5 f.

53. Fr. 67 A, 1 f.

54. Fr. 1.

55. Fr. 6.

56. Cf. O. Reverdin and others in "Archiloque," *Entretiens de la Fondation Hardt*, 10 (1963), 285 f.

57. Fr. 64.

58. *Od.* 11, 477–503.

59. Fr. 60; cf. Page, "Archiloque," (quoted in n. 56), 159, 214 and G. Devereux, *Cl. Quart.*, 15 (1965), 179, n. 9.

60. *Il.* 3, 203 f.

61. *Il.* 5, 801.

62. *Isthm.* 3/4, 69. Richmond Lattimore draws my attention to an interesting parallel in Clement of Alexandria's *Protrepticus* (II 29, 7, on p. 23 of vol. I of Stählin's edition): ʿΙερώνυμος δὲ ὁ φιλόσοφος (fr. 34 Hiller) καὶ τὴν σχέσιν αὐτοῦ ὑφηγεῖ τοῦ σώματος μικρὸν φριξότριχα ῥωστικόν. Δικαίαρχος δὲ(fr. 54 Wehrli)   σχιζίαν νευρώδη μέλανα γρυπὸν ὑποχάροπον τετανότριχα.

63. Fr. 84.

64. Fr. 58.

65. Frs. 67 A, 74.

66. Fr. 94.

67. *Pyth.* 2, 55. Pindar's own practice was perhaps not quite as different from that of Archilochus as his tone here might suggest; cf. ll. 83 f. of the same poem.

68. Fr. 1, 5–6.

69. *In* "Archiloque" (quoted in n. 56), 117 f.

70. Fr. 1; cf. *Il.* 9, 186–189.

71. Fr. 130.

72. Fr. 31, 17.

73. Fr. 58.

74. Fr. 16.

75. Frs. 39, 261, 361.

76. First printed (with photographs) by R. Merkelbach in *Zeitschrift für Papyrologie und Epigraphik*, 1 (1967), 81 f.; now Alcaeus fr. 138 *in* Page, *Lyrica Graeca Selecta*, p. 75; for commentary, see *GRBS*, 9 (1968), 125 f.

77. See J. Trumpf, "Studien zur griechischen Lyrik," Diss. Cologne (1958), 8 f.

78. Fr. 6, 14; fr. 72, 13.

79. Fr. 348 1 (cf. frs. 67, 4; 75, 12; 106, 3).

80. Fr. 29.

81. Frs. 1 and 2.

82. Fr. 2, I f.; *Il.* 6, 146 f.

83. Fr. 2, 5 f.; *Il.* 12, 326 f.

84. Fr. 2, 15–16; cf. *Il.* 24, 527 f. (controversial even in antiquity).

85. Fr. 7; cf. Theognis 793–797; Pindar, *Pyth.* 11, 28 (see C. M. Bowra, *Pindar*, 1966, 187).

86. Frs. 12, 12 A, 13.

87. Fr. 29.

88. Fr. 1.

89. Fr. 1, 1 f.

90. 34 f.

91. Fr. 7.

92. Fr. 15.

93. Fr. 1, 29 f.

94. Fr. 3, 1–10. See Jaeger, *S. B. Berlin* (1926), 69 f. = *Scr. Min.*, I 315 f. = *Five Essays*, 78 f. (especially pp. 89–94). Jaeger in a memoir (*Scr. Min.*, I xxiv = *Five Essays*, 40) tells how after he had read this paper in Berlin Wilamowitz remarked that Solon's notion of *Dike* was just the same as Hesiod's. Jaeger's way of telling the story shows that he did not realise that Wilamowitz, as always, knew what he was talking about.

95. Fr. 24, 16.

96. Fr. 3, 30 f.

97. W. Jaeger, *Paideia*, I 89.

98. Fr. 9.

99. *Loc. cit.*, 29–32. See Walter F. Otto, "Tyrtaios und die Unsterblichkeit des Ruhmes," *Die Gestalt und das Sein,* 367 f. which provides an excellent corrective to Jaeger's treatment of the poet here and at *S. B. Berlin* (1932), 537 f. = *Scr. Min.*, II 75 f. = *Five Essays*, 103 f.

100. Fr. 6, 3 f.

101. *Paideia*, I 92.

102. Parents 131–132, 821–822; strangers 793–796.

103. 337–350, 363–364, 869–872.

104. 607–610, 851–854.

105. 155–160, 425–428, 659–666, fr. dub. 4.

106. 161–172, 617–618, 1187–1190.

107. 133–142.

108. 197–208.

109. 401–406, 587–590, 629–632.

110. 687–688.

111. 373–392.

112. 731–752.

113. 53–68.

114. E.g. 27–38, 411–412.

115. 69–72, 221–226, 415–418, 529–530, 697–698.

116. 59–60; cf. 411–412, 895–896, 1171–1176.

117. 429–432, 577–578.

118. 59–60.

119. 39–52, 151–154, 605–606, 833–836; cf. 541–542.

120. 365–366, 1025–1026.

121. 355–360, 393–400, 555–556, 657–658, 1029–1030, 1062 a–e, 1178 a–b.

122. 653–654.

123. 145–146, 149–150, 197–208, 315–318 (= Solon fr. 4, 9–12), 393–400, 866–868.

124. 173–182.

125. 145–148.

126. *MR*, 78.

127. Fr. 37; see p. 48.

128. 1079–1080.

129. *Pyth.* 9, 95.

130. Frs. 15, 76.

131. Frs. 18, 74.

132. Fr. 2.

133. Frs. 16, 22.

134. Fr. 15, 4; 17, 19.

135. Fr. 1; cf. fr. 3, 36.

136. See Eduard Fraenkel, *Proceedings of the British Academy*, 28 (1942), 22–23.

137. Fr. 37 (542).

138. Ll. 27–29.

139. L. 33–35. For a different view of the poem, see Adkins, *MR*, 165 f.; 355 f.

140. Fr. 36 (541). Bowra, *Hermes*, 91 (1963), 257 f. followed me (*CR* n.s. 11, 1961, 19) in arguing for an ascription to Bacchylides. But W. S. Barrett, in a letter to me dated 12.6.61, observed that if ll.6–7 are dactylo-epitrite, then word end at ⦂ in ἐς τ]έλὄs οὔ γἄρ ελᾱφρὄν ⦂ ἐσθλὄν ἔμμἔν does not accord with the practice of Bacchylides as he describes it in *Hermes*, 84 (1956), 252.

141. L. 6 f.

142. Bowra, *Pindar*, 76.

143. *Pyth.* 3, 24 f.

144. *Ol.* 1, 59 f.

145. *Pyth.* 2, 21 f.

146. *Pyth.* 1, 15 f.; 73 f.

147. *Ol.* 13, 7.

148. Fr. 215 (a), 1.

149. *Nem.* 9, 15.

150. *Pyth.* 2, 87; though when Pindar says (*Pyth.* 11. 53) "I find fault with the fate of tyrannies," he means not that he disapproves of tyrants but that he has no wish to be one. See David C. Young, "Three Odes of Pindar," *Mnemosyne*, Suppl. IX (1968), 9 f.

151. *Pyth.* 4, 140.

152. *Ibid.*, 284, *Ol.* 7, 91; cf. *Pyth.* 8, 12.

153. Fr. 159; cf. *Pyth.* 8, 15.

154. *Isthm.* 9, 5; cf. *Ol.* 2, 6.

155. E.g. *Nem.* 10, 54; 78.

156. *Pyth.* 1, 94; *Pyth.* 6, 40; *Paean* 6, 131; *Pyth.* 11, 54.

157. *Isthm.* 7, 44.

158. *Ol.* 2, 76, *Pyth.* 73. Cf. *Nem.* 10, 12, of Talaus and Lynceus.

159. See *Maia* n.s. iii, Anno 19, 1967, 211 f.

160. Fr. 169; see M. Gigante, Atti del xl Congresso di Papirologia, 1966, 286 f.

161. *Works and Days*, 276–278.

162. *Pyth.* 1, 41; *Ol.* 9, 28.

163. *Nem.* 6, 1 f.

164. Herodotus I 31, 1 f.

165. See H. W. Parke and D. E. W. Wormell, *History of the Delphic Oracle*, II, pp. 59–60.

166. Theognis, 425–428; Pindar fr. 157 (in whose context Silenus probably expressed this sentiment); Sophocles, *OC*, 1211 f. See Vahlen, *Gesammelte Philologische Schriften*, I, 126 f.

167. See Parke and Wormell, *op. cit.*, I, 379.

168. Herodotus, 6, 86 1.

169. Parke and Wormell, *op. cit.*, 380.

170. Fr. 22.

171. Fr. 1, 7–8.

172. See Helen North, "*Sophrosyne*: Self-knowledge and Self-restraint in Greek Literature," *Cornell Studies in Classical Philology*, 35 (1966); cf. G. J. de Vries, *Mnemosyne*, s. 3, vol. 11 (1943), 81 f. Miss North accounts for the increased importance of this concept during the seventh and sixth centuries in terms of the sudden changes of fortune which she finds especially characteristic of this period. But we cannot really be sure that changes of fortune were commoner then than, say, during the ninth and eighth centuries; and the occurrence in Homer of terms like πινυτός, πεπνυμένος, ἐχέφρων should warn us against too easy acceptance of such an explanation.

173. *GI*, 36.

174. *Ibid.*, 30.

NOTES TO CHAPTER III
(Pages 55–78)

1. *GI*, 29.
2. *Op. cit.*, 30.
3. *Il.* 24, 605 f.
4. *GI*, 30.
5. *Od.* 4, 181.
6. *Od.* 23, 210 f.
7. *Od.* 8, 564 f.; cf. 13, 125 f.
8. Cf. A. W. Gomme, *The Greek Attitude to Poetry and History* (1954), 82.
9. *GI*, 30.
10. Fr. 1.
11. Fr. 3; cf. frs. 8 and 10.
12. *GI*, 30; cf. De Sanctis, *Storia dei Greci* (1939), II 216.
13. *Ibid.*, 42; cf. n. 55 on p. 56.
14. See Dodds, *GI*, 50, with literature there quoted. Doubtless A. Dihle, *Philologus*, 106 (1962), 207 f. is right in holding that Herodotus' treatment of the idea of *nomos* and of the formalisation of popular ethics reflects sophistic influence. But his mind was formed before he came into contact with the influence in question; and as Dihle himself points out (see in particular p. 214 f.), much of the sophists' work consisted in the rationalisation and systematisation of generally held beliefs and concepts. See p. 129 below for the argument that Protagoras and other sophists preserved more of the archaic world outlook than is generally allowed.
15. In the history of Greek literature published in *Die Kultur der Gegenwart,* ed. P. Hinneberg (2d ed., 1907), 58. In the third edition of 1912 (p. 97) this judgment is modified; see also Wilamowitz, *Glaube,* II 205 f.
16. See section 30 ("Herodot als Historiker") of his article s.v. "Herodotos" in *R.-E.* Suppl. II (p. 467 f.).
17. O. Regenbogen's important article, "Herodot und Sein Werk; Ein Versuch" first printed in *Die Antike,* 6, 1930, 202 f., now in his *Kl. Schr.,* 57 f. and in W. Marg's *Herodot: Eine Auswahl aus der neueren Forschung* (*Wege der Forschung,* 26; 2d ed., 1965, 57 f.) marks a turning-point; a similar point of view is expressed in M. Pohlenz' *Herodot, der erste Geschichtschreiber des Abendlandes* (1937), especially in the chapter headed "Die Deutung des Geschehens" (p. 91 f.), and H. R. Immerwahr, *Form and Thought in Herodotus* (1966), see ch. I.
18. See in particular H. Strasburger, "Herodots Zeitrechnung," *Historia,* 5 (1956), 129 f. = Marg, *Herodot,* 688 f.
19. See A. Momigliano, "The Place of Herodotus in the History of

Historiography," *History*, 43 (1958), 1 f. = *Secondo Contributo alla Storia degli Studi Classici* (1960), 29 f.; a German version is in Marg, *Herodot*, 137 f. Cf. the same author's "Erodoto e la Storia Moderna," *Aevum*, 31 (1957), 74 f. = *Secondo Contributo*, 45 f. Cf. Strasburger, *op. cit.*, 5 = 579: "Seine historische Sehweise ist die der älteren Griechen überhaupt, in ihrer weise reif bzw. jener wirklichkeit entsprechend und nicht eine bemängelnswerte Kindheitsstufe der unsrigen."

20. See H. Erbse, *Festschrift B. Snell* (1956), 209 f.; cf. H. R. Immerwahr, *TAPA*, 87 (1956), 243–247; H. F. Bornitz, *Herodot-Studien* (1968), 139 f.

21. I 5, 3 f.

22. Kurt von Fritz, *GG*.

23. K. Latte, "Die Anfänge der griechischen Geschichtsschreibung," in *Entretiens de la Fondation Hardt*, IV (1956), 1 f.

24. For the proper appraisal of his arguments his whole section on Herodotus and particularly the parts entitled "Lydische Geschichten und Geschichte" (208 f.), "Geschichte und Geschichten in den drei letzten Büchern des Werkes Herodots" (243 f.) and "Die Entstehung des Herodoteischen Geschichtswerkes und die Entwicklung Herodots zum und als Historiker" (442 f.) should be examined.

25. 7, 8 f,; see von Fritz, 244 f.

26. 7, 10 a f.

27. 247 f.

28. I, 53 f. Devereux writes, "The Xerxes dream is a wish-fulfilment dream, psychologically very plausible. To avenge Marathon is an *obligation;* to outdo his father in so doing is a compulsion. In that sense the dream is akin to the Queen's dream in Aeschylus' *Persians*. Artabanus' dreaming the same dream as Xerxes while sleeping in the royal bed proves that a King of Persia had no choice in the matter."

29. 7, 46 f., especially 50 f.

30. I, 206 f.

31. 8, 67 f.

32. I, 34, I. Cf. Gomme, *op. cit.* (in n. 8), 110.

33. 3, 133 f.

34. 3, 30, 33, 80.

35. So, at any rate, Themistocles calls him (8, 109, 3).

36. See above, p. 28.

37. I, 131.

38. 2, 53.

39. See I. M. Linforth, "Named and Unnamed Gods in Herodotus," *Univ. Calif. Publ. Class. Philol.*, vol. 9, no. 7, 201 f., especially p. 218 f.; cf. G. François, "Le polythéisme et l'emploi au singulier des mots θεός, δαίμων," *Bibl. de la fac. de phil. et lettres*, Liège, 147 (1957).

40. 1, 89.

41. 1, 207.

42. 7, 129; see also Linforth, *op. cit.*, 217.

43. 8, 129.

44. 9, 101.

45. 3, 80 f. Herodotus does not, as is commonly supposed, say (I, 60) that the Greeks have long been freer from nonsense than the barbarians; he says the opposite. See Burkert, *Rh. Mus.*, 106 (1963), 97–98, after Rosa Lamacchia, *Atene e Roma*, 4 (1954), 87 f. The old error is still found in L. Edelstein's posthumous work, "The Idea of Progress in Classical Antiquity" (1967), 47–48.

46. Very likely Herodotus was acquainted with the climatological theories known to us from περὶ ἀέρων ὑδάτων τόπων and other early Hippocratic works; see Wilhelm Nestle, *Vom Mythos zum Logos*, 2d ed., 225.

47. I, 155 f.

48. 6, 11 f.

49. 7, 102, 1.

50. Note, for instance, the story (9, 82 f.) of how after Plataea Pausanias caused a Persian dinner to be prepared as it would have been for Mardonius so that the Spartans might compare the Persian way of eating with their own.

51. 9, 108 f.; see Erwin Wolff, "Das Weib des Masistes," *Hermes*, 92 (1964), 51 f. = Marg, *Herodot*, 668 f.; also H. Bischoff, "Der Warner bei Herodot," Diss. Marburg, 1932, 78 f. = Marg, *Herodot*, 681 f.

52. 9, 114 f.

53. 9, 122.

54. See H. Strasburger, "Herodot und das perikleische Athen," *Historia*, 4 (1955), 1 f. = Marg, *Herodot*, 574 f. "Herodotus thinks in terms of divine punishment and *hybris* as long as he deals with the Persians," writes Friedrich Solmsen, *Class. Philol.*, 40 (1945), 123, "but when he comes to the Greeks gives them full credit for their *aretai* and achievements." I think Herodotus' attitude is far less partisan than this suggests.

55. Dodds, *GI*, 30.

56. 1, 30 f.

57. 7, 46.

58. Solon fr. 22.

59. *GI*, 42. Cf. Eduard Meyer, *Herodots Geschichtswerk* (1899), 259: "eine Frage, weshalb das Schicksal es so verfügt, die Annahme einer sittlichen Verschuldung des in Unglück gestürzten ist völlig ausgeschlossen."

60. *Loc. cit.*, (n. 21); cf. Strasburger, *op. cit.*, 17 = 598: "Für Herodot sind die meisten geschichtlichen Erscheinungen Kundgebungen eines

göttlichen Willes, Aüsserungen, die ihm geheimnisvoll und unheil-
schwanger erscheinen, mindestens solange noch nicht das Ende einer
bestimmten Schicksalskette sichtbar scheint."

61. 1, 32, 1.

62. 3, 40 f.

63. 7, 10 E.

64. 7, 46, 4.

65. 8, 109, 3.

66. 1, 32, 4.

67. 1, 34, 1.

68. 7, 10 E, *ad fin.*

69. 8, 109, 3.

70. 6, 86.

71. 6, 84, 3.

72. 7, 133 f.; cf. Thuc. 2, 67.

73. 8, 77 (1.2 of the oracle).

74. *Pyth.* 10, 20.

75. *Isthm.* 7, 38.

76. Aeschylus, *Persae*, 361; Pohlenz, *Herodot*, p. 111.

77. *Agamemnon*, 921, 946–947.

78. See Lloyd-Jones, "The Guilt of Agamemnon," *CQ* n.s. XII (1962),
187 f. I do not know whether it is my fault that N. G. L. Hammond, *JHS*,
85 (1965), 42 f. supposes that I think that "Agamemnon is seen as a puppet, of which the strings are pulled by Zeus." In Aeschylus, as in Homer,
even though a human action is prompted by a god, the human actor is
responsible.

79. *IA*, 1089–1097; contrast Dodds, *GI*, 31.

80. *GI*, 35.

81. *GI*, 54, n. 39.

82. *Od.* 15, 256 f.; Antiphon, *de caede Herodis*, 82 f.; see *GI*, 36, and n.
40 on p. 55.

83. *Ibid.*, 36.

84. *Ibid.*, 40.

85. *Ibid.*, 44 f.

86. *Ibid.*, 45 f.

87. *Ibid.*, 48.

88. K. O. Müller, *Eumenides* (1833), 136–137.

89. See Giuliana Lanata, *Medicina Magica e Religione Popolare in
Grecia fino all' Età di Ippocrate*, Rome (1967), 40 f.

90. Aeschylus, *Eum.*, 62–63.

91. *Il.* 24, 718 f.

92. W. Burkert, *Rh. Mus.*, 105 (1962), 36 f.

93. Kinkel, *Epicorum Graecorum Fragmenta*, p. 211; see Burkert, *op. cit.*, 39, with n. 14.

94. *Od.* 15, 225 f.

95. See Hesiod fr. 37 Merkelbach-West; cf. fr. 261 *ibid.*; for the Melampodia, see Kinkel, *op. cit.*, p. 151 f. and Ingrid Löffler, *Die Melampodie: Versuch einer Rekonstruktion des Inhalts, Beiträge zur klassischen Philologie*, ed. R. Merkelbach, Meisenheim am Glan, Heft 7, (1963).

96. See G. Murray, *The Rise of the Greek Epic* (1907, 3d ed. 1926), 12 f., 317 f.; Nilsson, *GGR* I², 107 f.; V. Gebhard, "Die Pharmakoi in Ionien und die Sybakchoi in Athen," Diss. Amberg, 1926 and in R.-E. s. vv. "Pharmakos" and "Thargelia"; cf. O. Masson on Hipponax, frs. 5-10.

97. Rohde, *Psyche*, 174 f.

98. See the summary of the poem's content by Proclus (Allen, Homeri Opera V, pp. 105–106); Bethe, *Der Troische Epenkreis*, pp. 167–168—pp. 19–22 of the 1966 reprint).

99. ΣD on *Il.* 2, 336 (Dindorf I, p. 102; not in Erbse's great edition *ad loc.*; not printed in full in Merkelbach-West, *Fragmenta Hesiodea*, pp. 22–23).

100. See Aeschylus fr. 314 (b) and (c) Mette (p. 113).

101. Fr. ii Allen (Homeri Opera V, p. 115).

102. H. W. Parke and D. E. W. Wormell, *History of the Delphic Oracle*, 2d ed., I 8.

103. *Ibid.*, 346. R. R. Dyer, *JHS*, 89 (1969), 38 f. will not convince the unbiassed reader of Aeschylus, *Eum.* 280–283 and 1038–1039 that Apollo purified Orestes anywhere but at Delphi.

104. *GGR* I², 91–92. Cf. L. Moulinier, *Le pur et l'impur dans la pensée des grecs d'Homère à Aristote* (1952), 33.

105. *Il.* 1, 11 f.

106. Devereux writes, "What legally is collective responsibility is magically pollution, or the risk of pollution, and is 'guilt' in moral terms."

107. *Ibid.*, 311–316.

108. *Il.* 3, 56–57.

109. See R. Hirzel, *Die Strafe der Steinigung*, in Abhl, Leipzig, 27 (1909), 25 f.

110. See Lloyd-Jones, *GRBS*, 9 (1968), 137; cf. C. M. Robertson, *BSA*, 62 (1967), 11, which I did not see until my article was with the printer. I hold to my view of the nature of the oath sworn by Ajax; to the authorities quoted in my n. 13, add R. Hirzel, *Der Eid* (1904), 41 f. and K. Latte, *Heiliges Recht* (1920, repr. 1964; see his index s.v. "Eid"), and see L. Gernet, *Anthropologie de la Grèce Antique*, 1968, 245.

111. Fr. 354 Mette; more evidence in R. Muth, *Träger der Lebenskraft* (1954), 31.

112. See Rohde, *Psyche*, 582 f.

113. *Eum.* 417.

114. See Nilsson, *GGR* I², 100 f.; Dodds, *GI*, 20, n. 33; Otto, *GG³*, 193–194. Dodds, *GI*, 21, n. 37 rejects Rohde's theory that the Erinyes were originally ghosts, partly because in all Homeric instances except one (*Od.* 11, 279 f.), the claims which they support are those of living persons. I think this simply shows that, as we know in any case, the concept of the Erinys had already evolved some way from its origins by Homer's time.

115. *Il.* 9, 454.

116. *Il.* 9, 571; 21, 412; *Od.* 2, 135.

117. *Il.* 15, 204.

118. *Il.* 19, 259 f.

119. *Il.* 19, 418. This passage is by itself enough to show how far the original conception of the Erinyes has developed by the time of Homer.

120. *Il.* 9, 566 f.

121. *Il.* 19, 87.

122. *Il.* 15, 204.

123. *Il.* 21, 412.

124. *Od.* 17, 475.

125. *Works and Days* 240–241.

126. This was already noted by Rohde, *Psyche*, 180: "The Homeric poems know nothing of any religious purification of those who have incurred the stain of blood. Analogous occurrences in the religious usage of allied peoples make it, however, almost impossible to doubt that the notion of religious uncleanness belonging to a man who has had any dealings with uncanny powers was of primeval antiquity among the Greeks, too. It can only have been suppressed in the Homeric view of the matter; just as that view suppressed the usages of expiation."

127. See Dodds, *GI*, ch. V *passim;* on the relation of "Orphism" to sin and punishment, see Latte, *ARW*, 20 (1920/21), 281 f. = *Kl. Schr.* 23 f.

128. The notion of a kind of "expurgation" in the Homeric tradition is advanced by Murray, *The Rise of the Greek Epic*, 120 f.; cf. F. Dirlmeier (cited in n. 24 on p. 172). We have found something like it in the passage of Rohde quoted in n. 126 above. "Der Begriff," says Latte, *ARW*, 20 (1920/21), 260. f. = *Kl. Schr.* 7 f., speaking of pollution, "der zu dem anthropomorphen Götterglaube dieser (= Homeric) Kreise nicht passte, wird wohl ganz bewusst gemieden sein. Denn es kann keinem Zweifel unterliegen, dass dieser ganze Vorstellungskomplex schon un seines primitiven Charakters willen in älteste Zeit zurlückgeht, obwahl das Dunkel, das über

dieser Periode der griechischen Religionsgeschichte liegt, uns die genauere Kenntnis verhüllt."

129. Cf. Burkert, *Rh. Mus.*, 105 (1962), 52: "Wenn auch die Welt Homers in wörtlichsten Sinn voll von Göttern ist, so sind doch diese Götter des Dämonisch-Numinosen in erstaunlichem Masse entkleidet; ihrer Epiphanie fehlt das mysterium tremendum, und ebenso ist die Welt der Toten entmachtet, und nur nebenbei sind einmal Demeter, Dionysos oder die Erinyen genannt. Eben damit wird freilich deutlich dass diese dunklen Mächte durchaus vorhanden sind; die Welt des Epos ist in dieser Beziehung ungreifbar-vielschichtig." Cf. G. Lanata, *op. cit.* (n. 27), 27 f.

130. In my article, "The Guilt of Agamemnon," *CQ* n.s. 12 (1962), 187 f., I tried to show how this applies to the curse of Thyestes in the *Agamemnon* of Aeschylus.

131. On the relation between the ancient belief in pollution and the developed conception of guilt, see Latte, *ARW*, 20 (1920/21), 278 f. = *Kl. Schr.*, 21 f.; on the scepticism about pollution sometimes expressed in tragedy, see *ibid.*, 283 f. = 24 f.

132. For the presence of tragedy, in a certain sense, in the *Iliad*, see Erwin Wolff's review of B. Snell's *Aischylos: Die Handlung im Drama* in *Gnomon* 5 (1929), 386 f.

NOTES TO CHAPTER IV
(Pages 79–103)

1. See F. M. Cornford, *From Religion to Philosophy* (1912, repr. 1957); cf. *Principium Sapientiae* (1952, repr. 1965). When Jaeger expressed the same view in his *Theology of the Early Greek Philosophers* (1947), it was hardly as new to English-speaking readers as he and Lesky *(History of Greek Literature*, 162, n. 8) evidently supposed; see W. Hamilton, *Cl. Rev.*, 64 (1950), 106 f.

2. See U. Hölscher, *Anfängliches Fragen*, (1968), 40 f.; cf. Kirk and Raven, *The Presocratic Philosophers*, 90–91.

3. See Kirk and Raven, *op. cit.*, 95; G. E. R. Lloyd, *Polarity and Analogy; Two Types of Argumentation in Early Greek Thought* (1966), 233–234.

4. See 12 *VS* frs. 2–3.

5. 12 *VS* fr. 1.

6. Devereux is reminded of Durkheim's view that man's conception of the world and of the supernatural is a projection of his image of his own society. G. E. R. Lloyd, *op. cit.* (n. 3, above), 213, writes: "Anaximander refers not to the *supreme power* of an autocratic king (such as Zeus is, in Homer and Hesiod) but to the *rule of law*, which regulates the relation-

ships between several factors which are *all of equal status*." I do not understand how he knows that the factors are "all of equal status"; it seems to me that some might have more *time* than others; and I do not see how he knows that Time, the "assessor" is compared to Law rather than to a king who enforces laws. In the interesting discussion of the use of social and political images in the fourth chapter of his book, Lloyd seems to me to make too much of the distinction between the "arbitrary decisions of a wilful ruler" (e.g. Zeus; see p. 224) and the later political notion of impersonal justice. He writes, for example, that "the social upheavals of the sixth century are, *of course,* reflected in Heraclitus' conception of the universality of war and strife" (my italics). I should have thought war and strife were so common to human life at all periods that the conditions of Heraclitus' own time were not especially relevant. Even in the *Iliad*, Zeus governs in accordance with a kind of law, based though his power is upon superior force.

7. Fr. 24, 3. Jaeger, *S. B. Berlin* (1926), 78 f. = *Scripta Minora* (1960), I 315 f. = *Five Essays* (1966), 77 f., thinks it significant that Solon stresses the operation of the divine justice through natural processes and not through divine interference with the course of nature; cf. G. Vlastos, *Cl. Phil.*, 41 (1946), 65 f. Yet for early writers the distinction between natural processes and such "interferences" with the course of nature as plagues and famines did not exist. Certainly Solon and later writers lay increasing stress on the operation of divine justice through the actions of men themselves; in doing so, they were carrying further a tendency present already in the epic, and no such radical break with the past as these writers posit is involved. The "political imagery" used by presocratic philosophers is not taken from contemporary politics; rather, it is taken from religion, which had used a kind of political imagery from the earliest times (see p. 6 f. above).

8. Vlastos, *Cl. Phil.*, 42 (1947), 174, credits Anaximander and his successors with having naturalised justice. "Justice," he writes, "is no longer inscrutable *moira*, imposed by arbitrary forces with incalculable effect, nor is she the goddess Dike, moral and rational enough, but frail and unreliable. She is now one with the ineluctable laws of nature herself." To me *Moira* in the early period seems less inscrutable and Dike less frail than they do to Vlastos, and the change seems correspondingly less abrupt.

9. The point is well brought out by C. H. Kahn, *Anaximander and the Origins of Greek Cosmology* (1960).

10. See especially chs. 2–4 (W. H. S. Jones, *Hippocrates* II, Loeb Library, 140 f.; cf. Giuliana Lanata, "Medicina Magica e Religione Popolare in Grecia fino all' Età de Ippocrate," 1967. On the sense of "the divine" in this work, see H. W. Miller, *TAPA*, 84 (1953), 2, n. 4.

11. "Das Göttliche ist für ihn der Naturvorgang selbst": Wilhelm Nestle, *Hermes*, 73 (1938), 8 = *Griechische Studien* (1948), 526. Thus for the author of περὶ ἀέρων ὑδάτων τόπων all πάθεα are equally human and all are equally divine (74, 14 f.); see H. Diller, *Philologus*, Suppl. 26, Heft 3 (1934), 55, and cf. G. Vlastos, *Phil. Rev.*, 54 (1945), 581.

12. περὶ ἀγμῶν ch. 1 (Jones, *op. cit.*, III, 94); cf. ch. 37 (*op. cit.*, 182).

13. περὶ ἀγμῶν ch. 7 (Jones, *op. cit.*, 112); cf. περὶ ἀγμῶν ch. 62 (Jones, *op. cit.*, 350).

14. περὶ ἀγμῶν ch. 7.

15. See above, p. 77.

16. See Burkert, *Rh. Mus.*, 106 (1961), 160 f.; but note the reservations of Hölscher, *op. cit.*, 85, n. 244.

17. 21 *VS* fr. 23, fr. 25.

18. See Kirk and Raven, *op. cit.*, 171–172.

19. 21 *VS* fr. 15, fr. 16.

20. Frs. 23–26.

21. See Otto, *GG*[3], 237–239; cf. *idem, Gestalt und Sein*, 124. "Gods lose all individual character by the attribution of perfection," writes Devereux, "another attribution of perfection to god is another step towards atheism." See his "Mad Gods" in *Studi e Materiali di Storia delle Religione*.

22. 21 *VS* fr. 11.

23. See in particular his speech at *Il*. 8, 18 f.

24. *Il*. 1, 5.

25. See above, ch. 1.

26. Fr. 1, 1 f.

27. *Works and Days*, 266, 252 f.

28. *Ibid.*, 48; contrast *ibid*. 105, *Theogony*, 613.

29. See G. S. Kirk, *Heraclitus: The Cosmic Fragments* (1954), 392 f.

30. *Ibid.*, 307 f.

31. E.g., of Homer (22 *VS* 42·= 30 Marcovich), Hesiod (40 = 16, 57 = 43), Archilochus (42 = 30), Pythagoras (40 = 16, 81 = 18, 129 = 17), Xenophanes and Hecataeus (40 = 16).

32. 5 = 86.

33. 14 = 87.

34. 96 = 76.

35. See Kirk, *op. cit.*, 44.

36. 5 = 86.

37. 22 *VS* 14 A; but this may not be genuine (see Marcovich, p. 465).

38. 15 = 50.

39. 32 = 84.

40. 11 = 80.

41. 64 = 79.

42. 93 = 14.

43. 52 = 94.

44. 80 = 28.

45. 102 = 91.

46. 43 = 102; cf. 31 = 85.

47. 114 = 23.

48. 78 = 90.

49. 85 = 70. Agamemnon in the *Iliad* erred, according to Nestor, "through yielding to his *thymos*" (9, 109–110); so did Achilles (*ibid.*, 496, 629, 636–637).

50. 119 = 94.

51. 1 = 1 (see Kirk, *op. cit.*, 43 f.); 2 = 23 (see *ibid.*, 57 f.).

52. See Kirk, *op. cit.*, 188 f.

53. 29 = 95.

54. 24 = 96.

55. 104 = 101.

56. L. Golden, *In Praise of Prometheus* (1966), ch. v *passim*, attaches much importance to the argument.

57. 160 f.

58. See Eduard Fraenkel's commentary, *ad loc.* (II 99 f.); cf. Eduard Norden, *Agnostos Theos*, 144 f.

59. 22 *VS* 32 = 84 M.

60. Fr. 105 Mette.

61. Fr. 667 Mette.

62. 22 *VS* fr. 40 = 16 M. B. Gladigow, "Aischylos und Heraklit," *Archiv für die Geschichte der Philosophie*, n.s. 44 (1962), 225 f. finds close links between these authors. By his method one could prove anything.

63. See Friedrich Solmsen, *Hesiod and Aeschylus* (1949).

64. *P.V.*, 187.

65. *Works and Days*, 259.

66. *Agam.* 183.

67. Fr. 530 Mette; see p. 99 below.

68. *Il.*3, 278f. 19, 250 f.; 19, 250 f.; see Dodds, *GI*, 137 and n. 10, p. 158 and Nilsson, *GGR* I², 677, n. 4.

69. *Agam.* 750 f.

70. Fr. 273, 15–16. Now that we can read the quotation in its original context, we can see how unfairly Plato (*Rep.* 380A) treated Aeschylus. "But Plato never wanted to be fair to Aeschylus": Eduard Fraenkel, *Proc. Brit. Acad.*, 28 (1941), 5.

71. *Agam.* 180.

72. 22 *VS* 11 = 80 M.

73. Stated explicitly in the Ghost's last speech, 821–822; cf. 808, 827 f.

74. *Pers.* 94 f.; cf. 762 f.

75. 109 f.

76. 745: 809 = 11.

77. Note especially 782 f., 790 f.

78. 353 f.

79. The fact needs stressing, since H. D. Broadhead in his commentary (Cambridge, 1960) failed to make use of Richmond Lattimore's important treatment of the subject; see *Classical Studies in Honor of W. A. Oldfather,* Univ. of Illinois (1943), 82 f.

80. 852 f.; See A. H. Coxon, *Cl. Quart.,* 8 (1958), 50.

81. See Schadewaldt, *Hermes,* 71 (1936), 25 f. = *Hellas und Hesperien*[2] (1970), I 308 f.

82. Athenaeus VIII 347 E.

83. See Deichgräber, *GGN* (1938/39), 231 f.

84. See below, p. 120.

85. See Lloyd-Jones, "The Guilt of Agamemnon," *Cl. Quart.,* 12 (1962), 187 f.

86. Apollo himself has warned Orestes of this; see *Cho.* 271 f.

87. See Stesichorus fr. 40 Page.

88. 490 f.; for the correct interpretation of the opening words, see K. J. Dover, JHS, 77 (1957), 230 f.

89. 517 f.

90. 523 f.

91. Dover, *op. cit.,* 233 takes a less simple view.

92. 690 f.

93. 696 f.

94. *Aristoteles und Athen* (1893), II 329 f.

95. See Dodds, "Morals and Politics in the Oresteia," *Proc. Cambridge Phil. Soc.* (1960), 19 f.

96. *Cho.* 258 f.; 302 f. The usurpers are tyrants: *Agam.* 1365, 1635 f., 1664 f.

97. Cf. Rohde, *Psyche,* 178: "It is true that the state directs the blood-feud required of the relatives of the dead man along constitutional channels that do not contravene the laws of the community; but it does not in the least intend to abolish the fundamental idea of the ancient family vendetta." See D. M. MacDowell, *Athenian Homicide Law in the Age of the Orators,* esp. the first two chapters.

98. Eur., *Or.* 491 f. See K. von Fritz, *Die Antike und Moderne Tragödie,* 1960, 113 f.

99. "Untersuchungen zum gefesselten Prometheus," *Tübinger Beiträge zur Altertumswissenschaft,* 9 (1929); cf. Schmid-Stählin, *Griechische Literatur-geschichte* I ii 193, 281 f.

100. Reinhardt, *Aischylos als Regisseur und Theologe.* (1949), 27 f.; Lloyd-Jones, *JHS*, 76 (1956), 55 f. At p. 65 of that article, l.7 f., I would now delete the words from "numerous" to "Kratos," which betray a failure to distinguish between gods and personified abstractions used in allegory. Also I would not now speak as I did then of the "naive dramaturgy" of the *Eumenides*. Aeschylean drama has its own canons, which are not those of later tragedy. Poetry may be simple and archaic without ceasing to be profound. Cf. *L'Antiquité Classique*, 33 (1964), 373.

101. Cf. Rose Unterberger, "Der gefesselte Prometheus des Aischylos," *Tübinger Beiträge zur Altertumswissenschaft*, 45 (1968), 138: "In der Promethie hat er sich zur Aufgabe gemacht, die Konstituierung der Weltherrschaft des Zeus als einer Herrschaft der Gerechtigkeit in ihrer Genese darzustellen. Er versucht dabei nicht, Zeus zu 'rechtfertigen,' und erst recht der späte Betrachter muss sich hüten, dergleichen zu unternehmen. Zeus ändert seine Politik, nicht mehr und nicht weniger."

102. See 168 f.; 516 f., 755 f., 907 f. The story about Thetis is also told by Pindar, *Isthm.* 8, 26 f., where it is Themis herself who utters the prophecy.

103. See frs. 332–333 Mette.

104. Probus *ad Verg., Ecl.* 6, 43 hunc quidem uolturem Hercules interemit, Prometheum tamen liberare, ne offenderet patrem, timuit. Sed postea Prometheus Iouem a Thetidis concubitu deterruit, pronuntians quod ex his nasceretur qui ipsis dis fortior futurus esset. Ob hoc beneficium Iuppiter eum soluit. Ne tamen impunitus esset, coronam et anulum gestanda ei tradidit. D. S. Robertson, *JHS*, 71 (1951), 154 is surely correct in saying that "it cannot be doubted that Weil was right to connect the plot of the *P. Solutus* with [this passage]."

105. 1026 f.

106. 1053.

107. Καὶ περαιωθεὶς ἐπὶ τὴν ἤπειρον τὴν ἀντικρὺ κατετόξευσεν ἐπὶ τοῦ Καυκάσου τὸν ἐσθίοντα τὸ τοῦ Προμηθέως ἧπαρ ἀετὸν ὄντα Ἐχίδνης καὶ Τυφῶνος. καὶ τὸν Προμηθέα διέλυσε δεσμὸν ἑλόμενος τὸν τῆς ἐλαίας καὶ παρέσχε τῷ Διὶ Χείρωνα θνῄσκειν ἀθάνατον ἀντ' αὐτοῦ θέλοντα.

108. 2, 5, 4 ἐκεῖθεν δὲ πρὸς Χείρωνα συνέφυγον [οἱ Κένταυροι]. . . . καὶ τούτῳ περιπεπτωκότας τοὺς Κενταύρους τοξεύων ἵησι βέλος ὁ Ἡρακλῆς. τὸ δὲ ἐνεχθὲν Ἐλάτου διὰ τοῦ βραχίονος τῷ γόνατι τοῦ Χείρωνος ἐμπήγνυται. ἀνιαθεὶς δὲ Ἡρακλῆς προσδραμὼν τό τε βέλος ἐξείλκυσε καὶ δόντος Χείρωνος φάρμακον ἐπέθηκεν. ἀνίατον δὲ ἔχων τὸ ἕλκος εἰς τὸ σπήλαιον ἀλλάσ εται. κἀκεῖ τελευτῆσαι βουλόμενος καὶ μὴ δυνάμενος ἐπείπερ ἀθάνατος ἦν ἀντιδόντος Διὶ Προμηθέως τὸν ἀντ' αὐτοῦ γενησόμενον ἀθάνατον ουτως ἀπέθανεν. F. Stoessl, *R.-E.* 23, 1 (1957), 679 suggests προμηθέ⟨α Ἡρακλέ⟩ως. I now find my solution of this problem anticipated by Gustav Grossmann, *Promethie und Orestie* (1970), 63 n. 84.

109. Participial phrases with γίγνεσθαι such as γίγνεσθαι ἀντί τινὸς in the sense of "to take someone's place" are not infrequent in Hellenistic Greek; see Robertson *op. cit.* (n. 104 above), 150 f.

110. It is best to approach the problem of the trilogy without deluding ourselves that metrical or stylistic statistics can furnish a reliable date for the *Prometheus*. We have not enough of Aeschylus for any guess based on such methods to command assent, as the case of the *Suppliants* ought to have reminded all of us. Wilamowitz, *Aischylos: Interpretationen* (1914), 242 and Pohlenz, *Die griechische Tragödie*, II² (1961), 35 dated it after Aeschylus' first Sicilian visit because of the account of the eruption of Etna, but before the *Sphinx*, produced in 467, because of the mention of Prometheus in fr. 235 Nauck and before Sophocles' *Triptolemus*, produced in 468, because of the supposed imitation of the *Prometheus* in that work; thus they arrive at the date 469. As will appear presently, this would well suit my own theory; but there is doubt about the argument by which it is arrived at.

111. Since R. Westphal published his *Prolegomena zu Äschylos' Tragödien* in 1869.

112. Note Σ on *P.V.* 511 ἐν γὰρ τῷ ἑξῆς δράματι λύεται.

113. The others are in the scholion on *P.V.* 94 (see frs. 340–341 Mette, and see pp. 150–151 of Murray's Oxford text, 2d ed.; for the catalogue, see p. 375 of that work) and in Gellius, 13, 19, 4.

114. See F. Focke, *Hermes*, 65 (1930), 263–270.

115. 320 D f.

116. 332 C; cf. 323.

117. 88*VS* fr. 25 = fr. 1 Nauck (*TGF*, 2d ed., p. 770).

118. Fr. 6 Nauck (*ibid.*, p. 813 f.); see Dodds ap. Lloyd-Jones, *JHS*, 76 (1956), 57, n. 24.

119. Hesiod, *op.* 255; *P.V.* 187.

120. P. Oxy. 2256 fr. 9 (A) = fr. 282 in my appendix to the Loeb *Aeschylus*. The occurrence of ὀτιή (1. 12), found in Euripides, *Cyclops*, 643 but not in tragedy, hardly suffices to prove it to be a satyr-play.

121. Fr. 535 Mette = fr. 281 Lloyd-Jones. In l.7, Lobel now suggests ἐμβολαῖς. ἐμβολαί are the passes through which a mountain-surrounded country may be entered and where φρούρια are placed; see, e.g. Xenophon, *Hell.* 5, 4, 48.

122. Eduard Fraenkel, "Vermutungen zum Aetna-Festspiel des Aeschylus," *Eranos*, 52, 1954, 61 f. = *Kleine Beiträge zur klassischen Philologie*, I, 249 f. His conjecture has found favor with Pohlenz, *Die griechische Tragödie* II² (1961), 223 and Lesky, *History of Greek Literature*, 320. See also Q. Cataudella, "Tragedie di Eschilo nella Siracusa di Gerone," *Atti del*

Congresso Internazionale sulla Storia della Sicilia Antica (Kokalos X-XI, 371 f.).

123. Vita Aeschyli 9 ἐλθὼν τοίνυν ἐς Σικελίαν ἱέρωνος τότε τὴν Αἴτνην κτί ζοντος ἐπεδείξατο τας Αἰτναίας οἰωνιζόμενος βίον ἀγαθὸν τοῖς συνοικίζουσι τὴν πόλιν. Cataudella, *op. cit.*, 386 may be right in taking this to mean "a (morally) good life."

124. *Aischylos, Die Tragödien und Fragmente* (1832; 2d. ed., 1842), II 311. Cf. E. J. Kiehl, *Mnemosyne*, 1 (1852), 365; Leopold Schmidt, *Quaestiones Epicharmeae*, 1 (1866), 55; A. O. F. Lorenz, *Leben und Schriften des Koers Epicharms* (1864), 84.

125. *Griechische Literaturgeschichte* (1884), III 311–312.

126. *Hermes*, 65 (1930), 259 f.

127. D. S. Robertson, *Proc. Cambridge Philol. Soc.*, (1938), 9 f. suggested that Aeschylus may have died before the trilogy was finished, and that some of the odes may have been supplied by one of his sons, Euphorion and Euaion, or his nephew, Philocles.

128. A. von Mess, *Rh. Mus.*, 56 (1901), 167 f. argued that Pindar and Aeschylus had a common epic source; so also O. Schroeder (p. 6) and R. W. B. Burton (p. 98) in their commentaries on the *Pythians*. Focke (p. 267) thinks Aeschylus followed Pindar, as did Wilamowitz, *Aischylos: Interpretationen* (1914), 121, n. 1 and Wilhelm Schmid *GLG*, I iii 292, n. 3.

129. See note 110 above.

130. P. Oxy. 2257, fr. 1 = fr. 26 Mette = fr. 287 Lloyd-Jones.

131. One should beware of translating μέρος as though plays of Aeschylus were regularly divided into "acts"; the earliest instances of such division known to us occur in the New Comedy.

132. Fr. 27 Mette; see Fraenkel, *op. cit.*, 62 =249 and K. Ziegler, *R.-E.* XVIII iii (1949), 99 f. (s.v. "Palikoi").

133. The Laestrygones are placed in Sicily by Hesiod, *Catalogues*, fr. 150, 26 Merkelbach-West and by Thucydides 6, 2.

134. Leontini is given as their home by Theopompus (115 FGH 225 ap. Polyb. 8, 11, 13 (see Walbank's commentary, II 83); Strabo I, 20 (cf. 22, 40); Polyaenus 5, 6; Pliny, N.H. 3, 89; Solinus 2, 26; Σ Od. 10, 86; Eustathius 1640, 15 = Paraphr. et Σ Lycophr. 659, 956; Silius Italicus 14, 33 and 125; Hesychius s.v. "Λεοντῖνοι" (II 566 Latte).

135. Lycophron 662–663 calls the Laestrygones "the remnant left by the arrows (*sc.* of Heracles); a scholion on 662 (ed. Scheer II, p. 220) says that Heracles shot the Laestrygones, who had attacked him, while driving back the cattle of Geryones, and that their territory is now Leontini.

136. Diodorus 4, 23 f.; on his way through Sicily with the cattle, Hera-

cles fights a battle with the Sicans near Syracuse and is honoured at
Leontini. One can see why the Sicilian patriot Diodorus should prefer
not to mention the connection of the Laestrygones with this area. I agree
with Cataudella, *op. cit.*, 387 f., that the παῖς μάργος of fr. 282, l. 31 is
more probably Ares (cf. D. S. Robertson, *Cl. Rev.* n. s. 3, 1953, 79 f.) than
Heracles (Phanis Kakridis, *Eranos*, 60, 1962, 111 f.). Without bringing in
the trial of Halirrhothius, as Robertson wished to do, one can easily
imagine how Ares may have been subdued by Dike.

137. See Otto, *GG*[3], ch. VI, "Gott und Mensch."

NOTES TO CHAPTER V
(Pages 104–128)

1. *Greece and Rome*, 13 (1966), 37 f.

2. O. Hey, *Philologus*, 83 (1927), 1 f. and 137 f., P. W. Harsh, *TAPA*,
76 (1945), 47 f.; K. von Fritz, *Antike und Moderne Tragödie*, 1 f.; R. D.
Dawe, *HSCP*, 72 (1968), 89 f.

3. *Poetics* 1453 B 28 f.

4. See von Fritz, *op. cit.*, 7.

5. Notably A. W. Schlegel, *Über dramatische Kunst und Literatur*, 1
(1809), 180; see Reinhardt, *Sophokles* (1933; 3d ed., 1947), 267.

6. 707 f.

7. 977 f.

8. 906 f.

9. *Op. cit.*, 128 f.

10. Dodds, *op. cit.* (n. 1 above), 42–44; von Fritz, *op. cit.*, 67 f.; W.
Schadewaldt, *Hellas und Hesperien*[2], I 466–467.

11. Dodds, *op. cit.*, 44–47.

12. See H. Patzer, *Die Anfänge der griechischen Tragödie* (1962), 89 f.

13. Dodds, *GI*, 193 quotes with approval the remark of Wilamowitz,
Glaube II 233, that "one cannot think that either Aeschylus or Euripides
would have cared to entertain a sacred snake." I believe that Aeschylus
would have been greatly honoured, and I very much doubt whether

Euripides would have been reluctant. In any case, to dismiss the whole Asclepius cult as an imposture would be to fail to do justice to some aspects of a very complex problem; see the third chapter, "Temple Medicine," of L. and E. J. Edelstein, *Asclepius: A Collection and Interpretation of the Testimonies* (1945), II 138 f. (After writing this note, I found that L. Edelstein himself had protested against the unkindness to Asclepius; see *The Idea of Progress in Classical Antiquity*, 56, n. 1.)

14. Dodds, *op. cit.*, p. 46.

15. *Psyche*, 426 f.

16. *Hermes*, 34 (1899), 56.

17. *Op. cit.*, 146; cf. H. Funke, *Die sogenannte tragische Schuld*, Diss. Cologne (1963), 73 f.

18. C. H. Whitman, *Sophocles: A Study in Heroic Humanism* (1951), 16. On p. 229 he writes, "Like all the men of his time, except perhaps Euripides, Sophocles ceased to look for justice to Zeus or the gods, or the inanimate world in general. He found it in man's own soul."

19. Among modern scholars, Sir Maurice Bowra is a rare exception. "Sophocles," he writes (*Sophoclean Tragedy*, 370), "accepts the ultimate justice and wisdom of the gods. He would agree with Theognis that they act according to their own plans, and he would add that these plans were just. He does not always make their reasons clear, but he assumes that they have reasons."

20. 863 f.

21. 823.

22. On unwritten laws, see the second chapter of V. Ehrenberg's *Sophocles and Pericles*.

23. The chief difficulty of the antistrophe is presented by its opening words, ὕβρις φυτεύει τύραννον (873). They look like a direct reference to Oedipus; yet an attack upon monarchy as such is paralleled nowhere in the play; in tragedy in general, the word τύραννος means an absolute ruler without pejorative implications. Nor does it make sense that the Chorus of Theban elders, so loyal to Oedipus to the last, should accuse him, even obliquely, of Hybris at this point. I suggest that we have here an instance of the common early Greek habit of speaking of Hybris, Koros and other similar concepts in genealogical terms; see notably *Agam.* 750 f., with the commentaries, and also the passages quoted in n. 24. ὕβρις φυτεύει τύραννον would then mean "the child of Hybris is a tyrant." The late Eduard Fraenkel, with whom I had a long and enjoyable discussion of this problem, agreed that Hybris must be spoken of genealogically, but found it hard to extract the required sense from the words as they stand. He therefore suggested reading, ὕβρις φυτεύει τύραννον ὕβριν, "Hybris begets a Hybris that is a tyrant," placing a stop after the word ὕβριν.

24. Solon, fr. 3, 7–9; Theognis 153; Pindar, *Ol.* 13, 10 f.; Herodotus 8, 77, 1.

25. 883 f.

26. The punctuation proposed for this stanza by Schadewaldt, *op. cit.* (n. 10), 288 f. is rightly rejected by H. Friis Johansen, *Lustrum* (1962/7), 243 and by J. C. Kamerbeek at *Wiener Studien*, 79 (1966), 87 and in his commentary, ad loc. Schadewaldt takes the whole stanza as a single period consisting of three parallel if-clauses interrupted by two parentheses (889–890 κακὰ . . . χλιδᾶς and 893–894 τίς ἔτι ποτ' . . . ἀμύνειν). But apart from the resulting awkwardness of the γὰρ in 895, the second parenthesis following so soon after the first would give a most unwelcome effect of jerkiness.

27. 369 f.

28. θυμοῦ ("recc.") is accepted by Wilamowitz and by Dain-Mazon; Schadewaldt, *op. cit.*, 479–483, argues for θυμῶν. The defenders of θυμοῦ accept Musgrave's εὔξεται for ἔξεται in 894, Schadewaldt the less probable ἔρξεται: he renders "Wer wird sich bewahren, in solchen Dingen schliesslich noch—als ein reiner Mensch bewahren, wer den Anprall der schlimmen Wallungen, der Leidenschaften, der Begierden und wilden Wünsche von seiner Seele abwahren können." Best read θυμοῦ and render "pride" or "passion"; it is upon the θυμός that Ate operates. On the word θυμός in the *O.C.*, see M. Pohlenz, *Die griechische Tragödie* II², 141.

29. 895.

30. Kamerbeek, *op. cit.* (n. 26, above), 89 and in his commentary.

31. For a bibliography of the question, see I. Errandonea, *Hermes*, 81 (1953), 130–131 and (in greater detail) *Univ. Nac. de la Cuid. Eva Perón Inst. de Leng. Clas., Textos y Estudios*, La Plata, iii, 1952. Although this ingenious scholar's view of the *OT* is very different from mine, we agree about the importance of the family curse.

32. *Sofocle,* Messina and Florence (1935; repr. 1965).

33. So, e.g. T. B. L. Webster, *An Introduction to Sophocles* (1936), 31 (unaltered in the 1969 edition, despite Dodds, *GI*, 53, n. 25); Lesky, *TDH*, 123. Even Bowra, whose view of justice in Sophocles is so different from that of most other moderns, denies the importance of curses (*Sophoclean Tragedy*), 88, 163.

34. *Greece and Rome, l. c.* 41; see n. 33, above.

35. See R. P. Winnington-Ingram, *Proc. Cambridge Philol. Soc.*, 183 (1954/5), 20 f. = *Sophokles*, ed. H. Diller, *Wege der Forschung*, 95 (1967), 400 f.; cf. H. Friis Johansen, *Classica et Mediaevalia*, 25 (1964), 8 f. Though stressing the importance of Dike in the *Electra,* I certainly do not mean that the play has a "happy ending," in which all the difficulties of its characters are resolved; see H.-J. Newiger, *Arcadia*, 4 (1969), 143–150.

36. 110 f.

37. 173 f.
38. 245–250.
39. 473 f.
40. 489 f.
41. 498 f.
42. 995 f.
43. 49 f.
44. 379–380.
45. 583 f.
46. Aeschylus, *Septem,* 720 f.
47. 599–603.
48. 603.
49. *Il.* 19, 86–87; see p. 22 above.
50. *Agam.* 205 f., especially 222–223.
51. 604 f.
52. 611–614.
53. See Lloyd-Jones, *CQ,* n.s. 7 (1957), 19.
54. *Agam.* 773–780.
55. *Ant.* 615.
56. 620 f.
57. *Op. cit.* (n. 53 above), 20; Perrotta, *op. cit.,* 75.
58. See Aeschylus, *Pers.* 93–100.
59. 332 f.
60. 781 f.; see von Fritz, *AMT,* 227 f.
61. Gerhard Müller, *Sophokles, Antigone* (1967), 15 rightly observes that it is strange that Reinhardt failed to recognise this; see his "Chor und Handlung bei den griechischen Tragikern" in *Sophokles,* ed. H. Diller (1967), 212 f.
62. 852 f.
63. Lesky, *Hermes,* 80 (1952), 91 f. = *Gesammelte Schiften* (1966), 176 f., unwilling to admit without a parallel that προσέπεσες . . . ποδί can mean "has stumbled into," brushes aside the simple and elegant conjecture that occurred independently to E. Bruhn (in his revision of Schneidewin-Nauck's commentary) and to J. U. Powell, *CQ,* 21 (1927), 176, which is to change πολύ to ποδί. Perrotta, *op. cit.,* 78 says all that need be said, except that he adopts Schneidewin's ποδοῖν. Cf. Aeschylus, *Agam.* 381–384 and *Eum.* 583 f.
64. 857 f.
65. Hegel's interpretation is now thoroughly discredited; see Gerhard Müller, *Sophokles, Antigone* (1967), 10 f.
66. *Op. cit.,* 113, cf. P. Friedländer, *Die Antike,* 1 (1925), 309 = *Studien zur antiken Literatur und Kunst* (1969), 145.
67. 76–77.

68. 86–87.

69. 93 f.

70. 543 λόγοις δ' ἐγὼ φιλοῦσαν οὐ στέργω φίλην.

71. *Op. cit.*, 120. Cf. H. Weinstock, *Sophokles*[3], 136. I cannot agree with Bernard Knox (*The Heroic Temper,* 107) that "the source of her heroic spirit is revealed . . . as purely personal."

72. 603. Pohlenz, *op. cit.* (n. 28 above), 84 says that this line does not prove Antigone to have been "ein willenlose Werkzeug" of the curse. Of course not, but does it prove that she was not its victim?

73. 872–875. Pohlenz (*loc. cit.*) seems to find this inconsistent with 856 πατρῷον δ' ἐκτίνεις τιν' ἄθλον; he forgets that persons under a curse are betrayed by their own rash judgment.

74. 96–97, 502–505.

75. 817 f.; cf. 692–699.

76. *Agam.* 1304–1305; cf. Euripides, *Alc.* 150–155.

77. Several scholars have been exercised by the problem of why Antigone perishes (e.g., Pohlenz, *op. cit.* I[2], 195, von Fritz, *AMT,* 5 f.); none has satisfactorily explained it. "Antigones Untergang," wrote Wilhelm Schmid (*GLG* I ii, 1934, 356–357), "ersche in einfach als Auswirkung des alten Fluches, vielmehr als Opfer für eine heilige Sache." Why not as both?

78. 220 f.

79. 226.

80. 237 f.

81. 254–258.

82. 266–267.

83. 510 f.

84. So Wilamowitz, *Geschichte der griechischen Literatur,* 349. I am not denying the relevance of the considerations adduced by Lesky, *Hermes,* 80 (1952), 100 f. = *Ges. Schr.* 184 f.

85. 548. The attempt of I. M. Linforth, *Univ. Calif. Publ. Class. Philol.,* vol. 16, no. 6 (1951) to minimize the importance of religion in this play is justified only in so far as some have written as though it were Christian religion.

86. So most recently Adkins, *MR,* 106; but as he himself writes (p. 99), the distinction between wilful, accidental and justifiable homicide seems to have been drawn even in the laws of Dracon. About Dracon, I would be as cautious as D. M. MacDowell, *Athenian Homicide Law in the Age of the Orators* (1963), 6 f.; but the distinction was certainly drawn in the law of Sophocles' time.

87. Naturally the requirements of the plot may have played a part in determining the attitude towards pollution which is adopted here.

88. 100–101.

89. 236 f.

90. 595–597.

91. 939 f.

92. 964–965. A. Wasserstein, *Bull. de l'Assoc. G. Budé*, 4th ser., 2 (1969), 189, gives a salutary warning against the view that the *O.C.* has a "happy ending."

93. Aeschylus, *Septem*, 742 f.

94. *Greece and Rome*, 13 (1966), 41.

95. 711 f.

96. 787 f.

97. See Perrotta, *op. cit.*, 203 (against Wilamowitz, *Hermes*, 34, 1899, 55 and *Griechische Tragödien*, i 14).

98. See above, p. 87.

99. See Stoll in Roscher's *Lexicon*, s.v. "Chrysippos," 902 f. and Lamer in *R.-E.*, xii. i, 476 f.

100. *Die Äschyleische Trilogie*, 354 f.; *Der Epische Cyclus*, i 94.

101. *Thebanische Heldenlieder* (1891), ch. 1.

102. *Oidipus* (1915), I, ch. v, 149 f.

103. The extract from "Pisander" given in the scholion on Eur. *Phoen.* 1760 must be used wth caution; see L. Deubner, *Abh. Pr. Akad.* (1942), no. 4 and F. Jacoby, *FGH*, I a, Nachträge zum Kommentar, 544 (on no. 16).

104. See Welcker, *Die Äschyleische Trilogie*, 359; *Der Epische Cyclus*, I 94; II 316; Hermann on Aeschylus, *Septem*, 813.

105. See P. Oxy. 2256 fr. 2 = fr. 169 Mette.

106. R. G. Dawe, *Proc. Cambridge Soc.*, 189 (1953), 40, n. 2 inclines to the same view; cf. Schadewaldt, *Hellas und Hesperien*[2], I 444–446.

107. Deubner, op. cit. (n. 103 above), 10, n. 5. The "homosexual substratum" in the myth has interested psychologists; see Devereux, *Int. Jour. Psychoanal.*, 34 (1953), 132 f. and D. Kouretas, *Ann. Méd. d'Athènes*, 2, nos. 5–6 (1963).

108. See frs. 228–229 Mette.

109. It is hardly safe to conclude with Wilamowitz, *SBPA* (1925), 46 = *Kl. Schr.* ii 61 that the story of Poseidon's rape of Pelops in the First Olympian Ode was Pindar's own invention.

110. Cf. Perrotta, *op. cit.*, 203; see also Zielinski, *Philol.* n.s., 9 (1896), 493 f. and Bruhn in the introduction to his revision of the Schneidewin-Nauck *O.T.*, 24 f.

111. 1184–1185.

112. 1329–1330. See Reinhardt, *op. cit.*, 270 (on text at 145). Apollo dominates the action as he does in the *Electra* (see Reinhardt, p. 149). This is "a strange way in itself of looking at oracles," says Adkins, *MR*, 98; the point is that Apollo has not merely predicted, but has caused what

has happened to happen. In case anyone supposes that I think Oedipus was only a puppet in the hand of Apollo, I had better explain once more that Apollo's action, in my view, does not diminish Oedipus' responsibility.

113. 690–691.

114. 800–802.

115. 911 f.

116. 1360.

117. 1382–1383; see Jebb's note on 1382.

118. See G. M. Kirkwood, *A Study of Sophoclean Drama* (1958), 75.

119. See von Fritz, *AMT*, 14.

120. 1180 f. Devereux refers to his "Some Political Functions of the Oedipus Myth in Early Greece," *Psychoanal. Quart.*, 32 (1963), 205 f.

121. *Agam.* 1341–1342.

122. E.g., by Pohlenz, *op. cit.*, ii² 92, who exaggerates the significance of 1.8; for the right view, see Kranz, *Stasimon*, 205 and Perrotta, *op. cit.*, 200.

123. See n. 32 above.

124. Aristotle, *Poetics*, 1451 B 25; Antiphanes fr. 191. I do not see that Eur. *Hipp.* 451–456 throws much light on this question; the speaker is a character in a tragedy, set in the heroic age.

125. 569; cf. 624 f., 849–851, 1229–1230, 1235, 1288–1289, 1299 f.

126. 434 f.

127. 189.

128. 1291 f.

129. 1008 f.

130. 504 f.

131. 147–150.

132. 837 f.

133. 201 f.

134. 944 f.

135. 824 f.

136. 1080 f.

137. 1302–1303; cf. 1191. See Eur. *Phoen.* 930–1018; as Jebb on *Ant.* 1303 says, the Menoeceus of the *Phoenissae* is the same person as the Megareus of the *Antigone*.

138. 453, 479, 490–491, 664, 724 f., 1430. Sophocles has the acutest sense of locality; consider the importance of Troy and its surroundings (and also Salamis) in the *Ajax*, Cithaeron in the *O.T.*, the region of Oeta in the *Trachiniae* as well as the *Philoctetes*, Colonus in the *O.C.*

139. Note l. 670; cf. *Trach.* 1174 f.

140. 676 f.

141. See 405–453; cf. 562–563.

142. 604 f., 1337 f.

143. 1426.

144. Cf. Wilamowitz, *SBPA* (1925), 51 = *Kl. Schr.* V ii, 69.

145. 714 f.; see above, p. 97.

146. 1174 f. On the legend of Heracles death, see M. Mühl, *Rh. Mus.*, 101 (1958), 106 f., especially 120 f.

147. *Sophoclean Tragedy*, 159 f.; cf. Pohlenz, *op. cit.*, I², 208 and II², 89–90; see also F. J. H. Letters, *The Life and Work of Sophocles* (1953), 192–193. I cannot agree with I. M. Linforth, *op. cit.* (n. 85 above), 266 that the final scene is "an allied piece which, though attached to the play, does not cohere."

148. *Greece and Rome*, 13 (1966), 46. He continues, "No one answers it. I can only suppose that the poet had no answer to give."

149. 1275 f. These lines belong to the Chorus; see Kranz, *Stasimon*, 205; Lesky, *TDH²*, 145, n. 1.

150. Poeas, according to Apollodorus ii 7, 7; others mention Philoctetes (see Frazer on Apollodorus *ad loc.*, i 270–271).

151. "'Justice' is one rendering of the word *Dike*, and sometimes it is not too far wrong": H. D. F. Kitto, *Sophocles as Dramatist and Philosopher* (1958), 47. His whole discussion of *Dike* is excellent.

NOTES TO CHAPTER VI
(Pages 129–155)

1. 889 B f.; see Friedrich Solmsen, *Plato's Theology* (1942), 28 f., 132 f.

2. See Peter Rau, "Paratragodia," *Monogr. Klass. Altertumswissen.*, 45 (1967), 43 n. 60, 158.

3. See Diogenes Laertius II 12 (59 *VS* II, 6); Plutarch, *Pericles* 32; *Nicias* 23; 59 *VS* A 19, 20. Cf. A. B. Drachmann, *Atheism in Pagan Antiquity* (1922) and Guthrie, *HGP* II 268.

4. Note, for example, the injunction to sing a hymn at a banquet at fr. 1, 9 f.; see C. M. Bowra, *Problems in Greek Poetry* (1953), 12.

5. See von Fritz, *GG*, I i, 70 f. "Das für den Beweis der Relativität moralischer Anschauungen wichtige ethnographische Material ist von Protagoras und seinen Gesinnungsgenossen gesammelt worden: von ihnen ist es zu Herodot . . . gelangt"; W. Kranz, Hermes, 69 (1934), 228 = *Studien zur antiken Literatur und ihren Nachwirken*, 119.

6. Philostratus, *Vit. Soph.* i, 10, I (= 80 *VS* A2); cf. Wilhelm Nestle, *Vom Mythus zum Logos*, 252; von Fritz, *R.-E.* XXIII.1 (1956), 907; Guthrie, *HGP*, III 262–263; and in particular C. W. Müller, *Hermes*, 95 (1967), 158–159.

7. 80 *VS* B I. Cf. K. Reinhardt, *Parmenides* (1916; repr. 1959), 242 f.

8. Von Fritz, *op. cit.* (n. 6 above), 914–917. Cf. E. A. Havelock, *The*

Liberal Temper in Greek Politics (1957), 252–254 (and *passim*). Guthrie, *HGP*, III 188 f. (cf. 170 f.) gives a history of the problem; he takes what I believe to be the wrong view.

9. Plato, *Protagoras*, 32 A f.; see above, p. 98.

10. See K. R. Popper, *The Open Society and Its Enemies* (1945), I 51 f.; cf. F. M. Cornford, *Plato's Theory of Knowledge,* 80 f. and Havelock, *op. cit.* (n. 8 above), 29, 31.

11. Just so the anonymous περὶ νόμων parts of whose work Pohlenz showed to have been preserved in the twenty-fifth speech of Demosthenes makes each νόμος a gift of the gods (Dem. 25, 20; see F. Heinimann, *Nomos und Physis,* 150). (See Addenda.)

12. W. K. C. Guthrie, *In the Beginning* (1957), 92 complains that G. B. Kerferd, *JHS,* 73 (1953), has taken the myth of divine intervention literally; Protagoras, he insists, was an agnostic. The point seems to be important only if one thinks of "agnosticism" in modern terms. G. Vlastos, *Phil. Rev.* 54 (1945), 580 rightly speaks of "the well-established practice of Ionian rationalism to salvage religious terms so long as (a) they can be adapted to the exigencies of naturalistic logic and (b) they do not inhibit rationalist critics of magic." See Guthrie, *HGP,* III 234–235; see also the excellent detailed discussion of Protagoras' attitude to the gods by C. W. Müller, "Protagoras über die Götter," *Hermes,* 95 (1967), 385 f.

13. See Jaeger, *The Theology of the Early Greek Philosophers,* 180 f.

14. 68 *VS* B 30. Dodds, *Euripides, Bacchae²,* 104–105 is surely right in denying that Prodicus was an atheist; Guthrie, *HGP,* III 242 thinks otherwise.

15. See Guthrie, *HGP* III 478 f. In general, see D. McGibbon, "The Religious Thought of Democritus," *Hermes,* 95 (1967), 385 f.

16. 68 *VS* B 264 μηδέν τι μᾶλλον τοὺς ἀνθρώπους αἰδεῖσθαι ἑωυτοῦ μηδέ τι μᾶλλον ἐξεργάζεσθαι κακύν, εἰ μέλλει μηδεὶς εἰδήσειν η οἱ πάντες ἄνθρ ωποι· ἀλλ' ἑωυτὸν μάλιστα αἰδεῖσθαι, καὶ τοῦτον νόμον τῆι ψυχῆι καθεστά ναι, ὥστε μηδὲν ποιεῖν ἀνεπιτήδειον. Cf. B 244 αυλον, κἄν μόνοῖ ἦις μήτε λέξηις μήτε ἐργάσῃ· μάθε δὲ πολὺ μᾶλλον τῶν ἄλλων σεαυτὸν αἰσχύνεσθαι· See C. E. Freiherr von Erffa, "ΑΙΔΩΣ und verwandte Begriffe in ihrer Entwicklung von Homer bis Demokrit," *Philologus,* Suppl. 30, 2 (1937), 197–198; cf. Guthrie, *HGP,* II 494.

17. To take a recent example, Lesky, "Der Kampf um die Rechtsidee im griechischen Denken" (Ἑλληνικὴ Ἀνθρωπιστικὴ Ἑταιριά, Κέντρον Ἀνθρωπ ιστικῶν Σπουδῶν, σειρὰ δευτέρα, Μελεταὶ καὶ Ἐρευναι 18, 1968, 15 writes, "Protagoras hat es so vermieden, die staatliche Ordnung und mit ihr das Recht dem Relativismus preiszugeben, aber unmöglich könnte das eine Lösung für längere Dauer bedeuten, unmöglich könnte ein Weitergreifen von Fragen verhindert werden, die nun die Axt an die Wurzeln der tradi-

tionellen Rechtsauffassung legten." As classical scholars so often do, he is taking Plato's word for it, and in a single bland sentence taking for granted the rightness of one side in a philosophical controversy that is even now a burning question. From this point his polished summary of the history of the problem glides smoothly on to the achievements of Plato and Aristotle and to the eventual triumph of the Church.

18. See Proper, *op. cit.* (n. 10 above), ch. 5 *passim*. "Justice is now a human device," writes Vlastos, *Class. Phil.*, 42 (1947), quoting Democritus frs. 172–173, "It applies to the acts and relations of conscious beings. It is not arbitrary, for it is rooted in the necessities of man's nature and environment. But neither does man find it in the universe as such; it is a product of civilization and art. Justice is only the form which the immanent order of nature achieves in the works of man. Justice is natural, but nature is not just." If we keep in mind the nature of ancient concepts of the divine, we see that this would not prevent Democritus from regarding justice as god-given.

19. Aristophanes, *Clouds* 889–1114.

20. 87 VS B 44. See Guthrie, *HGP* III 107 f., and G. B. Kerferd, *Proc. Cambridge Philol. Soc.*, 184 (1956/7), 26 f. Kerferd's opinion that "the papyrus fragments throughout are discussing the view of others and that Antiphon's own views only appear incidentally if at all" will not be easily refuted.

21. 88 VS B 25, fr. 1, p. 770 Nauck, *TGF²*.

22. *Suppl.* 201 f.

23. Cf. Drachmann, *op. cit.* (n. 3 above), 45–46. Guthrie's view (*HGP* III 243) that "The speech is a fairly obvious device of the author's for promulgating an atheistic view without giving too much offence" is scarcely verifiable without a knowledge of the context, and seems to me intrinsically unlikely.

24. Cf. K. J. Dover in *Fifty Years (and Twelve) of Classical Scholarship* (1968), 127–128: "The case for its scepticism (that of the audience of the Old Comedy), rests primarily on its tolerance of the discomfiture of Poseidon in *Birds* and the discreditable antics of Dionysus in *Frogs*. Yet the conclusion that Athenian society in the late fifth century was in general sceptical of traditional religion is not easily reconciled with the evidence from other sources, and rests on a failure of the imagination. To understand pre-Christian religious attitudes requires a great imaginative effort, and those who make it are commonly regarded as impostors by those who cannot. The intimate association of the gods with the fabric of ordinary Greek life is something which might be better understood by a Papuan than by a bishop, and perhaps best of all by the medieval Christian, whose humour was full of casual blasphemy and prompt to interweave the comic

and the tremendous. The fact is that the Greek gods understood laughter; at the right time and place they could take a joke." See P. Friedländer, "Lachende Gotter," *Die Antike*, 10 (1934), 209 f. = *Studien zur antiken Literatur und Kunst* (1969), 3 f.

25. See the story told by Plutarch, *Pericles* 6; (59 *VS* A 16).

26. Xenophon, *Memorabilia* I, 4, 2 f.

27. Lysias fr. 73 Thalheim (= 53 Scheibe); see Dodds, *GI*, 188.

28. See, for example, *Laws* 907 D f.

29. Von Fritz, R.-E., *op. cit.* (n. 6 above), 909–911; cf. Drachmann, *op. cit.* (n. 3 above), 39. Dodds, *GI*, 189 takes a different view; see his ch. 6, "Rationalism and Reaction," for an excellent statement of the kind of view against which I am arguing.

30. For Diagoras, see F. Jacoby, *Abhandlungen der Deutschen Akademie der Wissenschaften zu Berlin, Kl. für Sprachen, Literatur und Kunst* (1959), 3; see the review by F. Wehrli, *Gnomon*, 33 (1961), 123 f. and the sensibly cautious treatment by L. Woodbury, *Phoenix*, 19 (1965), 177 f. Cf. Guthrie, *HGP*, III 236 f.

31. Dodds connects the emergence of several cults at Athens towards the end of the fifth century with the reaction at that time against the enlightenment in which he believes. But since it was at this time that Athens became a great centre, we should expect exotic religions to flourish there from this time on. Dodds (*GI*, 194, also n. 93, p. 204) believes that the magical practice called *defixio* became common only during the fourth century, and at the time he wrote fifth-century examples were rare. But since then Miss L. H. Jeffery, *BSA*, 50 (1955), 72 f. has listed a number of fifth-century examples.

32. *Laws* 904 B μεμηχάνηται δὴ πρὸς πᾶν τοῦτο τὸ ποῖόν τι γιγνόμενον ἀεὶ ποίαν ἕδραν δεῖ μεταλαμβάνον οἰκίζεσθαι καὶ τίνας ποτὲ τόπους· τῆς δὲ γενέσεως τοῦ ποίου τινὸς ἀφῆκε ταῖς βουλήσεσιν ἑκάστων ἡμῶν τὰς αἰτίας, ὅπῃ γὰρ ἂν ἐπιθυμῇ καὶ ὁποῖός τις ὢν τὴν ψυχήν, ταύτῃ σχεδὸν ἑκάστοτε καὶ τοιοῦτος γίγνεται ἅπας ἡμῶν ὡς τὸ πολύ.

33. See Gilbert Murray, *Five Stages of Greek Religion*[2] (1930), 8 (preface to first edition of 1925). The phrase supplied the title of what was originally the third chapter, but in the second edition became the fourth; the chapter in question deals with the period between the end of the great period of Greek philosophy and the rise of Christianity.

34. Most lately put forward by Adkins, *MR;* see, for instance, p. 210 f., p. 220 f.

35. Thucydides 3, 53 f.

36. 5, 104; 112, 2.

37. 7, 77, 4; the whole speech is relevant.

38. See R. Syme, *Proc. Brit. Acad.*, 48 (1962), 39 f. for a powerful statement of this view; cf. H. Strasburger, *Saeculum*, 5 (1954) = *Thukydides*, ed. H. Herter (*Wege der Forschung*, 98), 451.

39. See I "Die Entdeckung der politischen Geschichte durch Thukydides," *Saeculum*, 5 (1954), 395 f. = *Thukydides*, ed. H. Herter (*Wege der Forschung*, 98), 412 f.; II "Thukydides und die politische Selbstdarstellung der Athener," *Hermes*, 86 (1958), 17 f. = *Thukydides*, ed. Herter, 498 f.; III "Die Wesenbestimmung der Geschichte durch die Antike Geschichtsschreibung," *S. B. Frankfurt* (1966), no. 3, 71 f. Cf. von Fritz, *GG*, I i 779 f.

40. In the second of the articles quoted in n. 39.

41. I, 98, 4.

42. I, 73 f.

43. See G. E. M. de Ste. Croix, *Historia*, 3 (1954), 1 f. and the discussion that resulted.

44. 2, 63, 2.

45. 2, 64, 3.

46. 2, 64, 4; on Pericles' concern with honour, cf. O. Regenbogen, *Thukydides*, ed. Herter, p. 54.

47. 3, 37, 2, cf. 2, 63, 2; with 3, 38, 1, cf. 1, 140, 1.

48. II, ap. *Thukydides*, ed. Herter, p. 515, n. 47. See H.-P. Stahl, *Thukydides: Die Stellung der Menschen im geschichtlichen Prozess*, Zetemata, Heft 40 (1966), 12 f.

49. *Aevum*, 9 (1957), 74 f. = *Secondo Contributo alla Storia degli Studi Classici* (1958), 45 f.; *History*, 43 (1958), 1 f. = *Secondo Contributo* 29 f.

50. I, ap. *Thukydides*, ed. Herter, 446 f.; cf. III, *passim*—not only the section devoted to Thucydides but especially 62 f. Cf. H. Erbse, *Rh. Mus.*, 96 (1953), 38 f. = *Thukydides*, ed. Herter, 317 f.; *Antike und Abendland*, 10 (1961), 19 f. = *Thukydides*, ed. Herter, 594 f.

51. I, 23, 1.

52. I, 9 f. Cf. 1, 21, 1; 22, 4.

53. The narrative of events at Corcyra leading up to the outbreak of war in 431 begins asyndetically at I, 24, 1 with Ἐπίδαμνός ἐστι πόλις: we remember the beginnings of epic narratives like that of Glaucus at *Il.* 6, 152 ἔστι πόλις Ἐφύρη . . . . In the final battle in the Great Harbour at Syracuse, all manner of cries are heard on both sides while the battle lasts 'till at last the Syracusans and their allies put to flight the Athenians πρίν γε δὴ οἱ Συρακόσιοι καὶ οἱ ξύμμαχοι ἐπὶ πολὺ ἀντισχούσης τῆς ναυμαχίας ἔτρεψαν τοὺς Ἀθηναίους (7, 70, 5). Karl Reinhardt, *Vermächtnis der Antike*, 210, compares *Il.* 12, 436–437: ὣς μὲν τῶν ἐπὶ ἶσα μάχη τέτατο πτόλεμός τε, πρὶν γ'ὅτε δὴ Ζεὺς κῦδος ὑπέρτερον Ἕκτορι δῶκε Πριαμίδῃ. Many more such instances could be enumerated.

54. See Strasburger II, ap. *Thukydides,* ed. Herter, 528–529.

55. On this and other similar juxtapositions in Thucydides, see Gomme, *The Greek Attitude to Poetry and History,* 122 f., 142 f.

56. See Adkins, *MR,* 221 f.; cf. R. P. Winnington-Ingram, *BICS,* 12 (1965), 70 f.

57. 3, 45, 4 f.; see Regenbogen, ap. *Thukydides,* ed. Herter, 46 f.; cf. W. Müri, *Mus. Helv.,* 4 (1947), 251 f. = *Thukydides,* ed. Herter, 135 f. Those who regard Diodotus' arguments as an example of *Realpolitik* should see R. P. Winnington-Ingram's excellent treatment of the debate (*BIGS,* 12, 1965, 70 f.).

58. Fr. 1, 33 f.

59. *Hipp.,* 380 f.

60. *Il.* 9, 646; see p. 23 above.

61. *Il.* 9, 636–637; see above, p. 17.

62. Stahl, *op. cit.* (n. 48 above) may exaggerate the pessimism of Thucydides (so P. A. Brunt, *CR,* 17, 1967, 279 f. and H. Erbse, *Gymnasium,* 76, 1969, 393 f.); but he has shown how strongly the historian stresses the uncertainty of the future and men's failure to take account of it. Cf. Adam Parry, *BICS,* 16 (1969), 106 f.

63. P. A. Brunt writes *(Thucydides,* in the series *The Great Histories,* New York, 1963): "Many Greeks had thought that power produced *hybris* . . . and that hybris led to ruin. Some have read this view into Thucydides; Athenian injustice and cruelty met with retribution. This cannot be right; in fact he expressly ascribed the fall of Athens to acts of imprudence, which were indeed prompted by the greed and ambition of the leaders." But when Zeus punishes *hybris,* he does so by sending Ate to take away his victim's wits.

64. E.g. Wade-Gery, in *The Oxford Classical Dictionary* (1949), 902 writes of Thucydides, "Born in the anti-Pericles opposition, he followed Pericles with a convert's zeal"; cf. *Essays in Greek History,* 260; von Fritz, *GG,* I i, 540. See also Stahl, *op. cit.* (n. 48 above), 25 f.

65. As was argued by F. M. Cornford in *Thucydides Mythistoricus* (1907). This early work of Cornford has been neglected by scholars, perhaps because its incautious application of the Marxist theory of history drew down severe criticisms. It none the less contains ideas which if carefully worked out could have led to a study of the historian in many respects much superior to others current at the time. As to the sense in which the history of Thucydides is a tragic history, see the concluding paragraph of Strasburger II (ap. *Thukydides,* ed. Herter, 527–530).

66. Cf. Von Fritz, *GG,* I i 803–4. On p. 804 he writes of the modern interpreters of Thucydides "die meisten von ihnen den *einen* Aspekt des von Thukydides geschilderten Geschehens, also entweder den Glanz des

perikleischen Athen, wie er in der Leichenrede geschildert wird, oder den harten Realismus der athenischen Politik gegenüber den Bundesgenossen, hervorgehoben haben, obwohl doch die Absicht des Thukydides offenbar gewesen ist, beide Aspekte, wenn auch nicht die Verbindung zwischen ihnen, für seine Leser ganz deutlich sichtbar zu machen."

Some authorities, observing that in some places Thucydides speaks favourably but in others unfavourably of the Athenian Empire, seem to take it for granted that the apparent inconsistency is to be resolved in terms of the so-called "Thucydidean Question" by supposing that these were written at different times. Now even in places where we can be reasonably sure that a particular passage was written within a particular period, we can seldom be sure about its surrounding context, so that it is hardly surprising that the long and detailed discussion of the Question, though it has produced many valuable observations, has led to no agreement. But even if our prospects of finding out when each part of the history was written, and of convincing others that our findings are correct, were much brighter than they are, the assumption that an "inconsistency" of this kind must necessarily be explained along these lines seems to me unsafe. For an excellent account of the history of the "Thucydides Question," see von Fritz, *op. cit.*, 565-575.

67. Cf. G. de Sanctis, *Storia dei Greci* (1939), II 432-434.

68. I have argued that Thucydides wrote a tragic history, and to that extent treated his subject with a grand impartiality. But he dealt with recent happenings, and in many cases it is possible to learn something of his personal preferences. Not the worst government in his time at Athens, he says (8, 97, 2) was that of the Five Thousand, the moderate oligarchy which in 411 replaced the narrow oligarchy of the Four Hundred. That unusual expression of a personal view does not suggest that he was an advocate of extreme democracy, and this inference is supported by what he says of certain persons. He loathes Cleon; he utterly despises Hyperbolus; he has no respect for the Syracusan demagogue Athenagoras. He respects Nicias for his character, but not for his ability; he admires the oligarchic schemer Antiphon; and he is not wholly unsympathetic to the low-born intriguer Phrynichus. Many think he is too kind to Alcibiades, another who cannot be regarded as a thorough-going democrat. Apart from Brasidas, who was strictly a military man, and from the special case of Pericles, the person he most admires is the rival of Athenagoras, the Syracusan conservative leader Hermocrates.

With his family connections, it would have been surprising to find that the historian was an advocate of extreme democracy; related as he was to Miltiades, Cimon and Thucydides the son of Melesias (see Wade-Gery,

JHS 52, 1932, 205 f. = *Essays in Greek History,* 239 f. and Andrewes, *CQ* n.s. 9, 1959, 239 f.), he might have been expected to show the kind of sympathies that his work in fact reveals. Political parties in the modern sense did not exist in ancient Athens, where except in rare emergencies like the crises of 411 and 404 even those who disapproved of the state's decisions commonly took a hand in carrying them out. During the thirties and twenties, while imperialism was successful, it clearly met with little opposition, nor would a man of wealth, ability and influence and with the family connections of Thucydides have refused or been refused public office because he was not a whole-hearted adherent of the "government" of the time. One might expect an intelligent person born into this particular family about 460, as the historian was, to respect the character and abilities of Pericles without becoming his political adherent. It would hardly be surprising if Thucydides had had grave reservations from the first about the imperialist policy, which as late as the forties was detested by many members of the aristocracy with strong connections in other states from which the historian sprang. Such people set a high value upon *Hesychia,* "quiet" or "tranquillity," which Pericles and those like him might call *Apragmosyne,* "Inactivity." (See Wade-Gery, *l. c.* and V. Ehrenberg, *JHS* 77, 1947, 46 f.) *Hesychia* is the goddess praised in Pindar's last poem, the eighth Pythian ode, composed in 446 for a native of Aegina, the city lately defeated and soon afterwards destroyed by Athens; *Hesychia* is the quality recommended to the Sicilian cities as the ultimate political good in the great speech made by Hermocrates at Gela (Thucydides 4, 59 f.).

In his tragic history, Thucydides maintains a delicate balance between the advocates of *Hesychia* and those of *Realpolitik;* that explains why his personal sympathies are, and perhaps always will be, a matter for debate. But to me the work seems to contain several indications that in his private person he preferred *Hesychia,* as we should expect from a man of his origin and his connections.

69. "Euripides and His Age" first appeared in 1913 and is still being reprinted; its point of view was expressed also in the introductions to its author's famous translations. Its worst features were due to the influence of A. W. Verrall, a scholar whose fertility in ingenious speculation was fatally combined with an utter inability to sympathise with the mental attitudes of the past. Regrettably, this influence is not yet quite extinct, partly owing to the work of Verrall's disciple, G. Norwood.

70. See the introductions to his *Heracles* (1889; 2d ed., 1895) and his *Hippolytus* (1891).

71. *Tradition und Geist,* 236 = *Euripides,* ed. E. R. Schwinge (*Wege der Forschung* 89), 517 f. Much earlier, P. Friedländer, *Die Antike,* 1 (1926),

79 = *Studien zur antiken Literatur und Kunst,* 156 had drawn attention to Ibsen's influence on Wilamowitz' conception of Euripides.

72. On Euripides' real or supposed allusions to the politics of his time, see G. Zuntz, *Acta Congressus Madvigiani,* 1 (1958), 155 f. = *Euripides,* ed. Schwinge, 417 f.

73. "In den letzten Jahrzehnten hat sich die Einsicht durchgesetzt, dass die euripideische Tragödie nicht Weltanschauung diskutieren oder gar predigen, sondern einen Spannungszustand zwischen Mensch und Welt gestalten will, der im Fall des Euripides vorläufig am ehesten als eine Antinomie zwischen Rationalen und Irrationalen charaktisiert werden kann": H. Diller, *Abh. der Mainzer Akademie* (1955), 454 = *Euripides,* ed. Schwinge, 471.

74. A. M. Dale's remarks about rhetoric in the preface to her *Alcestis* (Oxford, 1954, xxvii f.) deserve careful attention. "The aim of rhetoric," she writes, "is Persuasion, πειθώ, and the poet is as it were a kind of λογογράφος who promises to do his best for each of his characters in turn as the situations change and succeed one another." Cf. Schwinge's introduction to the volume cited in n. 71 above.

75. Dodds, *GI,* 186.

76. *Hipp.* 380 ff.

77. Love and Aphrodite are the same thing, so that there is no point in claiming, with Lesky, "Euripide" (*Entretiens de la Fondation Hardt,* VI, 1960, 135) that Phaedra is explicitly denying a mythological explanation of her state such as the Chorus has just offered. Since Phaedra is expressing what amounts to the traditional view, there is no need to suppose with B. Snell, *Scenes from Greek Drama,* 47 f. and others that Euripides is here "polemicising" against the moral intellectualism of the Socratics, who held that no one consciously does wrong. See *Gnomon,* 38 (1966), 15.

78. *Il.* 1, 194–198. See Otto, *GG*[3], 49 ff. (cf. 180, 212) and *idem, Gestalt und Sein,* 133 f.

79. See above, p. 17.

80. Dodds, *GI,* 186.

81. *Medea* 1333; *Hipp.* 1379.

82. *Hipp.* 141 ff.

83. See her great speech in fr. 125 Mette; it is on p. 50 of Murray's Oxford text of Aeschylus (2d ed.). See also Aeschylus, *Suppliants* 1035–1037.

84. 860–1059. The scene is discussed by: Reinhardt, *Tradition und Geist,* 234; Lesky, *op. cit.* (n. 77 above), 129 f.; Adkins, *MR,* 124 ff.

85. 884–888. It is Hecuba who "erwägt . . . zweifelnd, ob der oberste Got nicht in Wahrheit mit der Ananke oder dem Nous identifiziert werden müsse," not Euripides, as W. Jens, *Euripides,* ed. Schwinge, 3 says.

See Devereux, *Psychoanalytic Quarterly*, 26 (1957), 378 ff. and *From Anxiety to Method in the Social Sciences* (1967), 344, n. 2 (cited with approval by Guthrie, *HGP*, III 230, n. 1).

86. See above, p. 84.

87. Devereux remarks, "The realist Hecuba invokes Zeus, the mythologically defensive Helen does not."

88. Ch. V *passim*.

89. See A. P. Burnett, *Class. Philol.*, 60 (1965), 240 ff. = *Euripides: A Collection of Critical Essays*, ed. Erich Segal (1968), 51 f.

90. Note the Cyclops' blasphemy at 320–321 and Odysseus' prayer at 350–355.

91. See 33; Io 1–4.

92. 236 f.

93. 766 f.

94. 876 f. (On the rejuvenation of Iolaus, see Devereux in *La Parola del Passato* (forthcoming).

95. 301 f.

96. *Electra* 699 f.; *Orestes* 811 f.; 982 f.; *Phoenissae* 801 f.; 867 f.; 1050 f.; 1504 f.; 1595 f.

97. 21–23.

98. 148, 158.

99. 160; cf. 168 f., 207 f.

100. 267.

101. 421 f.

102. 763 f.

103. 1389–1390.

104. 1391–1392.

105. 469 f.; 775 f.; 884 f.; 1240 f.; 1280 f.

106. See T. C. W. Stinton, *Euripides and the Judgment of Paris* (Suppl. Paper No. 11, Hellenic Society, 1965). "The choice of Paris," he writes (p. 63), "meant the rape of Helen, which brought down Troy and involved all Greece in its ruin."

107. *Hipp.* 120; *Bacch.* 1249; cf. 1346.

108. 212; 339 f.; 498 f.

109. 1313 f.

110. *AMT* (1962), 113 f.

111. 491 f.; see von Fritz, *op. cit.*, 147 f.

112. *Or.* 194; cf. *El.* 1190 f.; 1245–1246.

113. See K. Matthiessen, "Zur Theonoeszene der Euripideischen Helena," *Hermes*, 96 (1969), 685 f.

114. Andreas Spira, *Untersuchungen zum Deus ex Machina bei Sophokles und Euripides*, Diss. Frankfurt, Kallmünz (1960).

NOTES TO CHAPTER VII
(Pages 156–164)

1. cf. *L'Antiquité Classique*, 33 (1964), 372 f.

2. "W. F. Otto, *Die Götter Griechenlands* . . . eine Verherrlichung des griechischen Götterglaubens, welche die geschichtliche Entwicklung preisgibt": Nilsson, *GGR* I², 66. Nilsson refers to his reviews of the book at *DLZ* (1931), 1825 f. and (1932), 2065 f.

3. See Philip Merlan, "Aristoteles' und Epikurs mussige Götter," *Zeitschrift für Philosophische Forschung*, 21 (1967), 485 f.

4. "Die Welt, die sie nicht erschaffen haben, ist der Obhut der Götter anvertraut; sie leiten und lenken sie nach einheitlichem Plane. Die Welt ein Kosmos: diese Vorstellung, wenn sie auch erst eine philosophirende Zeit sich mit diesem, aus dem politischen Gebiete übertragenen Namen verdeutlicht, ist griechischer Auffassung von Jeher vertraut, griechischer Sinnesart wie mit Notwendigkeit auferlegt": E. Rohde, *Kleine Schriften*, II 322 (from his Prorectoral Address of 1894 entitled "Die Religion der Griechen"). (On *Kosmos* as a philosophical term see Jula Kerchensteiner, *Kosmos: Quellen-kritische Untersuchungen zu den Vorsokratikern*, Zetemata, Heft 30, 1962.)

5. See W. Kranz, "Der Logos Heraklits und der Logos des Johannes," *Rh. Mus.*, 93 (1950), 81 f. = *Studien zur antiken Literatur und ihrem Fortwirken* (1967), 389 f.

6. Pindar, *Ol.* 12, 1 f.; Sophocles, *Ichneutae* 73 Pearson = 50 Page (*Greek Literary Papyri*, 32). ("The papyrus has θεός": E. Siegmann ap. Fraenkel, *Aeschylus, Agamemnon* iii 675, n. 2.) The view of Chester G. Starr, *Hermes*, 95 (1967), 269 f., that in Pindar "that obscurely unpredictable force, Tyche, can determine success or failure, *apparently apart from divine will*" (my italics) rests on no very careful examination of the way this word is actually employed by Pindar.

7. Dodds, *GI*, 209.

8. See Dodds, *GI*, ch. VII, "Plato, the Irrational Soul, and the Inherited Conglomerate," *passim*, and also Dodds, "Plato and the Irrational," *JHS*, 65 (1945), 16 f.

Glossary

Agathos.   Good; see p. 2

Agon.   Contest, ordeal

Aidos.   Regard for others, respect, shame; see p. 22

Aitia (in Ionic, *Aitie*).   Cause, responsibility, guilt

Aitios.   Corresponding adjective to the above; see p. 22

Amechania (in Ionic, *Amechanie;* in West Greek dialects, *Amachania*). Helplessness; see p. 36

Apeiron.   Unlimited, boundless

Arete.   Excellence, goodness; used as corresponding noun to *Agathos,* q v.

Ate.   A temporary insanity, causing disastrous error, often sent by Zeus to mortals; frequently personified; see p. 16

Daimon.   At first a vague term denoting an unspecified god or, later, a divine or semidivine being.

(to) Daimonion.   A neuter abstract derived from the above, and standing to it as *(to) theion* does to *Theos.* (N.B. *To* is the definite article, which placed before the neuter form of an adjective makes it a noun.)

Deilos.   Bad, cowardly

Demos.   The people, often in the political sense of the term

Dikaios.   Just, righteous; corresponding adjective to *Dike*

Dike.   Justice, the divinely appointed order of the universe; often personified

Dikaiosyne.   Justice as a quality; see p. 165, n. 6.

Eris.   Strife, contention

Eros.   Love, desire; often used of strong desires which are not in the modern sense erotic

Eudaimonia.   Prosperity, good fortune; originally it implied having good relations with a *Daimon* or *Daimones*

Eunomia.   Having good laws, or law-abidingness; see p. 42

Hamartia. Mistake, crime; it is often hard to distinguish these two senses; see p. 104

Kakia. Evil, badness, cowardice

Kakos. Corresponding adjective to the above

Katharsis. Purification

Kosmos. Order

Logioi. "Men of words"; an early term for "wise men," "writers."

Logos. Word, story, train of thought, theory, reason

Magos (pl. *Magoi*). A Persian word denoting the class of priests called "Magi"; for its Greek use, see p. 72

Moira. Portion, share, and hence fate; personified from early times

Noos (*Nous*). Mind, intelligence

Philia. Friendship, dearness

Philotēs. Poetic equivalent of the above

Philos. Dear, friend (adjective often used as a noun)

Phrēn (pl. *phrenes*). Mind, sense

Phronein. To think, to have sense; corresponding verb to the above

Phthonos. Envy, jealousy; see ch. iv, *passim*

Polis. City, state, civic community

Psychē. Soul, spirit

Sophron. Sensible, prudent; see p. 53

(to) Theion. "The divine"; see *Theos* and cf. *(to) Daimonion*

Themis. Right, justice; see p. 166, n. 23.

Themistes (pl. of the above). Principles of justice; see p. 6

Theos. God; on the difference between the early Greek and other conceptions of divinity, see p. 3

Thymos. First impulse, later mind, purpose

Timē. Honour, particularly the honour due to anyone on account of his station

Tyche. Happening, *later* chance; see p. 162

Addenda

P. ix. R. Hirzel, *Themis, Dike und Verwandtes: Ein Beitrag sur Geschichte der Rechtsidee bei den Griechen* (1907, repr. 1966); V. Ehrenberg, *Die Rechtsidee im frühen Griechentum* (1921, repr. 1966); J. L. Myres, *The Political Ideas of the Greeks* (1927, repr. 1968); A. B. Cook, *Zeus* I (1914), II (1925), III (1940).

P. x. See now the criticism of Adkins by A. A. Long, "Morals and Values in Homer," *JHS* 90 (1970), 121 f. I sympathise, but think the gods enter more into Homeric ethics than Long (see p. 135) allows.

P. 11. Kirk points out that the belief that the gods caused wars in order to relieve the earth of excessive population existed also in Mesopotamian religion.

P. 45. The force of Otto's observation is little diminished by R. Harder, *Kleine Schriften* (1960), p. 191, n. 14.

P. 51. On the Cyclopes, see Kirk, *Myth: Its Meaning and Function in Ancient and Other Cultures* (1970), 164 f.

P. 69. The concept of envy is the subject of a special study by H. Schoeck, in *Der Neid: Eine Theorie der Gesellschaft* (1966); Eng. tr. by M. Glenny and B. Ross, *Envy: A Theory of Social Behaviour* (1969).

P. 77. It is interesting to note that the author of the latest scientific study of the concept of pollution, Mary Douglas, is more disposed than many others have been to connect pollution with ethics; see her *Purity and Danger: An Analysis of Concepts of Pollution and Taboo* (1966; Pelican ed., 1970), esp. ch. 8.

P. 81 (cf. p. 186, n. 18). It is significant that Parmenides gives the name Dike, as well as the name Ananke, to the goddess who keeps the keys of the paths of Night and Day, and who has such central importance in his system; see 28 *VS* 1 B, 9 f.; and cf. *ibid.* fr. 37 A and the other fragments there quoted. W. Burkert, *Phronesis* 14 (1969), 1 f. has shown that Parmenides in his proem employs standard mythology and not privately invented matter; see esp. pp. 10–11, and see Guthrie, *HGP* II, 346.

P. 84 (end of second paragraph). I do not, of course, mean to imply that Logos is secondary to Dike in Heraclitus, for whom Logos is a central concept.

P. 90. I long ago retracted what I said at *CQ* 9 (1959), 87 f.; see L. Golden, *In Praise of Prometheus* (1966), 59, n. 25.

P. 98 (second paragraph). Of the characters of the *Agamemnon* one only appears in the *Eumenides,* and she as a ghost.

P. 107, l. 9 f. See below, pp. 188–189, n. 100.

P. 126. Kirk remarks that many of the myths were in all likelihood familiar from oral tradition, and not simply from literature.

P. 139. On Cleon's echoes of Pericles, see Gomme, *JHS* 71 (1951), 78 = *More Essays in Greek History and Literature* (1962), 108, and Jacqueline de Romilly, *Thucydides and Athenian Imperialism* (1963), 163 f.

P. 157 (second paragraph). See now Kirk, *Myth* (cited in Addendum to p. 51), pp. 238–251 (one of the most interesting sections of this important book).

P. 160 (second paragraph). Kirk points out that Babylonian religion also is something between monotheism and polytheism.

P. 172, n. 24. Dirlmeier's article is now reprinted in *Ausgewählte Schriften zu Dichtung und Philosophie der Griechen* (1970), 68 f.

P. 173, n. 34. See F. Dirlmeier, ΘΕΟΦΙΛΙΑ-ΦΙΛΟΘΕΙΑ, *Philologus* 90 (1935), 57 f. and 176 f. = *Ausgewählte Kleine Schriften* (cited in Addendum to p. 172 above), 85 f.

P. 175, n. 84. The interpretation of *Il.* 24, 527 f. has been controversial since antiquity (see Leaf's note); Pindar, *Pyth.* 3, 81 f. seems to have accepted the view taken in my text.

P. 180, n. 45. Dodds writes that he is not convinced by Burkert's argument. " 'εἰ καὶ τότε γε,' he writes, 'even at this late date,' gives Herodotus' reason for calling the trick exceptionally silly. What is decisive, it seems to me, is the word ἀπεκρίθη. Herodotus thought the barbarian races were the oldest (2,2): hence he could speak of the Greek race 'separating itself off' from the barbarian, but *not,* I think, the other way round." Even if this is right, the fact that Herodotus felt respect for many "barbarian" religions and institutions is beyond doubt.

P. 187, n. 62. Not even the cautious argument of W. Rösler, *Reflexe vorsokratischen Denkens bei Aischylos* (Beiträge zur klassischen Philologie, ed. R. Merkelbach, Heft 37, 1970) has convinced me that there is any positive evidence that Aeschylus was seriously influenced by the philosophers.

Pp. 188–189, n. 100 (cf. p. 107, l 9 f.—the remarks about Aeschylus).

The relation of a poet's "thought" to his poetry is nowhere better handled than by T. S. Eliot in his paper on "Shakespeare and the Stoicism of Seneca" (*Selected Essays*, p. 126 f.). When Eliot writes (p. 136) "I can see no reason for believing that either Dante or Shakespeare did any thinking on his own," he did not mean that Dante or Shakespeare was stupid.

P. 190, n. 110. C. J. Herington, *The Author of the "Prometheus Bound"* (1970) now offers the best analysis so far of the indications of language, style and metre. He inclines to a date very late in the poet's life, but sensibly refrains from claiming certainty for this conclusion.

P. 193, n. 13. I do not mean that Dodds dismisses the whole Asclepius cult as an imposture; see Dodds, *GI,* 112.

P. 200, n. 11. I should have mentioned the doubts about the "Anonymous" raised by M. Gigante, ΝΟΜΟΣ ΒΑΣΙΛΕΤΣ (1966), 268–292 (cf. Guthrie, *HGP* II 75).

P. 208, n. 89. See now Mrs. Burnett's "Catastrophe Survived: Euripides' Plays of Mixed Reversal" (1971).

P. 209, n. 4. For the idea of a cosmos, see also W. Burkert, *Wissenschaft und Weisheit* (1969), 68–70.

P. 209, n. 6. See the excellent treatment of Tyche by John H. Finley, Jr., *Thucydides* (1947), 312 f. As he remarks, the term covers just that element of the incalculable supplied in Greek religion by the action attributed to the gods.

Index of
Modern Authors

Adkins, A. W. H., x; on the Greek notion of "goodness," 1–2, 136 (cf. 202 n. 34), 158; on morality in the *Iliad*, 7, 12–15; on justice in Theognis, 47; on the oracle in Sophocles, *O.T.*, 197 n. 112; on homicide, 196 n. 86; on Athenian ruthlessness, 204 n. 56; Addenda to p. x

Andrewes, A., 206 n. 68

Barrett, W. S., 176 n. 140
Benedict, R., 17
Bergk, T., 100
Bethe, E., 120, 182 n. 98
Bischoff, H., 180 n. 51
Bornitz, H.–F., 179 n. 20
Boulanger, A., 169 n. 44
Bowra, C. M., xi; on the *Iliad*, 168 n. 37; on the date of the *Aethiopis*, 169 n. 46; his specimens of "primitive" poetry, 173 n. 49; on Pindar, 49, 175 n. 85; on Simonides fr. 36, 176 n. 140; on curses in Sophocles, 194 n. 33; on Sophocles, *Tr.*, 127, 199 n. 47
Broadhead, H. D., 188 n. 79
Bruhn, E., 195 n. 63, 197 n. 110
Brunt, P. A., 204 n. 63
Burkert, W., on laments for the dead, 72; on Herodotus' attitude to "bar-

barians," 180 n. 45; on the lack of mystery in Homer, 184 n. 129; on Anaximander, 186 n. 16; Addenda to p. 81

Burnett, A. P., 208 n. 81; Addenda to p. 208

Burton, R. W. B., 191 n. 128

Calhoun, G. M., 171 n. 106
Campbell, J. K., 24
Cataudella, Q., 190 n. 22, 191 n. 23
Chantraine, P., 1, 6, 167 n. 23
Cook, A. B., ix, Addenda to p. ix
Cornford, F. M., 184 n. 1, 200 n. 10; on Thucydides, 204 n. 65
Coxon, A. H., 188 n. 80

Dain, A., 194 n. 28
Dale, A. M., 207 n. 74
Dawe, R. D., 192 n. 2, 197 n. 106
Defradas, J., 173 n. 36
Deichgräber, K., 171 n. 108, 188 n. 83
De Romilly, J., Addenda to p. 139
De Ste. Croix, G., 203 n. 43
De Sanctis, G., 170 n. 100, 178 n. 12, 205 n. 67
Deubner, L., 197 nn. 103, 107
Devereux, G., xi; on psychic coherence

General Index

Achilles: in the *Iliad* ch. I *passim,* esp. 10–23; in Aeschylus, 21, 121; in the *Aethiopis,* 73

Act divisions in Greek drama, 191 n. 23

Aegisthus: in the *Odyssey,* 28; in Aeschylus, 91, 94

Aeschylus, 84–103; his thought, 107, expurgation of myths in, 146; form and principles of Aeschylean tragedy, 159; Achilles trilogy, 21, 89; Danaid trilogy; 85, 90, 190 n. 110; Heliades, 86; Lycurgus trilogy, 85, 90; *Niobe,* 87, 187 n. 70; *Oresteia:* 90–95; *Ag.* 69, 89, 113–114, 123, 169 n. 47; *Cho.* 75, 77; *Eum.* 77; *Pers.* 69, 88–89; Prometheus trilogy, 95–103; *Prometheus Firekindler,* 98; Theban trilogy, 113, 119–121; frs. 281–282 Ll.-J. (*Women of Aetna?*), 35, 86, 99–100, 190 n. 121

Aethiopis, 73

Aetna (city), 100–101. *See also* Etna (mountain)

Agamedes, 52–53

Agamemnon: quarrel with Achilles, 10–23, 27–28; in Aeschylus, 69, 90–91

Agathos: main ethical term of praise, 2; alleged to connote competitive rather than cooperative qualities, 2; this allegation considered, *passim;* summing-up, 158; whether Athenian chauvinism due to inadequacy of such terms as, 136; in Alcaeus, 42;

in Theognis, 46–47. *See also Esthlos, Aristo, Aretē*

Agnosticism, 129–134; of Thucydides (?), 141, 144

Agyrion, 102

Aidōs: Achilles said to lack, 22; sent by Zeus to men, 98–99; in Sophocles, 112, 128; in Democritus, 131–132; in Euripides, 147–148; in sense of "respect," 147–148. *See also* Shame, Shame-culture

Aitia, 59. *See also* Causality, Causal chains

Aitios, 22. *See also* Aitia

Ajax: in Sophocles, 4, 116, 125; in Homer, 17–19, 23, 143

Alastor, 89, 147

Alcaeus, 41–42, 46

Alcibiades, 133, 139–140, 144

Alcman, 37

Alcmene, 142

Amasis, 68

Amechania. See Helplessness

Amestris, 66

Amphitryon, 153

Anaxagoras, 129–130; prosecution of, 133, 150

Anaximander, 79–81

Anger. *See Cholos,* Persian

Anthropomorphism: criticism mentioned by Herodotus, 64; criticised by Xenophanes, 81–83; not criticised